Evaluating Corporate Investment and Financing Opportunities

EVALUATING CORPORATE INVESTMENT AND FINANCING OPPORTUNITIES

A Handbook and Guide to Selected Methods for Managers and Finance Professionals

---

SHERMAN L. LEWIS

Q

QUORUM BOOKS

NEW YORK • WESTPORT, CONNECTICUT • LONDON

Library of Congress Cataloging-in-Publication Data

Lewis, Sherman L.
  Evaluating corporate investment and financing
opportunities.

  Includes index.
  1. Corporations—Finance.   2. Capital investments.
I. Title.
HG4026.L62   1986   658.1'5   86–623
ISBN 0-89930-144-4 (lib. bdg. : alk. paper)

Library of Congress Catalog Card Number: 86-623
ISBN: 0-89930-144-4

First published in 1986 by Quorum Books

Greenwood Press, Inc.
88 Post Road West, Westport, Connecticut 06881

Printed in the United States of America

The paper used in this book complies with the
Permanent Paper Standard issued by the National
Information Standards Organization (Z39.48-1984).

10 9 8 7 6 5 4 3 2 1

Contents

Preface

This book is directed to the practitioners of corporate finance and to all managers, consultants, teachers, students, and writers who are interested in this dynamic subject. The content is based on extensive experience in management, consulting, and teaching. The material contains sound ideas and concepts, supported by detailed technical applications illustrated with clear, practical examples.

Financial management consists of three principal parts—planning, investing, and financing. The *planning process* embraces both analysis of past performance and formulation of financial plans to meet company goals. The *investing process* includes profitability analysis for both short-term and long-term assets (capital expenditures). Uncertainty and risk are evaluated separately in relation to projected expenditures. The special subjects of bond refunding and merger are explored in separate chapters. The *financing process* contains definitions and valuation techniques for corporate securities and financial leases. The composition of capital structure is analyzed, with particular attention to the appropriate discount rate to measure project profitability. A final chapter explores the techniques for dealing with foreign currency transactions. These three processes are closely interrelated and must be handled concurrently and relative to varying future periods in a climate of constant change. Both investing and financing require simultaneous evaluation of profitability, risk, and liquidity.

Managers at all levels and in all functions of the company are better equipped to perform and advance to the extent that they comprehend the relationships of their responsibilities to finance. Financial managers need to understand operations, and operating managers need to understand finance. Financial managers are given a rigorous analysis of their financing activities and clear guidance on evaluation of profitability, liquidity, and risk. The related fields of macro-finance and personal finance are depicted only in relation to their interfaces with management finance. The viewpoint of company financial management is preserved. Operating managers are provided with a thorough, practical analysis of asset investment decisions, including the acquisition of other companies. All managers are concerned with financial statement analysis, the computation of profitability measures, and the evaluation of alternatives for financial planning. Specific techniques are presented with detailed examples.

Financial and accounting knowledge are needed to grasp the technical topics. Standard texts should be consulted for full exposition. Current literature should also be reviewed.

Financial accounting statements as prepared for public use are adapted in the text to meet the needs of management without exploration of the supporting standards and practices, referred to as GAAP (generally accepted accounting principles). Income taxes are dealt with where applicable, but there is no attempt to cover the current tax code or to deal with taxes in depth.

Careful distinction is made between financial profitability, the basis for analysis, and accounting profit as measured by GAAP; unfortunate discrepancies exist that must be evaluated.

The approach is entirely within the company and, accordingly, draws on all available data relevant to financial analysis. There is no coverage of financial statement analysis by outsiders for purposes such as credit evaluation or personal investment.

Decisions must be made within a given time frame and with limited information under rapidly changing conditions clouded by uncertainty. This calls for a pragmatic approach, with survival the ''sina qua non.'' The quest for ''optimizing'' decisions and ''maximizing'' profits is quixotic.

Each topic is presented in a manner to show the interrelationships of profitability, liquidity, uncertainty and risk, and survival. These are the main strands of the financial fiber and must enter into both investing and financing evaluations. Both short- and long-term effects must also be weighed.

Analysis, at best, can only be a tool to guide the decision-making process. Properly used, the appropriate methods can be invaluable, even indispensable in today's high competitive, technological, and fast-paced environment. But the role of judgment cannot be replaced or overruled by quantitative methods. Company goals, supported by strategy and policy, provide the primary criteria for the decision process.

The chapter sequence reflects one logical approach, but each chapter is largely self-sufficient so that other combinations of presentation are practical. The appendix contains the present value tables with abundant examples of their use.

PART 1

The Planning Process

The first chapter sets forth the basic definitions and analytic techniques for the financial statements, which are presented in a format designed for management use. All managers must understand the language of accounting for both clear thinking and effective communication: the detailed rules can be left to the specialist.

The financial statements are analyzed in detail in the second chapter to provide a basis for interpreting results and for the development of financial plans. Also, three major, controversial topics are explored.

The third chapter arrives at projected financial statements, expressing all operating and financial plans, to facilitate coordinated action and delegation of responsibility. Detailed analyses are given. Clear distinction is made between "funds" and "cash"—a continuing but avoidable source of confusion.

CHAPTER 1

Financial Management

ROLE AND CONTRIBUTION TO THE FIRM

BASIC FACTORS

Managerial finance is concerned with investments and financing, primarily for profit-making organizations. Investment in assets includes both short-term assets (working capital) and long-term assets, such as plant and equipment, long-term receivables and inventories, and stock in other companies. Financing deals with the sources of funds needed to operate the firm, such as capital stock, retained earnings, loans, bonds, and includes dividend policy. Investing and financing are closely related and determine a firm's success. Both are analyzed in terms of profitability, risk, and liquidity over time.

Management decisions are based on company goals, strategies, and policies, which are directed toward increasing the value of company stock; stock value is a combination of dividends and market price. These factors depend primarily on growth in revenues and profits—which are preferably steady and predictable—called the "quality of earnings." Growth depends on investment in assets, with funds provided by earnings (less any dividends), borrowings, and sale of stock. Market valuation of stock reflects the growth prospects for the company, together with the influence of industry and world developments.

Stock market prices also embody exposure to risk, which is a combination of operating risk and financial risk. *Operating risk* is the variability of earnings, defined as EBIT (earnings before interest and tax). The degree of variability, called "operating leverage," is based on fixed operating expenses. EBIT is also responsive to industry and world developments. *Business risk* is an alternate term for operating risk. *Financial risk* is the variability of income available to the common stockholders, or EBIT less interest, taxes, and preferred dividends. The degree of variability is called "financial leverage." Financial risk also includes fixed obligations for debt repayment, financial leases, pension plans, and royalties, because of possible insolvency and bankruptcy. The interaction of operating and financial risk is called "company risk."

Investors hold company stocks in proportions that meet their preferences for return and risk. *Return* refers to the yield (profit) provided by dividends and changes in market prices. *Risk* is company risk. Investments in stock and other assets are the subject of portfolio management. *Total market return* is the sum of all dividends and price changes. *Market risk* is the variability of returns. It is unitary because it cannot be diversified within that market. Investors can regulate portfolio return and risk by diversifying holdings among several companies. *Systematic risk* is the term used for market risk, and *unsystematic risk* refers to company risk.

Company managers make decisions based on their personal attitudes toward growth and risk, motivated by the desire to succeed, to hold their jobs, and to earn peer respect. Management, including the board of directors, cannot be guided by the preference of stockholders, except when the number is very small. The individual investor can readily shift stock holdings. Thus investors pick companies to meet their portfolio needs (the clientele effect). As a practical matter, management motives are necessarily personal but are not necessarily in conflict with stockholder interests. Frequently, management income and wealth are tied closely to company performance. How well managers serve stockholders is a moot, if not intractable, problem.

THE APPROACH AND CONTENT

This handbook covers the principal areas of managerial finance with emphasis on clear and practical examples and illustrations. The approach provides a grasp of numbers and analytical techniques to promote understanding of the concepts and their application to real problems.

It is important to recognize that the standard financial texts provide the full background and theory, as well as some topics omitted here such as bankruptcy, dividend policy, financial markets, financial institutions, income taxes, credit analyses, mathematical models, and international business. The subject of personal finance is also not included here, but financial securities are analyzed from the viewpoint of investors and lenders as related to the company. Economics and macro-finance are skirted here as well, except for observable linkage with financial decisions. For example, interest cost for firms is analyzed in depth but not the related monetary and fiscal policies or the term structure of interest rates.

PROFITABILITY, LIQUIDITY, RISK

Decisions in managerial finance require the simultaneous evaluation of three primary elements—profitability, both financial and accounting; liquidity; and risk. Time constraints are often present. The information availability is necessarily limited, imprecise, and often lacking. The future must be projected but remains uncertain. Personal fallibility and internal politics are inescapable.

This amalgam is the environment in which decisions must be made, but it is unrealistic to envision "profit maximization" or "optimum results" or the avoidance of "sub-optimization." Even after the event such judgments can seldom be made to any purpose.

However, relevant and practical analysis, properly made, can be a powerful tool to aid sound decision-making. The approach is: locate opportunities, define alternatives, carry out applicable analyses, make a judgmental decision. (Avoid the use of sophisticated tools to hunt for problems that show their power.)

INVESTING

The primary factors pertaining to investing are briefly described here and receive full attention for each topic in the ensuing chapters.

Profitability

Financial profit is the excess of cash gain (higher net revenue or reduced cost) over cash outlay (the cash flows) for the project life, discounted at the current cost of funds (the discount rate). The excess of the discounted cash over the current cash outlay is *net present value* (*NPV*) also expressed as a percentage rate of return, or yield. Proposals to make investments—projects—must be carefully defined for cash flows, economic life, and tax effects.

Financial profitability is the primary decision factor, but accounting profit must also be determined, based on company practices. They are different, often to a significant extent. The accounting results often show losses or very low profits in the first few years of project life. This reduces reported earnings and earnings per share (EPS) with a possible adverse effect on market valuation.

Investments include land, depreciable assets, expenses, and net current assets (cash, receivables, and inventory less related payables). Investments also include acquisitions with financial (capital) leases, purchase of other companies (mergers), long-term receivables and inventories, and bond refunds, and they include major expense programs such as product promotion, management training, research and development, public relations, and environmental improvement.

The term *capital expenditure* is used to embrace the planning and control of these projects, as well as the evaluation of asset retention and disposal.

Risk

Every investment project involves some degree of possible variation in the amount and timing of cash flows. Estimating the extent and probability of such variations provides a basis for better evaluation and for more effective communication among managers. The risk of loss, or failure to earn the minimum profit (the discount rate), is called the "downside risk"; the opportunity to do better is called the "upside potential." The responses of individuals to risk are highly subjective and are variable over time and as to types of risk and amounts. This is known as the "utility function." Risk aversion and risk tolerance affect all decisions to an unknown extent.

Projects are usually submitted for approval with a single set of calculations, or point estimates. If risk ranges and probabilities are not expressed there is great danger of accepting proposals that are too risky and rejecting others that are acceptable. The result could be significant increase in risk and reduction in profit.

Companies are characterized by their risk posture. Investors respond according to their risk preferences (utilities) but can diversify away company risk to the extent desired by portfolio management.

Liquidity

Liquidity depends on the continuing inflow of cash, in amount and timing, sufficient to meet all obligations for cash outlay. Variability of cash inflow that threatens liquidity can be guarded against by cash reserves, borrowing capacity, sale of stock, and disposal of assets. The possibility of insolvency imposes a restraint on management freedom of action, which may impair profitability, particularly for the long run.

Investment proposals must be evaluated for their effect on liquidity, as well as for profitability and risk. The required cash outlays are scheduled for the near term in (usually) predictable amounts, but the cash inflows extend into the future and may have a high degree of variability. Hence some profitable proposals may be foregone, or deferred, to preserve future liquidity.

FINANCING

Funds arise from several sources:

Operations—less dividends

Borrowing—all funds that incur interest and must be repaid (includes financial leases)

Sale of stock—preferred, with a dividend requirement; common—residual benefits— ownership; and treasury stock, which has been purchased

Asset disposal—sales less expenses and taxes

Working capital reduction—decrease of current assets; increase of current liabilities

The capital section of a balance sheet shows all borrowing and stockholder equity balanced in total by working capital (net current assets), fixed assets (property, plant, and equipment), investments, and other assets. The *capital structure* is the amount of debt and equity comprising total capital. (If current liabilities are added, the total is called "financial structure," but this total is not relevant.)

Decisions to borrow or to sell stock entail evaluations parallel to those for investments:

Profitability—cost of the funds, relative to available sources, and relative to intended use

Risk—possible inability to meet payment terms, with resulting insolvency and bankruptcy and their attendant costs

Liquidity—effect on cash flows in amount and timing

The financing and investing decisions are closely interrelated. Analytical methods can be useful, even critical, aids to judgment but must be used selectively in a practical and relevant manner.

FINANCIAL STATEMENT ANALYSIS

An overview of managerial finance is provided by the three principal financial statements:

Comparative Balance Sheets (also known as Statement of Financial Position). See Exhibit A.

Income Statement and Retained Earnings (also called the Profit and Loss Statement). See Exhibit B.

Funds Statement (officially, Statement of Changes in Financial Position). See Exhibit C.

These statements are prepared according to company accounting policies and practices. Published statements reflect generally accepted accounting principles (GAAP), as established by the Financial Accounting Standards Board (FASB), the Securities and Exchange Commission (SEC), and the American Institute of Certified Public Accountants (AICPA), and are attested to by independent public accountants.

The published formats reflect both regulation and custom. Careful restatement of format is essential for clear analysis, but no item should be omitted or altered. Each represents a valuation by management, supported by their accountants.

Comparative Balance Sheets

The customary form of presentation for the Comparative Balance Sheets has been modified for clarity of analysis, but all assets and liabilities appear. The comparative form is used for added insight and to lead into the Funds Statement.

The following commentary discloses the underlying transactions and their handling in the related statements by letter cross-reference: B—Income Statement and C—Funds Statement.

Net Current Assets—increase $35: C

Current Assets less Current Liabilities. (The term *working capital* is debatable and has been dropped.) Liabilities requiring repayment with interest are excluded from Current Liabilities and included under Debt. This reclassification is necessary for logical analysis of profitability and financial leverage.

Investment in Subsidiary—increase $10: C

Includes subsidiary earnings (equity method) of $15, in B—Other Income, less $5 dividend received. Net $10 in C—equity income from subsidiary.

Plant & Equipment—increase	$145 (1)
Depreciation allowance—increase	25 (2)
Net increase	$120 (3)

Exhibit A
Comparative Balance Sheets (in Thousands)

		Ending Balances		Increase	Cross-Reference
		Last Year	This Year	(Decrease)	to B & C
Net Assets					
Current Assets:					
Cash		$ 30	$ 51	$ 21	
Receivables—net		180	216	36	
Inventory		240	228	(12)	
		450	495	45	
Current Liabilities (excludes debt):					
Payables & Accruals		75	89	14	
Taxes Payable		30	20	(10)	
Dividends Payable		0	6	6	
		105	115	10	
Net Current Assets	Subtotal	345	380	35	C
Investment in Subsidiary	Subtotal	100	110	10	C
Plant & Equiment:					
Land		80	75	(5)	
Buildings		400	450	50	
Machinery & Equipment		500	600	100	
		980	1125	145	
Less Depreciation Allowance		440	465	25	
Net	Subtotal	540	660	120	
Goodwill	Subtotal	85	45	(40)	B, C
Deduct: Deferred Tax Liability	Subtotal	(70)	(95)	(25)	B, C
Net Assets	Total	$1000	$1100	$100	
Capital					
Debt (includes current portion):					
Bank Loan (16%)		$ 100	$ 140	$ 40	C
Notes Payable (18%)		0	50	50	C
Bonds Payable (10%)		300	260	(40)	C
Total Debt	Subtotal	400	450	50	
Equity:					
Preferred Stock (10%)		200	200	0	
Common Stock:					
Paid-in Total		195	215	20	C
Retained Earnings		205	235	30	B
Common Equity		400	450	50	
Total Equity	Subtotal	600	650	50	
Capital	Total	$1000	$1100	$100	

Asset Accounts	Land	Buildings	M & E	Total	
Opening balance	$ 80	$ 400	$ 500	$ 980	
Acquire	0	80	150	230	C
Sell—cost	− 5	− 30	− 50	− 85	
Net increase	− 5	+ 50	+ 100	+ 145	(1)
Ending balance	$ 75	$ 450	$ 600	$ 1,125	
Depreciation Allowance					
Opening balance	$ 0	$ 200	$ 240	$ 440	
Depreciation provided	0	30	60	90	C
Sell—book	0	− 30	− 35	− 65	
Net change	0	0	+ 25	+ 25	(2)
Ending balance	$ 0	$ 200	$ 265	$ 465	
Net opening balance	$ 80	$ 200	$ 260	$ 540	
Net ending balance	75	250	335	660	
Net increase	$− 5	$+ 50	$+ 75	$+ 120	(3)
Cash sales	$ 5	$ 30	$ 30	$ 65	
Net book balance	5	0	15	20	C
Gain	$ 0	$ 30	$ 15	$ 45	B

Goodwill—decrease $40: B and C
Amortization of cost based on evaluation of remaining value
Deferred Tax Liability—increase $25

Total income tax provision	$56 B
Tax liability (credit A/P)	31
Deferred—payable in future	25 C

The deferred amount is a future liability, with both timing and amount dependent on future events, such as the company's taxable income and liability per future tax codes. This account is an estimated future liability without explicit cost. It is omitted from Capital and is deducted in arriving at Net Assets, which are supported only by Debt and Equity.

Accrual accounting requires recognition of the income tax based on total taxable income according to GAAP. The tax return filed reflects tax code provisions that may allow greater deductions, or lesser revenue, thus reducing the tax currently payable. In the future, based on current expectations, the deductions will be smaller and revenue greater, to create a tax liability greater than that based on GAAP taxable income at that time. These differences are known as timing differences, which cancel out over time. Any difference between GAAP income and income not subject to income tax is called a "permanent tax difference" such as goodwill amortization.

Thus the deferred tax liability can have either a debit or credit balance but is planned to reach zero in time. The subject is controversial because the deferred amount is conjectural, subject to unpredictable future events. Elimination of this account would restore the balance to retained earnings.

Net Assets—increase $100

This is the amount that must be supplied by some combination of debt and equity.

Total Debt—net increase $50: C

Interest expense detail includes the following:

Bank Loan—$100 at 16% = $16
   (increase at year end, $40)
Notes Payable—$50 at 18% =   0
   (issued at year end)
Bonds Payable $300—at 10% =   30
   (payment at year end, $40)   —
                       $46 B

Memo: Debt included in Current Liabilities per published statement:

Last Year	Current	Non-Current	Total
Bank Loan	$ 80	$ 20	$ 100
Bonds Payable	40	260	300
	$ 120	$ 280	$ 400
This Year			
Bank Loan	$ 45	$ 95	$ 140
Notes Payable	—	50	50
Bonds Payable	40	220	260
	$ 85	$ 365	$ 450
	$ (35)	$ 85	$ 50

Preferred Stock   No Change
   Declared dividend $ 20   B & C

Common Stock
   Paid-in—increase $ 20   C
   Employee stock purchases at year end—800 shares at $25 added
      to 10,000 shares outstanding
   (Par Value and Excess Paid-in Capital accounts shown in pub-
      lished statements are combined.)

Retained Earnings—increase $ 30   B

Total Equity—increase $ 50

Capital—increase $ 100 $ 100
   Balanced by increase in Net Assets.

Income Statement and Retained Earnings

Exhibit B is condensed to suit financial, as compared with operating, purposes. Both EBIT and EBT (earnings before tax) are necessary for analysis.

The Retained Earnings section shows separately the Net Income available to common after deduction of the Preferred Dividend, with a separate entry for the Common Dividend.

Exhibit B omits, by design, infrequent (but often significant) events such as discontinued operations, extraordinary gains and losses (both unusual and infrequent for that company), and changes in accounting principles. Such items appear before net income and after income from continuing operations, net of tax effects, in published financial statements.

Exhibit B
Income Statement and Retained Earnings This Year (in Thousands)

			Percent	Cross-Reference to A & C
Sales		$2,100	100.00	
Cost of Sales		1,500		
Gross Margin		600	28.57	
Expenses		462		
Operating Profit		138	6.57	
Other Income (Expense):				
Subsidiary income	$15			C
Asset disposal gain	45			
Amortization—goodwill	(40)			A, C
		20		
EBIT		158	7.52	
Interest Expense		46		
EBT		112	5.34	
Income Taxes (payable 31, deferred 25)		56		C
Net Income		$ 56	2.67	C
Retained Earnings				
Net Income		$ 56		C
Preferred Dividend		20		C
Available to Common		36		
Common Dividend		6		C
Net Increase		30		A
Opening Balance		205		A
Ending Balance		$ 235		A

Funds Statement

Preparation of the Funds Statement requires record analysis, as designated on the statement for each item, together with the cross-references to A and B. The presentation form is modified from the published statement but without change of content.

All Financing is supported by the Equity and Debt details. All Investing is supported by Net Current Assets and Plant & Equipment. This approach highlights the basic financial activities of investing in assets and financing with debt and equity funds.

"Funds" and "Cash"

There is unnecessary confusion over the definition of *funds* as compared with *cash*. Funds are changes in the Balance Sheet (also known as Statement of Changes in Financial Position) as prepared by management in accordance with GAAP using accrual accounting. The change in Cash (increase $21) is necessarily included as part of the change in Net Current Assets (increase $35).

GAAP requires the inclusion of all accrual transactions. A statement of cash receipts and disbursements without regard to accrual transactions would serve no purpose for the public (or for management except as part of cash planning and control). A funds statement prepared on a "cash basis" must include all accruals, but a misleading format is used. A funds statement may be prepared on a "working capital basis" but again must include all accruals. Such presentations simply recast the accruals to show the selected item last. (In practice, most funds statements lack coherence and must be restated to aid comprehension.) Working capital is a controversial topic and is not relevant in terms of funds.

Technical adjustments omitted from the analysis include:

- Gain or loss on early debt extinguishment.
- Amortization of premium (discount) or debt (payable and owned).
- Capital stock issued as compensation.
- Long-term liability for deferred compensation, pensions, and retirement.
- Stock dividends omitted because no funds are involved. Declarations payable in cash or property are included when declared.

The Funds Statement is of primary significance to both investors and management. In a sense, it answers the question of what happened to the profits. Net income of $56 becomes Funds provided by operations, $201. This amount is available to resolve the basic questions of investing and financing. The choices made are shown in the rest of the statement.

Exhibit C
Funds Statement This Year (in Thousands)

			Cross-Reference to A & B
Financing			
Equity:			
Net Income		$ 56	B
Items not affecting funds:			
Add depreciation	$90*		
amortization—goodwill	40*		B
deferred taxes	25*		A, B
	155		
Deduct equity income from			B
subsidiary	$15		
less dividend received	5		
	10		A
Net		145	
Funds provided by operations		201	
Sale of stock		20*	A
		221	
Dividends declared:			
Preferred	20		B
Common	6		B
		26	
Net equity increase		195	
Debt:			
Bank loan	40		A
Notes payable (equipment)	50		A
Bond installment paid	(40)		A
Net debt increase		50	
Financing increase		$245	
Investing			
Net Current Assests		$ 35	A
Plant & Equipment:			
Building	$80*		
Machinery & Equipment	100*		
Equipment (notes payable)	50*		
	230		
Less (book values):			
Sale of land	$ 5*		
Other asset disposal	15		
	20*		
Net Plant & Equipment		210	
Investing Increase		$245	

*Developed from the records.

Equity

The Net Income of $56, from the Income Statement, is adjusted to a funds basis by adding $155 for book entries required by accrual accounting but not requiring current outlays. Depreciation and amortization are book allocations of costs. Deferred taxes are a future liability recognized currently according to GAAP. The equity income of $15 is the company's share in the subsidiary's earnings. The dividend of $5 is received and is deducted. The Net of $10 subtracted from the $155 leaves $145 to be added to the Net Income to determine the Funds provided by operations, $201. (The cash available is the cash balance of $51, an increase of $21 for the year.) Sale of stock is added, and Dividends are deducted (as declared whether or not paid) to arrive at the Net equity increase $195.

Debt

The changes in the Debt accounts net to a $50 increase. The combined Debt and Equity increase is totaled to $245, the amount of funds available for investing.
Net Current Assets—increase $35: A
Plant & Equipment—net increase $210.

Total fixed assets are acquired for $230, and disposals of $20 at book value are deducted. Details are shown in the Balance Sheet commentary. The Asset disposal gain of $45 is shown in B. Depreciation provision, a cost allocation over time, is not shown in this section—it appears in the Equity section.

The Investment Increase of $245 is composed of short-term assets, $35, and long-term assets, $210, all provided by the Financing increase of $245.

This chapter describes the principal financial statements briefly to provide a basis for both analysis and planning, presented in the next two chapters. The approach is based on all of the information in the company and how it is used for management purposes. No attention is given to the official requirements of published statements, per GAAP, or to information required by outside agencies, which specify the data needed.

CHAPTER 2

Financial Statement Analysis

BOOK AMOUNTS AND MARKET VALUES

This chapter's analysis of the financial statements (see Exhibits A, B, and C in Chapter 1) is concerned solely with the needs of management for internal control. Comparisons of actual results with budgets and standards are omitted for simplicity.

PROFITABILITY

ROA and ROE (Return on Assets and Return on Equity)

Part of the Income Statement (Exhibit B) reads:

EBIT	$158
Interest Expense	46
EBT	112
Income Taxes	56
Net Income	$ 56

EBIT (earnings before interest and tax) arises from operations and is independent of the financing sources. It is the same regardless of the amount of debt. However, it must be stated after tax (not shown above) because of the variable nature of the tax effect on differing kinds of transactions. Differences arise in profitability for the several components of EBIT and their related asset bases, to be shown later.

The following table restates the above schedule, plus other entries from Exhibit B:

	Before Tax	Tax	Net	Measurement Base (Exhibit A)	
EBIT	$158	$79*	$79*	Net Assets	(1)
Interest Expense	46	23*	23*	Debt	(2)
EBT	$112	$56	56	Total Equity	(3)
Preferred Dividend			20	Preferred Stock	(4)
Available to Common			$36	Common Equity	(5)

*Amounts supplied to provide a logical basis for measurement.

The base amounts need to be averaged for the year to relate properly to the period amounts:

		Basis
Retained Earnings:	$ 205	
	235	
	$ 440/2 = $220	Average

			Basis
Common Stock Paid-in Total (new stock sold at year end)	$ 195		Last Year
Common Equity	415	(5)	Subtotal
Preferred Stock—no change	200	(4)	No Change
Total Equity	615	(3)	Subtotal
Debt (all changes at year end)	400	(2)	Last Year
Net Assets—residual	$1,015	(1)	Total

In practice, these calculations are made monthly and call for exact and consistent rules.

The profitability schedule can now be written as follows:

	After Tax	Base	Percent	
EBIT	$79	(1) $1,015	7.783	ROA
Interest Expense	23	(2) 400	5.750	net interest rate
EBT	56	(3) 615	9.106	total equity
Preferred Dividend	20	(4) 200	10.000	dividend rate
Available to Common	$36	(5) $ 415	8.675	ROE

ROA (return on assets) measures the net profitability of assets for the year. This basic ratio is examined in detail later.

Net Interest Rate

Bank Loan—16%, net 8%

Bonds Payable—10%, net 5%

The net interest rate overall is 5.75%, above, but the bank loan has a negative leverage effect at net 8.00%, while the bonds at net 5.00% have a favorable effect. Combined, ROA of 7.783% is boosted to 9.106% by net interest leverage. The notes written at year end carry a rate of 18.00%, or net 9.00%, with a potential for depressing future ROA. Also, all rates and analysis could be made before tax if desired for communication, as follows:

Memo	Before Tax	Base	Before Tax		After Tax
EBIT	$158	$1,015	15.566%		7.783%
Interest—loan 16%	16	100	16.000	Negative	8.000
EBT—loan	142	915	15.519	Lower	7.760
Interest—bonds 10%	30	300	10.000	Positive	5.000
EBT—combined	$112	$ 615	18.212	Higher	9.106

The total equity net of 9.106% requires subdivision when there is a preferred dividend declaration (or even without the declaration for cumulative preferred).

Preferred Dividend Rate

The 10.00% rate is after tax because dividends, unlike interest, are not tax deductible. However, the preferred dividend requirement is the near equivalent of a fixed contractual payment. Failure to pay the preferred dividend could have serious adverse effects. This 10.000% rate reduces the 9.106% total equity rate to 8.675% for the common—ROE—or negative leverage.

ROE

The final earnings residual is 8.675%, compared with ROA of 7.783%, a small net favorable leverage. Leverage is analyzed later in depth. Fixed payment obligations are expected to provide positive leverage when incurred, but possible subsequent reduction in EBIT is the risk arising from operations. The obligation to meet fixed payments is the financial risk. Combined, the total risk affects net income and stock valuation by the market.

ROE is widely regarded as the single most important measure of profitability, both internally and externally. In practice, it is compared with both past and expected (planned) performance. ROE is also comparable with industry results. For example, industry ROE might be:

Upper quartile	17.84%
Median	10.12
Lower quartile	5.55

The company at ROE 8.675% is trailing the competition. ROE can be readily computed from published statements; ROA is difficult to determine but can be approximated.

EPS (Earnings per Share)

Earnings per share equal the net income available to common—$36,000— divided by the average number of shares outstanding for the year:

$$\$36,000/10,000 \text{ shares} = \$3.60 \text{ EPS}$$

At year end 800 shares were issued for $20,000 to employees for stock options. The EPS calculation will reflect this next year.

Note: When a company has outstanding securities that are "common stock equivalents," it must compute both primary EPS and fully diluted EPS. The calculations are technical, complex, and not fully resolved. Since they are not relevant to management, they are omitted from consideration here.

EPS requires careful interpretation and is not comparable with EPS for other companies. Assume a constant net income (NI) of 10% on equity and no dividends. EPS then increases 10% a year while ROE remains at 10%:

		Equity	EPS (100 shs.)
Balance		$1,000	
NI	10%	$ 100	$1.00
		1,100	
NI	10%	110	1.10
		1,210	
NI	10%	121	1.21
		$1,331	

If dividends (Div.) equal net income, equity remains unchanged, ROE is 10%, and EPS is constant at $1.

		Equity	EPS (100 shs.)
Balance		$1,000	
NI	10%	100	$1.00
Div.		− 100	
		1,000	
NI	10%	100	1.00
Div.		− 100	
		1,000	
NI	10%	100	1.00
Div.		− 100	
		$1,000	

With dividends at half of net income, and ROE 10%, the EPS increases 5%. The number of shares must be adjusted for stock dividends and stock splits—retroactively for comparisons.

Note: Some analysts compute a "cash EPS" as follows (Exhibit C):

Funds provided by operations	$201,000
less Preferred Dividend	20,000
Available to Common	$181,000

$181,000/10,000 shares = $18.10 "cash EPS"

This is a funds (not cash) number. It confuses liquidity with profitability. It is of no use to management and is decried by the accounting profession.

Book Values

At year end, book value of common was $450,000 and 10,800 shares were outstanding = $450,000/10,800 shares = $41.67 book value per share. This is a construct of accrual accounting and has no particular financial import. It is sometimes computed in reference to market price.

Per share calculations are as follows:

$$\text{EPS } \$36{,}000/10{,}000 \text{ shares} = \$3.60$$

$$\text{Div. } \$6{,}000/10{,}000 \text{ shares} = \$0.60$$

$$\text{Div./EPS} = \$0.60/\$3.60 = 16.7\% = \text{payout ratio}$$

$$(\text{Also } \$6{,}000/\$36{,}000 = 16.7\% \text{ payout ratio.})$$

Market Values

Stock market prices fluctuate constantly in response to economic and industry developments, as well as company prospects. Prices quickly reflect all available information—the efficient market concept—and are not predictable. Past prices contain no indication of future prices (random walk). Insiders with private knowledge of the company may trade to their advantage, but this is illegal and closely monitored.

Assume that the company stock is selling at $30.00, which is 72% of book value ($30.00/$41.67). Total market value is: 10,800 shares at $30.00 = $324,000.00. Book value is $450,000.00 (also 72%).

The market rate of earnings is:

$$\text{EPS } \$3.60/\$30.00 = 12\%$$

The P/E ratio (price to earnings) is:

$$\$30.00/\$3.60 = 8.33 \ (12\% \text{ reciprocal})$$

The dividend yield is:

$$\$0.60/\$30.00 = 2\%$$

These ratios are comparable with those in other companies and are used for stock valuation.

If the market requires a rate of return (yield) of, say, 16% on this stock, then 16% of $30.00 = $4.80. Deduct the $0.60 dividend, and the balance of $4.20 is the expected price increase, or 14% ($4.20/$30.00). The required yield of 16% is a 2% dividend rate plus a 14% growth rate. The stock market price responds to the pressures of investors requiring more or less yield, based on their portfolios.

Preferred stock at 10.00% sells at $100 only if the market rate is 10.00%. If the market is 12.50%, the price is $80:

$$\$10/\$80 = 12.50\%$$

If the market rate is 8.00%, the price is $125:

$$\$10/\$125 = 8.00\%$$

At $80, the preferred total market value is $160,000, compared with $200,000 book value.

Bond values also respond to the market. Because the amount of bond interest remains fixed, the bond price falls when market interest rates rise (and bond prices rise when rates fall).

If the market rate is 14% for 8 year, 10% bonds, the price falls to $815 (f = discount factor, PV = present value; see Appendix for details):

	Contract	8 years, 14% f	PV
Principal	$1,000	0.351	$351
Interest—10%	100	4.639	464
Market price or present value			$815 (81.5%)

Check: market interest $140 − contract interest $100 = $40 × f 4.639 = 185 discount (18.5%).

The company bonds payable of $260,000 at year end have a market value of $211,900 ($260,000 × 81.5%), or $212,000.

A weighted average cost of capital can be computed on book amounts or market values.

Books:

			After Tax
Bank Loan—16%	$140 =	$22.4 or	$11.2
Notes Payable—18%	50 =	9.0 or	4.5
Bonds Payable—10%	260 =	26.0 or	13.0
	$450		$28.7

Thus $28.7/$450.00 = 6.378% = weighted average interest rate after tax.
   Summary:

Total Debt	$ 450	40.9% × 6.378% =	2.609%
Preferred Stock	200	18.2 × 10.0 =	1.820
Common Equity	450	40.9 × 16.0 =	6.544
	$1,100	100.0%	10.973%

The Book Value rate is 10.97%.

With market values (the Bank Loan and Notes Payable are assumed to have a market equal to Book Value).

			After Tax
Bank Loan—16%	$140 = $22.40 or		$11.20
Notes Payable—18%	50 = 9.00 or		4.50
Bonds Payable—14%	212 = 29.68 or		14.84
	$402		$30.54

Thus $30.54/$402.00 = 7.597% or 7.600% weighted average interest rate after tax.

The calculations can be summarized as follows:

Total Debt	$402	45.4% × 7.60% =	3.450%
Preferred Stock	160	18.0 × 12.50 =	2.250
Common Equity	324	36.6 × 16.00 =	5.856
	$886	100.0%	11.556%

The market value rate is 11.56% (cf. 10.97% book rate).

These results are close. Use of book or market values is controversial, and the value of either result is questionable. The subject is explored in depth in Chapter 12, "Capital Structure."

LIQUIDITY

Liquidity is a matter of cash timing—the ability to meet scheduled outlays, plus some reserve, for an indefinite period. (*Solvency* is a technical term referring to the satisfaction of all legal obligations from available assets.) Liquidity is managed by cash planning, described in the next chapter.

Five ratios relate to liquidity:

D/E (Debt to Equity Ratio)

This year: $450/$650 = 69.2%

Last year: $400/$600 = 66.7%

An alternative, though undesirable, is the ratio of debt to total capital:

This year: $450/$1,100 = 40.9%

Last year: $400/$1,000 = 40.0%

The equity amount includes both preferred and common because all debt claims have preference. With any surplus, the preferred has preference over the common.

D/E can also be measured by the ratio of book debt (as above) to equity value at market. Using market values of $160 preferred and $324 common, or $484, the ratio for this year is $450/$484 = 93.0%, compared with D/E 69.2% on the book basis.

Interest Coverage

EBIT $158/Interest Expense $46 = 3.43 times (there are $3.43 of EBIT for every dollar of interest. It is usually expressed as "times interest earned 3.43" with no sign).

If EBIT drops from $158 to $46, interest is still covered ($46/$46 = 1 time). EBT would then be zero and tax zero. EBIT below $46, or negative EBT, would indicate very low earnings (accrual) but would not necessarily indicate inability to pay (cash). A banker (or manager) is primarily interested in the assurance of cash flow adequate to meet repayment terms, regardless of the book profit. The interest payment could also be related to the funds provided by operations $201 (Exhibit C), but this is not cash. The company uses cash planning to ascertain its ability to pay cash obligations as they become due.

Fixed Charge Coverage

This ratio may include fixed payments such as preferred dividends, financial lease payments, pension annuities, and sinking funds. Using only the preferred dividend of $20, which requires earnings of $40 because it is not tax deductible:

EBIT		$158
Interest Expense	$46	
Preferred Dividend	40	86 = 1.84

Current Ratio

This is the ratio of Current Assets (CA) to Current Liabilities (CL), including the current portion of Debt (D).

This year: CA		$495	
CL	$115		
+D	85	200	= 2.48
Last year: CA		450	
CL	105		
+D	120	225	= 2.0

The Debt amounts are the current portion of debt, not shown on the Balance Sheet but included in the commentary, Chapter 1.

Acid Test Ratio

CA includes only Cash and Receivables (Inventory is omitted):

	This Year	Last Year
Cash	$ 51	$ 30
Receivables	216	180
	$267	$210
CL	200	225
Ratio	1.33	0.93

These ratios are comparable with past performance, planned ratios, and industry data, if available and reliable. The measures are useful primarily to outsiders and are of little use to management.

RISK

Liquidity affects the market value of stock because of the costs of insolvency and bankruptcy—financial risk. Operating, or business, risk rests on the variability of EBIT. The effect of company risk on market value is moderated because investors can, at small cost, minimize individual company risk by diversification of investment among several companies and industries. A portfolio can be managed to provide the desired combination of yield and risk. However, the market (systematic) risk remains. This complex area is part of personal finance.

Managers evaluate operating and financial risk in terms of company goals, strategies, and policies. Investors respond to company performance and prospects in their demand for the stock—the clientele theory. However, if a company changes its risk posture perceptibly, some investors will be impelled to sell and others to buy, shifting their portfolios at some expense. Risk analysis and evaluations are presented in Chapter 6.

ROA ANALYSIS

The ROA for all operations, as developed above, is:

$$\frac{\text{EBIT after tax}}{\text{Average assets}} \quad \frac{\$ \quad 79}{\$1,015} = 7.783\%$$

The ROA equation introduces sales of $2,100 (Exhibit B):

$$\frac{\text{Sales}}{\text{Average assets}} \quad \frac{\$2,100}{\$1,015} = 2.069 \text{ turnover}$$

$$\frac{\text{EBIT net}}{\text{Sales}} \quad \frac{\$\ \ \ 79}{\$2,100} = 3.762\% \text{ profit margin}$$

$$\text{ROA} = 2.069 \times 3.762\% = 7.783\%$$

The turnover ratio shows sales dollars per dollar of assets—$2.069 per $1.00. The profit percentage shows net profit dollars per hundred dollars of sales—$3.762 per $100.00 (or $0.03762 per $1.00). The turnover ratio directs attention to obtaining more sales from the same assets, or the same sales with less assets, to increase turnover. The profit percentage reflects the combined effect of pricing, volume, and expense control.

For internal analysis of operations the asset base should exclude:

	Last Year	This Year	Average
Investment in Subsidiary	$ 100	$ 110	$ 105
Goodwill	85	45	65
Deferred Tax Liability	(70)	(95)	(70)
Net to exclude	115	60	100
Balance Sheet totals	1,000	1,100	1,015
Net Asset balance	$ 885	$1,040	$ 915

The profit to be used for internal analysis should be the operating profit of $138 (disregarding other income and expense of $20), or $69 net.

$$\text{ROA} = \frac{\$\ 69}{\$915} = 7.54\%$$

The ROA equation (NA = Net Assets; S = Sales; Pr. = Profit) is:

$$\frac{S}{NA} \quad \frac{\$2,100}{\$\ \ 915} \times \frac{\text{Pr.}}{S} \frac{\$\ \ \ 69}{\$2,100} = \frac{\$\ 69}{\$915} = 7.54\%$$

$$\text{Turnover } 2.295 \times 3.286\% \qquad\qquad = 7.54\%$$

Actual performance can be compared with plans. Assume the following for illustration:

$$\text{Plan} \quad \frac{S}{NA} \quad \frac{\$2,000}{\$1,000} \times \frac{\text{Pr.}}{S} \quad \frac{\$\ \ 100}{\$2,000} = \frac{\$\ \ 100}{\$1,000} = 10\%$$

$$2 \quad \times \qquad\qquad 5\% \qquad\qquad = 10\%$$

$$\text{Actual} \quad \frac{S}{NA} \quad \frac{\$2,100}{\$1,200} \times \frac{\text{Pr.}}{S} \quad \frac{\$\ \ 84}{\$2,100} = \frac{\$\ \ 84}{\$1,200} = 7\%$$

$$1.75 \quad \times \qquad\qquad 4\% \qquad\qquad = 7\%$$

Sales increased $100, but NA increased faster—$200—to reduce turnover. Profit dropped $16 with a sales increase to lower the rate to 4%. Combined, the 7% result is 30% under the 10% plan. These figures suggest the need for better asset control and improved expense control.

With the same plan, better results would be:

$$\frac{S}{NA}\ \frac{\$2,100}{\$1,000} \times \frac{Pr.\ \$\ 126}{S\ \ \$2,100} = \frac{Pr.\ \$126}{NA\ \$100} = 12.6\%$$

$$2.1 \times 6.0\% \qquad\qquad\qquad = 12.6\%$$

Company segments can be analyzed with the ROA equation: subsidiaries, divisions, profit centers, product lines, customers, exports, distribution methods, foreign operations. Such analysis should follow responsibility lines and be applied to the extent that causative determination can be made of sales, assets, and profits. Reasonable approximation may be useful, but allocations should not be used.

Assume that a company operates with three divisions (A, B, C) and an executive office (E.O.):

Plan	A	B	C	Total	E.O.	Company
Sales	$1,000	$700	$300	$2,000	$ 0	$2,000
NA	$ 300	$350	$150	$ 800	$200	$1,000
Turnover	3.33	2	2	2.5	—	2
Profit	$ 45	$ 35	$ 30	$ 110	$(10)	$ 100
%	4.5%	5.0%	10.0%	5.5%	—	5.0%
ROA	15.0%	10.0%	20.0%	13¾%	—	10.0%

For the company to achieve 10%, the divisions must produce 13¾% in total.

Actual	A	B	C	Total	E.O.	Company
Sales	$970	$770	$360	$2,100	$ 0	$2,100
NA	$350	$350	$200	$ 900	$150	$1,050
Turnover	2.77	2.2	1.8	2.33	—	2.0
Profit	$ 59	$ 49	$ 32	$ 140	$(14)	$ 126
%	6.08%	6.36%	8.89%	6.67%	—	6.00%
ROA	16.85%	14.00%	16.00%	15.55%	—	12.00%

The company achieved 12.00% (plan 10.00%), and the divisions realized 15.55% (plan 13¾%).

A—Higher ROA—turnover down—profit % up

B—Higher ROA—turnover up—profit % up

C—Lower ROA—turnover down—profit % down

The division results are subject to further ROA analysis to the extent deemed constructive. ROA turnover control rests on the individual assets.

INDIVIDUAL ASSETS

This year balances are as follows:

Cash

Exhibit A shows a balance of $51,000. Cash balances fluctuate daily and require close planning and control to insure liquidity for current needs, plus a reasonable reserve. Excess cash balances over expected needs can depress ROA; some sacrifice of profit is made to reduce risk. Sufficiently large excess balances may be put into short-term marketable securities to earn some return, less transaction costs. Methods are available to reduce collection float (and increase payment float), tailored to meet company needs.

Receivables

Total receivables of $221,666 carry an allowance for doubtful accounts of $5,666 (2.55%) based on collection experience, or net $216,000.

The number of days in receivables is:

$$\frac{Sales}{Days} \ \frac{\$2,100,000 \ (\text{all on credit})}{360 \ (\text{other days may be used})} = \$5,833.33 \text{ sales per day}$$

$$\frac{Receivables}{Sales \text{ per day}} \ \frac{\$221,666.00}{\$5,833.33} = 38 \text{ days}$$

or

$$\frac{\$221,666}{\$2,100,000/360 \text{ days}} = \frac{360 \times \$221,666}{\$2,100,000} = \frac{\$79,800,000}{\$2,100,000} = 38 \text{ days}$$

This analysis assumes, in effect, that sales occur evenly throughout the year (and are not seasonal) and that all credit is granted on the same terms. The result can be compared with both the past and the planned number of days in receivables.

If the credit terms call for payment 30 days after purchase, no discount (30 net), the excess 8 days over 30 in the 38-day figure can be accounted for by mail and handling time, plus overdue balances.

Sales must be segregated by cash and by credit terms. Seasonal sales require separate analysis. For instance, if December sales are $221,666, the number of days in receivables is 31 (not 38 as above). Conceivably, the number of days in sales is even less, assuming the daily sales are:

December 31	$21,666
December 30	40,000
December 29	40,000
December 28	40,000
December 27	40,000
December 26	40,000
A total of 6 days in receivables	$221,666

Aging of the receivables is often necessary. With terms of 10 days, EOM (end of month), the following is true:

At Year End	Monthly Sales	Receivable	
December	$150,000	$150,000	all current
November	120,000	40,000	20 days overdue
October	100,000	20,000	50 days overdue
Prior	—	11,616	
		$221,666	

Accounts receivable credit balances may occur and should be separately disclosed to avoid understatement of the amounts to be collected.

The problem, at bottom, concerns the status of individual accounts. For example:

Customer #632, Balance $608		
December	$ 50	paid late—discount not allowed
November	100	request for price concession on "PIPS"
October	300	return of "POPS" not authorized
Older	158	record dispute—file missing
Total	$608	

This type of account calls for decisive action.

Another troublesome problem, not unusual, is the customer with past-due balances who continues to receive shipments:

Customer #236, Balance $2,800		
December	$ 500	current
November	800	past due one month
October	400	past due two months
Older	1,100	past due over two months
Total	$2,800	

The last payment was received August 20. Thus the number of days in receivables is a statistic that may conceal more than it reveals.

Inventory

The inventory balance is $228,000. Turnover measures (M = 000) are:

$$\text{Based on sales} \quad \frac{\$2,100M}{\$\ 234M} = 8.97 \text{ Turnover on sales}$$
$$\text{Year average}$$

$$\frac{(240M + 228M)}{2} = 234M$$

$$\text{Based on cost of sales} \quad \frac{\$1,500M}{\$\ 234M} = 6.41 \text{ Turnover on cost at sales}$$
$$\text{Year average}$$

$$\text{Number of days} \quad \frac{360}{6.41} = 56 \text{ days in inventory at cost}$$
$$\text{Turnover}$$

The many sub-categories of inventory must be analyzed separately. Seasonality must be considered. Results can be compared with past and planned amounts.

Effective inventory control rests on operational planning and close monitoring. Factors include planned usage, EOQ (economic order quantities), quantity discount, lead time, vendor dependability, variability of sales demand by time periods and by products, production runs, product perishability, and danger of obsolescence. Surplus stocks, damaged goods, and obsolete items should receive constant attention and prompt action.

CURRENT LIABILITIES

Current liabilities of $115,000 are shown in Exhibit A. Payables and Accruals have a balance of $89,000.

All invoices should be entered net of any discounts. A missed discount should be charged to a separate financial account (with zero budget). The distribution of invoices to accounts on the net basis neutralizes the effect of discounts on cost.

All bills should be paid within the terms given to foster good vendor relations. Cash discounts almost always provide a favorable rate of saving compared with borrowing. If the terms are 2%/10 days, net 30, for a $100 invoice, then $98 can be paid in 10 days or the full $100, 20 days later:

The annual rate is: $2/$98 × 360 days/20 days = 2.04% × 18 times = 36.72%. This is the equivalent annual interest rate for using $98 for 20 days, much higher than loan rates.

Vendor selection rests on many factors of which price and terms are only a part. Thus the accounts payable balance does not lend itself to any useful ratio. Payable balances change constantly. Debit balances should be segregated. There is no explicit cost; hence the term *spontaneous credit* may be used.

Current Liabilities are deducted from Current Assets for financial purposes because only the net amount needs to be financed.

Accruals differ from payables only in the particular that no bill has been received but the expense has been incurred. Examples are utility services and payrolls.

Taxes Payable

Taxes Payable of $20,000 includes balances for taxes, both those payable based on returns filed and estimates for all types of taxes. Tax accruals are also included.

Dividends Payable

The balance is $6,000. Dividends declared by the board of directors, for both preferred and common, are charged to Retained Earnings and credited to this account. A legal liability exists. When payment is made, the account is charged.

NET CURRENT ASSETS

The balance is $380,000. The Net Current Assets balance is governed by its constituent elements. It is the amount that must be financed through debt and equity.

INVESTMENT IN SUBSIDIARY

The balance is $110,000. The Investment in Subsidiary account is debited with the subsidiary's earnings of $15,000, which are credited to a separate account—subsidiary income—and dividends of $5,000 are credited to the investment account. This treatment is known as the "equity method." Thus the account has increased by $10,000 net. The yield is $15,000 divided by the average investment of $105,000, or 14.3% before tax. However, the after-tax rate is:

Income	$15,000	100.00%
85% tax exclusion	12,750	
Taxable (15%)	2,250	
Tax at 50%	1,125	7.50%
Net	1,125	
Add back 85%	12,750	
Gain after tax	$13,875	92.50%
After tax yield	$13,875/$105,000 = 13.21%.	

This compares with the ROA for operating assets of 7.54% and for the company 7.78%. Thus this account raised ROA by 0.24% (7.78% − 7.54%). This illustrates the need to make all analysis net of tax and for careful definition of the ROA components.

PLANT & EQUIPMENT

Plant & Equipment	$1,125,000	
Less Depreciation Allowance	465,000	$660,000 net

Turnover ratios (P & E = Plant & Equipment) are:

$$\frac{\text{Sales}}{\text{Gross P \& E}} \quad \frac{\$2,100M}{\$1,125M} = 1.87$$

$$\frac{\text{Sales}}{\text{Net P \& E}} \quad \frac{\$2,100M}{\$ \ 660M} = 3.18$$

These ratios show sales dollars per dollar of fixed assets—gross or net—based on book amounts, usually historical cost. They are comparable with past and planned ratios, but such ratios are of questionable value.

Effective control rests on the capital expenditure program that guides all acquisitions and disposals. All fixed assets in use should be evaluated periodically for retention, replacement, or disposal. Analysis thus rests on current acquisition costs and disposal values. Book values are not relevant to the control process (but enter into calculation of gain or loss on disposition). Chapter 4 provides details.

Depreciation is the allocation of cost over useful life. Several methods are permissible. Depreciation is analyzed later in this chapter.

Restatement of book cost either to a current acquisition cost basis or by price-level adjustment to reflect inflation is not relevant to management. It is a current requirement for the published statements of larger companies, also discussed later in this chapter.

GOODWILL

The Goodwill balance of $45,000 is the cost of purchased goodwill attributable to the future, based on current management evaluation. When acquired, amortization is scheduled within a maximum span of 40 years.

DEFERRED TAX LIABILITY

The Deferred Tax Liability of $95,000 arises because income tax provision must be based on accrual income. If currently taxable income is less, the tax on the difference is credited to this account. In time, taxable income exceeds accrual income (reversal), and the excess of the actual tax over the accrual tax is charged to this liability account. These differences are known as "timing differences" and are said to "turn around." An example is the use of accelerated depreciation for tax returns and straight-line depreciation on the books. Permanent differences, such as goodwill amortization, reduce accrual income but are not tax deductible and are excluded from tax provision.

The actual future liability depends on unknown future events, such as the company's income and the tax code. The account may have a debt balance. It has no explicit cost, like Current Liabilities, so it is deducted to arrive at the amount that must be financed—Net Assets.

INCOME STATEMENT

The condensed form of Income Statement (Exhibit B) is sufficient for most financial purposes. Comparisons with past and planned results are desirable but are omitted here for convenience.

The primary concern of financial management is to insure that adequate systems of control exist and are being used effectively. Direct responsibility rests with operating management. Internal auditors and systems designers are essential to both groups. The public accountants evaluate the system of internal control (both accounting and management control systems) including the role of the internal auditors.

The Operating Profit—$138,000—reflects all continuing operations, with definable organization responsibility, supported by relevant details such as products, markets, customers, and sales channels. Other transactions (non-operating) are included in Other Income (Expense) to arrive at EBIT (earnings before interest and tax) of $158,000.

Net Income—$56,000—is from continuing operations in this case because the statement excludes relatively rare but often significant events: discontinued operations, extraordinary items, change in accounting principles, and error correction. Such items are expressed net of income tax.

Separate EPS is required, when applicable, for income from continuing operations and net income. Primary and fully diluted EPS may also be required.

A statement of Retained Earnings is included with Exhibit B to support the Balance Sheet and disclose all dividend declarations. Available to Common of $36,000 is used for ROE. Also, note that ROA is based on EBIT $158,000, less tax, or $79,000, which does not appear separately on the statement.

Relatively specialized equity type items are omitted: revaluation of long-term securities to market, foreign currency translation adjustments, error correction, and appraisal valuations.

When there are numerous transactions affecting the equity accounts, a separate (fourth) statement may be prepared.

FUNDS STATEMENT

The format in Exhibit C focuses on the interaction of financing—through equity and debt—and investing—in short-term and long-term assets. All items are coded to show source—Exhibits A and B—and amounts obtained by record analysis. Comparison with past and plan are omitted for simplicity.

This statement highlights the critical management decisions of asset investments by type and financing through debt and equity sources, less dividends. Both areas involve the balancing of profitability, risk, and liquidity in terms of company goals, strategy, and policy.

Funds provided by operations—$201,000—are available for management disposition, a significant number that is far different from the (accrual) net income of $56,000. The sale of stock—$20,000—less the preferred dividend of $20,000 leaves a balance of funds ($201,000) as a basis for a discretionary common Dividend, which is $6,000. The net equity increase of $195,000, plus an additional $50,000 from increased debt, provides a total of $245,000.

The total of $245,000 is summarized by principal type of investment. Capital expenditures of $230,000 are offset by the book value of disposals. The asset disposal gain of $45,000 is shown on B.

It is illuminating to consider several possible scenarios relative to investing and financing:

1. Pay no dividend and reduce debt. Would reduce leverage on ROE and improve liquidity. ROA unchanged.
2. Pay higher dividend and increase debt. Would increase leverage on ROE and reduce liquidity. ROA unchanged.
3. Pay no dividend and increase investments. If all acceptable investments have already been included, this is not an option.
4. Pay higher dividend and reduce investments. The approved investments are needed to meet sales and profit goals. Benefit of higher dividend questionable.
5. An increase in debt to support larger investment is not needed because all acceptable investments have been included. A debt decrease at the expense of approved investments would improve liquidity at the expense of growth goals.

The effect of these scenarios on the price of stock is speculative, depending on the market's perception of the results relative to profitability, risk, and liquidity. The decisions may also be guided by the ownership position (both stock and options) of members of the board of directors.

The question of a new common stock issue would be evaluated in terms of capital structure and goals, as explained in Chapter 12. This is a major, and infrequent, decision involving large amounts and heavy expenses.

Liquidity must be carefully monitored on a timely basis. As results occur and prospects change, plans may have to be revised relative to dividends, borrowings, and investments. Borrowing terms may change and new investment opportunities could develop.

Quarterly, or monthly, fund statements showing results compared with plan are needed from all management segments of the company.

THREE DEBATABLE TOPICS

The Interest Method for Depreciation

Depreciation expense is the allocation of the cost of a depreciable asset over time. The expense is included in product cost for production assets and in period expense for all other assets. Certain methods are allowed by GAAP and the tax code. The interest method, not sanctioned by GAAP, is the procedure that would record depreciation on the books in a manner consonant with that used for investment analysis to determine NPV and yield. For example, consider an asset cost, $29,906; five-year life; no salvage; annual cash gain, $10,000; and interest, 20%, as follows:

Year	Annual Gain	20% on Balance	Principal Reduction	Principal Balance, $29,906
1	$10,000	$ 5,981	$ 4,019	$25,887
2	10,000	5,178	4,822	21,065
3	10,000	4,213	5,787	15,278
4	10,000	3,056	6,944	8,334
5	10,000	1,666	8,334	0
	$50,000	$20,094	$29,906	

The $50,000 total gain recoups the outlay of $29,906 and provides $20,094 more, at a constant annual rate of 20% on the reducing principal balance. The principal reduction column is the equivalent of depreciation. The amounts increase while interest (20% on the balance) decreases. This is known as the "level payment method," generally used for mortgages. For financial purposes, the entire life is dealt with as a single period.

Yield, or interest, can be determined without the detail schedule, using present value tables:

$$\$29,906/\$10,000 = f \ 2.9906; \ 5 \text{ years} = 20\%$$

Approved accounting methods include:

SL (straight line): $29,906/5 years = $5,981.20 per year, or 5 years at 20% per year.

SYD (sum-of-the-years-digits) Short-cut method: 1 plus 5 = 6 × 2½ = 15; $29,906/15 years = $1,993.733 = for year 5 only:

Year	Fraction	Dollars
1	$\frac{5}{15}$	9,969
2	$\frac{4}{15}$	7,975
3	$\frac{3}{15}$	5,981
4	$\frac{2}{15}$	3,987
5	$\frac{1}{15}$	1,994
		29,906

DDB (double declining balance): SL = 20%. DDB = 40%. Year 1 is 40% of $29,906 = $11,962.40. Year 2 is 40% of ($29,906 − $11,962) $17,944 = $7,178. Year 3 is 40% of ($17,944 − $7,178) $10,766 = $4,306. The balance is now $6,460 ($10,766 − $4,306), which is booked by SL at $3,230 each year to achieve full write-off.

Tax Code

Frequent changes are made in the tax code, but one tax proposal for a future year is used for illustration, with computations omitted, in the following table.

Schedule of Annual Depreciation by Five Methods

Year	Interest	SL	SYD	DDB	Tax Code Amount	Tax Code Percent Applied to $29,906
1	$ 4,019	$ 5,981	$ 9,969	$11,962	$ 5,383	18%
2	4,822	5,981	7,975	7,178	9,868	33
3	5,787	5,981	5,981	4,306	7,476	25
4	5,944	5,981	3,987	3,230	4,786	16
5	8,334	5,982	1,994	3,230	2,393	8
	$29,906	$29,906	$29,906	$29,906	$29,906	100%

The Net Assets balance each year is $29,906 less depreciation to date.

Use of the interest method on the books would provide much less depreciation in the earlier years and help to eliminate the troublesome problem of reconciling financial profitability (yield), used to make investment decisions, with book amounts (ROA), used to measure performance. This is explored in Chapter 4 relative to the accounting rate of return.

The interest and SL methods are compared for Year 1 and Year 5.

	Year 1		Year 5	
	Interest	SL	Interest	SL
Gain	$10,000	$10,000	$10,000	$10,000
Depr.	$ 4,019	$ 5,981	$ 8,334	$ 5,981
Balance	$ 5,981	$ 4,019	$ 1,666	$ 4,019
Asset	$29,906	$29,906	$ 8,334	$ 5,981
Yield	20.0%	13.4%	20.0%	67.2%

The interest and DDB methods are also compared for Year 1 and Year 5:

	Year 1		Year 5	
	Interest	DDB	Interest	DDB
Gain	$10,000	$10,000	$10,000	$10,000
Depr.	$ 4,019	$11,962	$ 8,334	$ 3,230
Balance	$ 5,981	−$ 1,962	$ 1,666	$ 6,770
Asset	$29,906	$29,906	$ 8,334	$ 3,230
Yield	20.00%	− 6.56%	20.00%	209.60%

These schedules illustrate the problem that affects all ROA analysis. For instance, old plants are more fully depreciated and have lower asset bases and higher ROA's that are misleading.

Companies generally take the highest deduction allowed by the tax code to minimize current tax payments. The government fiscal policy is to encourage capital investment. Later tax payments are higher, but the difference constitutes interest free capital. At the same time, many companies use SL depreciation on the books and for financial reports, to show higher income in the early years of asset life. Financial analysis is made with the actual tax amounts to determine accurate cash flows by years necessary to compute true yields.

The accounting concept, illusory at best, is to try to specify the actual loss in "value" attributable to usage on a periodic basis and to "match" revenue and expense. The financial approach is to measure profitability based on the discount rate, for both proposed asset acquisition and retention of owned assets, calculated for the single period of estimated life.

Inflation and Analysis

The handling of inflation in financial analysis is easier said than done. Investment decisions require estimates of cash flows for all periods and for each item, for example, labor hours and wages, material quantities and prices, utility charges, taxes, insurance, rent, freight, travel, supplies, communication, sales commission, advertising, promotion, and fees.

The estimated future cash flows should include a factor for price change, or inflation, for each item for each year, but cash flow estimates are difficult at best. Current cash outlays are determinable and do not require adjustment. The discount rate used to express future dollars in terms of present dollars is the current borrowing rate less the current tax rate and also need not be adjusted.

The current interest rate for a given company and period includes a basic rate (real rate) of, say, 5%; a rate for expected inflation of, say, 6%; and a risk differential of, say, 4%, for a total of 15%. U.S. Treasury bonds might be 11%, the prime rate 12%, and the company rate 15%. With a current marginal tax rate of 6% (40% of 15%), the discount rate is 9% (60% of 15%). Higher discount rates depress the amount of profitable investments, slowing down growth.

In practice, estimating future cash flows is often an approximation that may require expression in ranges with probabilities, with no explicit separate recognition of inflation.

Book profits are said to be overstated, using historical costs, when charges based on current replacement costs for depreciation and inventories would be higher (they could also be lower). Investment decisions are not affected because they relate to the future. The only link is the use of current cash disposal value for an asset to be replaced, net of taxes.

Some 1,500 companies are currently required to publish memorandum computations adjusting book results for inflation (using CPI-U [Consumer Price Index for urban consumers]), referred to as "constant dollars," and for current replacement costs, called "current dollars." This trial is to explore the possible usefulness of such estimates to the investing public. Results to date are anomalous. The information is not useful for management decisions. Some companies, however, do recognize in their dividend policies the need of stockholders to keep up with inflation.

Capitalization of Interest

Interest expense is deducted from income as incurred (accrual basis). It is a period expense related to financing only. It is a major part of liquidity analysis and governs the effect of leverage on ROE. A primary ratio is EBIT/interest expense.

The FASB now requires, under certain circumstances, that interest be charged directly to assets, rather than expense, such as inventories and construction costs. The rules are detailed, complex, arbitrary, subject to interpretation, and controversial. (FASB approval was by a minimum margin.)

Any capitalized interest becomes a part of the asset cost and appears in cost of sales over time without separate identity, as material cost and depreciation. The amount of interest in these expenses is not disclosed, but disclosure is to be made for the total amount of interest incurred and the amount capitalized. Interest expense currently capitalized could be restated for analysis, but the amount of capitalized expense included in current expenses would be indeterminate. This ruling rests on the faulty premise that interest is an operating outlay rather than the cost of money.

An example of financial analysis with all interest expensed is (D/E = Debt/Equity; NI = Net Interest):

	Debt (15%)	$ 80	
	Equity	120	D/E $80/$120 = 67%
	Capital	$200	
1.	EBIT	$ 48	$48/$12 = 4 interest coverage
	Interest (15% of $80)	12	
	EBT	36	
	Tax	18	
	NI	$ 18	$18/$120 = 15% ROE
			($48 − $24) $24/$200 = 12% ROA

If half the interest is capitalized:

2.	EBIT	$ 48	$48/$6 = 8 (cf. 4)
	Interest	6	
	EBT	42	
	Tax	21	
	NI	$ 21	$21/$120 = 17.5% ROE (cf. 15%)
			$24/$200 = 12.0% ROA—no change

Thus, interest coverage doubles, ROA is unchanged, and ROE increases from 15.0% to 17.5%.

As the capitalized interest is expensed over time, in unknown amounts, EBIT is decreased. If it is assumed that, in a given period, EBIT is reduced by write-off of interest charges of $6, and total new interest incurred of $12 is capitalized for $6 and $6 expensed:

3.	EBIT ($48 − $6)	$ 42	$42/$6 = 7 (cf. 8)
	Interest	6	
	EBT	36	
	Tax	18	
	NI	$ 18	$18/$120 = 15.0% ROE (cf. 17.5%)
			$21/$200 = 10.5% ROA (cf. 12.0%)

Compared with the first example, ROE remains 15.0% but ROA drops from 12.0% to 10.5%, a higher leverage ratio.

Finally, if $6 of interest is expensed but no interest is capitalized:

4.	EBIT	$ 42	$42/$12 = 3.5
	Interest	12	
	EBT	30	
	Tax	15	
	NI	$ 15	$15/$120 = 12.5% ROE
			$21/$120 = 10.5% ROA

An alternative economic concept has sound logic—capitalize the cost of all debt and equity at a fair rate of return on total capital. In theory, any income over this amount would be economic profit—and competition would be attracted—and shortfalls would indicate failure to remain competitive. It is not clear how the capitalization rate would be determined or how the entries would be made. There is no apparent advantage over the present determination of ROA and ROE, which are directly comparable with the returns for other companies and industry groups as well as with company profitability goals.

Interest capitalization is one of numerous accounting attempts to introduce financial concepts into the records unnecessarily, complicating accounting and confusing analysis, without discernible benefit to the public.

CHAPTER 3

Financial Planning

MAKING CHOICES FOR THE FUTURE

PROJECTED INCOME STATEMENT AND RETAINED EARNINGS

Exhibit I shows the projected amounts for next year compared with this year (Exhibit B, Chapter 1), the increase or decrease, all with percentages based on sales. The final column is the percentage of change. Projection of the Balance Sheet and Funds Statement are given in Exhibits II and III. These projections are the result of careful preparation throughout the company but are subject to evaluation by top management before acceptance as approved financial plans.

Sales are projected to increase by 19.0% to $2,500. Cost of Sales at standard is given separately to show the margin increase from 30.0% to 31.0%. Standard costs are the basic measure of product cost and provide a history reflecting both changing prices of inputs (inflation) and productive efficiency (utilization of capacity, learning curve, rate of output per man-hour). Standard product costs are used to determine product profit margins, a measure of marketing performance. The incremental margin change is relatively large—up $145, 36.3% of the sales increase ($400). Thus the sale change percentage of 19.0% yields 23.0% at the standard margin.

Production costs are measured at standard, as shown, but a prudent allowance for variance is made for financial purposes, projected at $25. All other expenses drop from 22.0% to 20.0% on sales but increase by 8.2%. Operating Profit becomes 10.0% of Sales, and the $112 increase is a high 28.0% on incremental sales, or an increase of 81.2% over this year. The projection is ambitious. It is designed to provide a measure of performance by operating management and is also the basis for financial planning.

Other Income and Expense decline slightly, but EBIT increases by 67.1%, or 26.5% on incremental sales. Interest Expense increases from 2.1% to 2.6%, a 39.1% rise. Thus EBT to sales increases from 5.4% to 8.0%, which is 22.0% incrementally. Taxes are kept at 50.0% of EBT (a combination of both actual and deferred tax provisions). Projected Net Income is 4.0% of sales and 11.0% of the increment—a jump of 78.6%. This plan requires the determination of the asset support required, and ROA can then be determined, as shown later.

Retained earnings show the obligatory Preferred dividend of $20. Available to common rises to $80 and provides for a large Common dividend—$30, or five times the current $6 rate. Thus the net increase in equity is $50.

This projection rests on the validity of the $250 Operating Profit—10.0% of sales. If this were to remain at the current rate of 6.6%, there would be $165 (6.6% of $2,500) or $85 less than the projection of $250. Plans for investment and dividends would be jeopardized. However, performance could also be better than expected due to greater product demand and more efficient production. Thus performance must be closely monitored, expectations revised, and plans changed periodically. Contingency plans prepared in advance are a prudent way to achieve prompt and flexible response.

Exhibit I
Projected Income Statement and Retained Earnings (in Thousands)

	(Exhibit B) This Year		Projected for Next Year		Increase (Decrease)		Percentage of Change
Sales	$2,100	100.0%	$2,500	100.0%	$400	100.0%	19.0
Cost of Sales—at standard	1,470		1,725		255		17.3
Margin—at standard	630	30.0	775	31.0	145	36.3	23.0
Variances	30		25		(5)		
Gross Margin	600	28.6	750	30.0	150	37.5	25.0
Expenses	462	22.0	500	20.0	38	9.5	8.2
Operating Profit	138	6.6	250	10.0	112	28.0	81.2
Other Income (Expense):							
Subsidiary income	15		40				
Asset disposal gain	45		14				
Amortization—GW	(40)		(40)		(6)		
	20		14		(6)		
EBIT	158	7.5	264	10.6	106	26.5	67.1
Interest Expense	46	2.1	64	2.6	18	4.5	39.1
EBT	112	5.4	200	8.0	88	22.0	78.6
Income Taxes	56		100		44		
Net Income	$ 56	2.7%	$ 100	4.0%	$ 44	11.0%	78.6
Retained Earnings:							
Deduct Preferred dividend	$ 20		$ 20		$ —		—
Available to common	36		80		44		122.2%
Common dividend	6		30		24		400.0%
Net addition	30		50		20		66.7%
Opening balance	205		235		30		
Ending balance	$ 235		$ 285		$ 50		

Exhibit II
Projected Summary Balance Sheet (in Thousands)

Net Assets		(Exhibit A) This Year	Projected for Next Year	Increase (Decrease)
		Ending Balances		
Net Current Assets	Subtotal	$ 380	$ 400	$ 20
Investment in Subsidiary	Subtotal	110	120	10
Plant & Equipment		1,125	1,335	210
Less Depr. Allowance		465	535	70
Net	Subtotal	660	800	140
Goodwill	Subtotal	45	5	(40)
Deduct: Deferred Tax Liability	Subtotal	(95)	(125)	(30)
Net Assets	Total	$1,100	$1,200	$100
Capital				
Debt (includes current portion):				
Bank Loan (16%)		$ 140	$ 140	$ —
Notes Payable (18%)		50	50	—
Bonds Payable (10%)		260	220	(40)
Equipment Loan (14⅔%)		—	90	90
Total Debt	Subtotal	450	500	50
Equity				
Preferred Stock (10%)		200	200	—
Common Stock:				
Paid-in Total		215	215	—
Retained Earnings		235	285	50
Common Equity		450	500	50
Total Equity	Subtotal	650	700	50
Capital	Total	$1,100	$1,200	$100

RISK—ESTIMATING PROFIT RANGES

Projected operations reflect point estimates, which presumably lie within some range of possible outcomes. Revenue projections may be too optimistic or unduly conservative. Projected costs may harbor secret reserves or reflect a demanding level of efficiency too difficult to reach.

It is possible, but not necessarily practical, to establish revenue and expense ranges with probabilities in support of the point estimates. For example, if the point estimate is: $100 revenue less expense $60 equals $40 profit, and the

Exhibit III
Projected Funds Statement (in Thousands)

Financing	(Exhibit C) This Year		Projected for Next Year		Increase (Decrease)
Equity:					
Net income		$ 56		$100	$44
Items not affecting funds:					
Add depreciation	$ 90		$100		
amortization—goodwill	40		40		
deferred taxes	25		30		
	155		170		$ 15
Deduct equity income from					
subsidiary	15		40		
less dividend received	5		30		
	10		10		0
		145		160	15
Funds provided by operations		201		260	59
Sale of common stock		20		0	(20)
		221		260	39
Preferred dividends		20		20	0
		201		240	39
Common dividends		6		30	(24)
Net equity increase		$195		$210	$15
Debt:					
Bank loan	$ 40		$ 0		$(40)
Notes payable	50		0		(50)
Bonds payable	(40)		(40)		0
Equipment loan	—		90		90
Net debt increase		50		50	0
Financing increase		$245		$260	$15
Investing					
Net Current Assets		$ 35		$ 20	$(15)
Plant & Equipment less disposals at	$230		$240		$(10)
book value	20		0		20
		210		240	30
Investing Increase		$245		$260	$15

revenue range is ± $20 and the expense range is ± $10, then there are nine outcomes to be evaluated, each with a probability of occurrence.

	Revenue	Expense	Profit	Probability	
	$120	$50	$70	5%	$ 3.5
	120	60	60	10	6.0
	120	70	50	10	5.0
	100	50	50	15	7.5
Point	100	60	40	20	8.0
	100	70	30	15	4.5
	80	50	30	10	3.0
	80	60	20	10	2.0
	80	70	10	5	0.5
				100%	$40.0

Thus the point profit of $40 has a ± $30 range ($10 to $70). The probable summary outcome at $40 equals the point outcome. (The ranges and percents are proportional for this example but in practice would be skewed.) The significant news is the 15% chance of a profit of $20 or less (and the 40% chance of $30 profit or less). This downside risk exposure usually outweighs any degree of upside potential; 15% chance of $60 profit or more.

This type of trial could be useful for evaluating ranges of possible results for new products and new markets. Personal risk attitudes that are expressed help to foster constructive communication and may lead to more thorough research and planning.

ANALYTICAL TECHNIQUES

Several useful analytical techniques are presented because of their broad applicability in planning and budgeting.

Break-Even Analysis (B/E)

The following is an example of break-even analysis:

	Units	at	Total	Percent
Sales (S)	600	$5	$3,000	100
Variable Cost (VC)	600	2	1,200	40
Variable Margin (VM)	600	$3	1,800	60
Fixed Costs (FC)			1,500	50
Profit (Pr.)			$ 300	10

Taxes can be introduced into the table but seldom have any effect on the purpose of the analysis at this stage.

Break-even refers to zero profit. In this example, with zero profit and FC $1,500, VM is $1,500. With VM unit at $3 each, the total is 500 units for zero profit, or $2,500 sales. VC varies directly with sales, and FC remains constant for all volumes.

	Units	at	Total	Percent
S	500	$5	$2,500	100
VC	500	2	1,000	40
VM	500	$3	1,500	60
FC			1,500	60
Pr.			$ 0	0

Break-even is 100 units less than 600, a safety margin of 16.7%.
   B/E can be calculated two ways:

$$\frac{FC}{VM}\ \frac{\$1,500}{\$\quad 3} = 500 \text{ units } (\times \$5 = \$2,500 \text{ sales})$$

$$\frac{FC}{VM}\ \frac{\$1,500}{60\%} = \$2,500\ (\div \$5 = 500 \text{ units})$$

The percentage method is necessary for product groupings where per unit sales and variable costs are not stated because they are statistical and not relevant.

B/E is convenient for a variety of problems in profitability analysis, including the elasticity of demand. Six examples are given, all compared with the original example.

1. What is the effect of reducing the price 10% ($5.00 to $4.50) and increasing units 20% (600 to 720)?

	Units	at	Total	Percent
S	720	$4.50	$3,240	100.0
VC	720	2.00	1,440	
VM	720	$2.50	1,800	55.6
FC			1,500	
Pr.			$ 300	9.3

Profit remains unchanged at $300. Sales are higher by 8.0% ($3,240 − $3,000 = $240). B/E = $1,500/$2.50 = 600 units. The safety margin is 120 units/720 units or 16.7%. More assets (receivables and inventories) may be needed, lowering ROA, as analyzed later.

2. What is the effect of reducing units 10% (600 to 540) and increasing the price 10% ($5.00 to $5.50)?

	Units	at	Total	Percent
S	540	$5.50	$2,970	100.0
VC	540	2.00	1,080	
VM	540	$3.50	1,890	63.6
FC			1,500	
Pr.			$ 390	13.1

S decreases but Pr. increases from $300 to $390. B/E is $1,500.00/$3.50 = 428.6 units. Safety margin is 540 − 428.6 = 111.4 units, or 20.6%.

3. What is the effect of increasing sales to 700 units and increasing FC to $1,800?

	Units	at	Total	Percent
S	700	$5	$3,500	100.0
VC	700	2	1,400	
VM	700	$3	2,100	60.0
FC			1,800	
Pr.			$ 300	8.6

Profit remains unchanged but sales increase. B/E is $1,800/$3 = 600 units, a safety margin of 14.3% (100 units/700 units). The added FC might be for sales promotion to obtain higher market share.

4. What is the effect of reducing VC from $2.00 to $1.60 by increasing FC by $300 to $1,800?

	Units	at	Total	Percent
S	600	$5.00	$3,000	100
VC	600	1.60	900	
VM	600	$3.40	2,040	68
FC			1,800	
Pr.			$ 240	8

The profit loss is $60 ($300 to $240). B/E is $1,800/$3.40 = 529.4 units. The safety margin is 70.6 units/600 units = 11.8%. This illustrates the topic of reducing VC by higher FC. To maintain the Pr. of $300, FC could only be $1,740 ($60 less), or VC would have to drop to $1.50 per unit. These parameters help to determine the more promising approaches.

5. To increase Pr. from $300 to $600, what increase in units is needed?

Pr.	$ 600
FC	1,500
VM	2,100
Unit VM	$ 3 = 700 units

The increase from 600 units to 700 units = 16.7%.

6. What price provides $600 Pr. with the same volume?

Pr.	$ 600	
FC	1,500	$2,100
Units		600 = $3.50 VM
		2.00 VC
		$5.50 Price

The sales price must increase 10% ($0.50/$5.00).

The B/E method is a practical and powerful tool for exploring price and cost interrelationships to illuminate desirable alternatives. However, the technique is linear, and all factors must be carefully defined. In the long run all costs are variable, and in the short run all costs are fixed. Definition of VC and FC is arbitrary, resting on many assumptions. The effect of volume changes is incremental. Higher volume lowers unit FC only up to a point; when added capacity is needed, unit FC will rise. Time frames must be assumed to derive VC and FC, and volume must remain in the range that is relevant. Budgets and standards used for product costing and expense control may require recasting to apply logically to the analysis. Each analysis requires individual attention, with all assumptions fully expressed.

Incremental Analysis—Operations

The incremental approach rests on analysis of the changes (increments) caused by the alternatives under study. There are three examples.

Example 1—Sell to a new class of customer with high credit risk?

	Increment
Sales	$12,000
Costs (variable and fixed)	8,000
Gross margin (GM)	4,000
Credit and collection	600
	3,400
Bad debts (20% of $12,000)	2,400
Profit (before tax)	$ 1,000
Receivables—90 days ($\frac{1}{4}$ of 360 days)	$ 3,000
Less bad debts (20% of $3,000)	600
Net receivables	2,400
Inventory increase	2,000
Assets increase	$ 4,400
ROA (before tax) $1,000/$4,400 =	22.7%

The result may be attractive for a borrowing rate below 22.7%, to the extent of the leverage and to the degree that the estimates are dependable. Estimated ranges for each item would permit risk evaluation.

The bad debt estimate reduces both profits and assets. Failure to reduce receivables would produce ROA of $1,000 divided by $5,000, or 20%. Analysis can also be made on the basis of receivables at cost by deducting the GM: net receivables of $2,400 (with profit) become $1,600 net at cost, for a total of $3,600 with the $2,000 inventory increase. ROA is then $1,000/$3,600 = 27.8%. Analysis should be logical, consistent, and material in amount, relevant to its purpose. Small changes can have large effects on the results.

Such analysis can disclose highly profitable market segments and also preclude ventures that are unsound. Existing segments can also be analyzed for retention, revision, or elimination. This two-front attack could have a dramatic impact on ROA—profit increase and asset decrease.

A brief outline of the possibilities follows:

	Now	Drop	Revised	And Add	New	Net Change
Sales	$10,000	−$2,000	$ 8,000	+$4,000	$12,000	+$2,000
GM	$ 1,000	+$ 500	$ 1,500	+$1,500	$ 3,000	+$2,000
Sales %	10.00%		18.75%	37.50%	25.00%	100.00%
Assets	$20,000	−$5,000	$15,000	+$5,000	$20,000	$ 0
ROA	5%		10%	30%	15%	—

Thus ROA is tripled—5% to 15%—with no increase in assets. Many combinations are possible.

Incremental analysis should be carried into all segments, and to the smallest measurable parts, on a regular basis to constantly monitor changing relationships and to seize new opportunities.

Example 2—An opportunity to enter into a private brand contract with a major company.

	Increment
Sales	$12,000
Cost	10,800
GM	1,200
Expenses	600
	600
Bad debts (none)	0
Profit (before tax)	$ 600
Receivables—30 days ($\frac{1}{12}$)	$ 1,000
Inventory increase	600
Assets increase	$ 1,600

ROA $600/$1,600 = 37.5% (before tax)

Sales are guaranteed by the customer, with a 10% GM. There is no credit risk and pay is prompt. Inventory is low because shipments can be made as goods are finished in shippable quantities.

The assumption of existing capacity is used for this high ROA, together with no better alternative use (opportunity cost). If capital expenditure is a requisite, the analysis to be used is given in Chapter 4.

Example 3—Extend credit terms from 30 to 72 days to all customers (a form of non-price competition). Increase sales 25% from $12,000 to $15,000.

			Increment
Sales:			
New		$15,000	
Present		12,000	$3,000
GM			1,200
Credit expense			400
			800
Bad debts:			
$15,000 at 12%		$ 1,800	
$12,000 at 10%		$ 1,200	600
Profit (before tax)			$ 200
Receivables:			
15,000—72d (1/5)		$3,000	
12,000—30d (1/12)		1,000	
		2,000	
Less bad debts ($360 − $100)		260	$1,740
Inventory increase			760
Asset increase			$2,500

ROA $200/$2,500 = 8% (before tax). This result is unattractive.

Profitability can be eroded by plans to increase assets, as above, without sufficient gain, for example, higher inventories to expedite delivery, shipments on consignment, liberal return policy, slack collection efforts, and billing delays.

Incremental Analysis—ROA

Three combinations demonstrate the method:

	Profit	**Assets**	**ROA**	
Present	$400	$2,000	20%	Base
Proposal (each based on present):				
1. Add	100	500	20	
Result	500	2,500	20	No change
2. Increase	150	500	30	
Result	550	2,500	22	Higher
3. Decrease	130	500	26	
Result	270	1,500	18	Lower

The following example shows the effect of a proposal with a lower ROA than now exists:

	Now	Proposal	Result
Profit	$ 600	$ 300	$ 900
Assets	$2,000	$1,500	$3,500
ROA	30.0%	20.0%	25.7%

The proposal offers 20.0% but lowers the average from 30.0% to 25.7%. However, the proposal is desirable if the borrowing rate is under 20.0%—positive leverage is provided.

Rejection of proposals that lower ROA overall but provide ROA over the borrowing rate impede profitable growth.

Another example illustrates a proposal with a still lower ROA:

	Now	Proposal	Result
Profit	$ 600	$ 100	$ 700
Assets	$2,000	$1,000	$3,000
ROA	30.0%	10.0%	23.3%

This proposal is not acceptable for a borrowing rate at 10% or over.

An additional calculation clarifies the analysis, using a 15% borrowing rate:

	Now	ROA	Proposal	ROA	Result	ROA
Profit	$ 600		$ 120		$ 720	
Assets	2,000	30%	600	20%	2,600	27.7%
Required (15%)	300	15	90	15	390	15.0
Profit Gain	300	15	30	5	330	12.7
Total	$ 600		$ 120		$ 720	

The 20% proposal provides a real profit gain of $30, despite the drop in ROA. When the profit gain is zero, ROA and the borrowing rate are equal. This method shows the gain over the borrowing rate in dollars and thus helps to demonstrate the real profit despite the resulting lower ROA.

Leverage Ratios

Operating and financial leverage ratios may be developed to determine profit increases attributable to assumed sales increases but only within the relevant range (time and volume governing the VC and FC assumptions).

Sales	$1,000
VC 40%	400
VM 60%	600
FC	400
EBIT	200
Interest	100
EBT (10%)	$ 100

$600/$200 = 3 times (DOL—degree of operating leverage)

$200/$100 = 2 times (DFL—degree of financial leverage)

$600/$100 = 6 times (DCL—degree of combined leverage)

Formula:

$$DOL\ (3) \times DFL\ (2) = DCL\ 6$$

With FC zero:

$$EBIT = \$600\ and\ DOL = 1\ time\ (\$600/\$600)$$

With Interest zero:

$$EBT = \$200\ and\ DFL = 1\ time\ (\$200/\$200)$$

With both zero:

$$DCL = 1\ time\ (\$600/\$600)$$

The above examples illustrate no leverage.

From a low base, increases are relatively high:

VM	$600	
FC	450	4 times DOL
EBIT	150	
Interest	125	6 times DFL
EBT	25	

($600/$25) = 24 times DCL

Application: If sales increase 20%, what is the EBT increase? 20% × 6 times DCL = 120%. Or, sales are up $200 and EBT is up $120. Proof is:

Sales	$1,200
VC 40.0%	480
VM 60.0%	720
FC	400
EBIT	320
Interest	100
EBT (18.3%)	220

Sales have increased $200 and EBT $120—120% on $100.
The new leverage ratios are:

$$\text{DOL } \$720/\$320 = 2.25 \text{ times}$$

$$\text{DFL } \$320/\$220 = 1.45 \text{ times}$$

$$\text{DCL } \$720/\$220 = 3.27 \text{ times}$$

The ratios change for each increment and get progressively smaller: In the example above, sales increase 50% × 6 times DCL = 300%.

Sales	$1,000	+50% or $500 =	$1,500
VM 60%	600		900
EBIT	200		500
EBT	100	+ 300% or $300 = $	400
DOL	600/200 = 3 times		900/500 = 1.8 times
DFL	200/100 = 2 times		500/400 = 1.25 times
DCL	600/100 = 6 times		900/400 = 2.25 times

It appears simpler and safer to make each incremental analysis on an independent basis, specifically tailored to the situation. The leverage ratio approach requires great care and does not seem to be worth the effort.

PROJECTED SUMMARY BALANCE SHEET

Net Current Assets—increase $20, in support of $400 sales increase. Individual accounts omitted.

Investment in Subsidiary—increase of $10 reflects equity in earnings of $40 shown in Exhibit I less $30 dividend.

Plant & Equipment—increase $210, and

Depreciation Allowance—increase $70. Both reflect a $30 reduction for fully depreciated equipment, so gross acquisitions are $240 and provision for depreciation, $100. The equipment sale at $14 (book value zero) appears in Exhibit I as Asset disposal gain.

Goodwill—amortized $40 down to $5 current value.

Deferred Tax Liability—$30 increase. Current tax liability, $70. Total tax provision, $100.

Net Assets—increase $100 to $1,200, balanced by $1,200 Capital.

Bank Loan—no change. Could include advances and repayments within the year.

Notes Payable—unchanged.

Bonds Payable—reduced by $40 for current instalment.

Equipment Loan—for $90 at midyear. Total Interest Expense of $64 on the Income Statement (Exhibit I) is calculated:

Bank Loan—16% on $140	=	$22.4
Notes Payable—18% on $50	=	9.0
Bonds payable—10% on $260	=	26.0
Equipment Loan—14⅔%		
on $90 (6 months)	=	6.6
		$64.0

Preferred Stock—unchanged.

Common Stock—unchanged for Paid-in Total. Increase in Retained Earnings, $50 (Exhibit I), based on $80 Available to common less $30 dividend.

Capital—increases $100—$50 Debt and $50 Common Equity—to $1,200.

Liquidity Evaluation

D/E Ratio	This Year	Projected
D	$450	$500
E	$650	$700
	69.2%	71.4%

There is a slight increase. Both D and E increased $50. The times interest earned ratio is:

	This Year	Projected
EBIT	$158	$264
Interest	$ 46	$ 64
	3.4×	4.1

The coverage is improved. If EBIT stays at $158 and interest is $64, the ratio is only 2.5—very low. However, estimated ranges for EBIT indicate a low of $192, or 3.0 ($192/$64), which is acceptable. If lower sales and profit develop during the year, loans and interest could be reduced to preserve liquidity.

The preferred dividend of $20 requires $40 earnings before tax. Adding $64 interest makes $104 fixed charges. The EBIT of $264 divided by $104 equals 2.54. For this year the ratio is 1.84, or $158 divided by $86 ($40 plus $46). Other fixed charges can be included if relevant.

The D/E ratio can also be based on the stock market values. If $700 book equity has a market value of $500 (71.4%), the ratio is D $500/E $500 = 100%. Also, the $264 EBIT may be increased by $160 for items not affecting funds (Exhibit III) to $424. The coverage ratio is 6.6, or $424/$64. The concern of management, however, is funds control first, followed by cash control, to be examined later.

The Current Ratio and the Acid Test Ratio are not computed because they mean little to management. They are used primarily by credit analysts who have access only to published amounts. The calculations rest on some arbitrary assumptions about the timing of asset conversion to cash and liability payments. The time period is usually one year. Bookkeeping cut-offs can have an impact. For example:

	Books	Add Late Invoice	New	Add Deferred Tax Liability	New
CA	$300	$100	$400	$200	$600
CL	$100	$100	$200	$200	$400
Ratio	3		2		1.5

The crux of liquidity is the continuing inflow of cash to meet planned needs plus a cushion to absorb temporary contingencies.

Profitability Analysis—ROA and ROE

Taken from Exhibit I:

	Before Tax	Tax	Net
EBIT	$264	$132	$132
Interest Expense	64	32	32
EBT	$200	$100	100
Preferred dividend			20
Available to common			$ 80

The measurement bases are Balance Sheet averages (Exhibit II):

Net Assets	$1,150
less Debt	475
= Total Equity	675
Preferred Stock	200
Common Equity	475

	Projected	This Year
ROA $\dfrac{EBIT}{Net\ Assets}$	$\dfrac{\$\ 132}{\$1,150} = 11.48\%$	$\dfrac{\$\ 79}{\$1,015} = 7.78\%\ ROA$
$\dfrac{Interest}{Total\ Debt}$	$\dfrac{\$\ 32}{\$475} = 6.74\%$	$\dfrac{\$\ 23}{\$400} = 5.75\%$ interest rate

The EBIT increase of $53 ($132 − $79) over net asset increase of $135 ($1,150 − $1,015, or $53/$135 = 39.3% incremental ROA—a big jump.)

	Projected	This Year
EBT Total Equity	$\frac{\$100}{\$675} = 14.81\%$	$\frac{\$ 56}{\$615} = 9.11\%$ equity rate
Incremental EBT Incremental Equity	$\frac{\$ 44}{\$ 60} = 73.3\%$	
Preferred dividend Preferred stock	$\frac{\$ 20}{\$200} = 10.0\%$	$\frac{\$ 20}{\$200} = 10.00\%$ preferred rate
ROE Available to Common Equity	$\frac{\$ 80}{\$475} = 16.84\%$	$\frac{\$ 36}{\$415} = 8.67\%$ *ROE*

The projected ROA of 11.48% becomes 14.81% total equity by interest leverage. Preferred leverage raises ROE to 16.84% or plus 5.36 points, far in excess of the current leverage from 7.78% to 8.67% (0.89 points).

The projection shows positive leverage for each item of debt, contrary to this year. The individual-item interest rates are 16.00%, 18.00%, 10.00%, 14⅔% (Exhibit II), before tax, and ROA of 11.48% net would be 22.96% before tax. The preferred also provides positive leverage at 10.00% compared with EBT 14.81% to provide 16.84% ROE.

The ROA equations are:

Projected:

$$\frac{S \quad \$2,500}{NA \ \$1,150} \times \frac{Pr. \ \$ \ 132}{S \quad \$2,500} = \frac{\$ \ 132}{\$1,150}$$

$$2.174 \qquad \times \ 5.28\% \qquad = 11.48\%$$

This Year:

$$\frac{S \quad \$2,100}{NA \ \$1,015} \times \frac{Pr. \ \$ \ 79}{S \quad \$2,100} = \frac{\$ \quad 79}{\$1,015}$$

$$2.069 \qquad \times \ 3.762\% \qquad = \ 7.78\%$$

Incremental:

$$\frac{S \quad \$400}{NA \ \$135} \times \frac{\$ \ 53}{\$400} = \frac{\$ \ 53}{\$135}$$

$$2.96 \qquad \times \ 13.25\% \qquad = 39.3\%$$

The incremental turnover rate times the incremental profit rate combine to provide an incremental ROA of 39.30%, moving the weighted average from 7.78% to 11.48%.

For operating analysis, the asset base should exclude Investment in Subsidiary, Goodwill, and Deferred Tax Liability, leaving an asset base of Net Current Assets and Plant & Equipment net (Exhibit II).

	This Year	Projected	Average
Net Current Assets	$ 380	$ 400	$ 390
Plant & Equipment—net	660	800	730
	$1,040	$1,200	$1,120

Projected operating profit should be used net of tax—$250 − $125 = $125. The ROA equation for operations is:

$$\frac{S}{NA} \; \frac{\$2{,}500}{\$1{,}120} \times \frac{Pr.}{S} \; \frac{\$\;125}{\$2{,}500} = \frac{\$\;125}{\$1{,}120}$$

$$2.232 \qquad \times \; 5.00\% \qquad = 11.16\%$$

Financial ROA (above) is:

$$2.174 \qquad \times \; 5.280\% \qquad = 11.480\%$$

The operations ROA should be decomposed into the lowest segments, or responsibility centers to which profits and assets can be identified or traced without allocation. To illustrate with three segments:

	Company Total	Home Office		Total Operations	Divisions 1	Divisions 2	Divisions 3
Profit	$ 132	− $ 7	=	$ 125	$ 90	$ 30	$ 5
Assets	$1,150	− $30	=	$1,120	$600	$300	$220
ROA	11.48%			11.16%	15.00%	10.00%	2.27%

Actual results can be compared with planned and prior performance. ROA may be carried down to lower centers of profit responsibility. Special ROA analysis can be made for categories such as products, customers, order size, and channel of distribution.

Interpretation must recognize the vagaries of accounting practice, such as historical amounts, allocations, accruals, and cut-offs. Performance evaluation rests on many factors outside of quantitative measurement and relates to long-term goals. A sharp distinction is needed between individual accountability and financial results—the best managers may have the worst divisions. Also, the figures can be manipulated and do not include actions not taken.

The effects of inflation, competition, and economic developments must be considered. However, aside from the question of management evaluation (subjective, political, variable) the central problem is investment (disinvestment), supported by financing to achieve goals relative to profitability, liquidity, and risk.

If the investment discount rate is, say, 8.00% net, all projects with yields over 8.00% increase profit (given acceptable risk and liquidity). Investments over 8.00% yield but under 15.00% would increase division 1 profits but lower ROA. For division 2, the range is from 8.00% to 10.00%. For division 3, investments yielding from 2.27% to 8.00% would increase ROA but are not acceptable. The objective is to make more profit than the cost of the funds to provide positive leverage and increase ROE. The alternative is to increase dividends so that the money is released for investment by the stockholders.

ROA analysis can be useful to aid both management evaluation of alternatives and the measurement of financial performance but only within the narrow and arbitrary limits of accounting practice that governs record keeping.

Risk Evaluation

The uncertainty of projected EBIT $264 affects both ROA and ROE—the greater the range, the greater the risk. It is constructive to estimate ranges and probabilities to illuminate possible developments. For example, with increments of $40 EBIT, you have:

EBIT ($)	144	184	224	264	304	344
After tax ($)	72	92	112	132	152	172
NA $1,150	(no range given for this example)					
ROA (on $1,150) (%)	6.26	8.00	9.74	11.48	13.22	14.96
Probability (%)	5	10	15	45	20	5

NA would change to some extent for changes in sales and in EBIT, with the effect of moderating the ROA ranges shown. The point estimate of ROA 11.48% is given a 45% chance. Upside potential of 25% goes to 14.96% ROA. Downside risk of 30% drops to ROA 6.26%.

If the ROA goal is 10.0%, these odds appear to be acceptable. With a 12.5% ROA goal, however, the odds are much longer. If it is necessary to reduce the ranges, some riskier projects would be eliminated, reducing both risk and profit, as well as growth—the classic trade-off that distinguishes managers and companies, as well as individual investors.

Companies are known for their risk posture. Overly conservative and overly risk-prone managers have their careers at risk if they are not successful.

Financial risk is affected by operating risk. The combination of the two is company risk; it varies considerably by companies within an industry and among industries. With high operating risk (toys) financial risk is low (little debt). With low operating risk (utilities) financial risk is high (large debt). If both are low, there may be an opportunity cost in the failure to use leverage. If both are high, the risk of insolvency is high. These effects on the market price of stock are moderated because investors can diversify away company risk (unsystematic risk) with relative ease and economy.

The example is continued for coverage ratios:

EBIT ($)	144	184	224	264	304	344
Interest ($)	64	64	64	64	64	64
Coverage ratio	2.25	2.88	3.50	4.12	4.75	5.37
Probability (%)	5	10	15	45	20	5

This appears acceptable if coverage over 3 times is the policy. With dropping EBIT, interest may also be reduced so that coverage is protected.

Introducing ROE, you have:

EBIT net	$72	$92	$112	$132	$152	$172
Interest net	32	32	32	32	32	32
Net Income	40	60	80	100	120	140
Preferred dividend	20	20	20	20	20	20
Available to Common	$20	$40	$ 60	$ 80	$100	$120
Common equity	$475 (no range given for this example)					
ROE	4.21%	8.42%	12.63%	16.84%	21.05%	25.26%
ROA (above)	6.26%	8.00%	9.74%	11.48%	13.22%	14.96%
Probability	5%	10%	15%	45%	20%	5%
Leverage difference:						
ROE − ROA	−2.05%	+0.42%	+2.89%	+5.36%	+7.83%	+10.30%
Ratio of ROE to ROA	0.67	1.05	1.30	1.47	1.59	1.69

There is about a 15% chance of small or negative leverage with 25% odds for extra high leverage.

All of the items could change with ongoing operations, and management can intervene or replan, if necessary. Perhaps the most flexible item is the dividend for common, which can be adjusted for liquidity protection. With less net income, equity is also less, but dividend reduction keeps the balance higher, and ROE is lower. Maintaining balance among all factors for profitability, liquidity, and risk as conditions change is an ongoing task calling for constant vigilance, flexibility, and judgment.

The estimates illustrated provide a degree of guidance to help resolve the planning decisions that are translated into budgets. Of great potential consequence, contingency planning is encouraged so that untoward events can be more readily handled. Actual results, both better and worse, are better understood when related to the ranges, moderating any tendency toward overreaction.

Financial planning requires some hedging to handle shocks and to preclude premature commitments to outlays for investments and dividends. Pressure for short-term results should be kept in perspective. Unrealistic goals should be avoided because they impair morale, lead to unsound decisions that penalize the future, and encourage "creative" accounting. It should be noted that control systems outside of accounting and finance are essential to guide performance in critical areas such as employee morale, maintenance, research and development, customer support, and market development.

PROJECTED FUNDS STATEMENT

In Exhibit III projected Net Income of $100 (accrual accounting) is increased by $160 for non-fund items, to provide $260—the *Funds* provided by operations. This is the amount of funds (not cash) at the disposal of management. No stock sale is planned. Preferred dividends of $20 will be paid. The projected balance of $240 will be used to pay Common dividends of $30, a large increase over the current $6, leaving $210 Net equity increase. Note that the $30 is related to the $240 available, as compared with the $100 Net income. Debt is projected to increase $50 net, to provide $260 in financing.

Investing is to increase Net Current Assets by $20 (includes cash) and fixed assets by $240, for a total of $260. This reflects a shift in emphasis—$15 down for Net Current Assets and $30 up for fixed assets. The capital expenditure budget is $240, compared with the current $230. Fully depreciated assets disposed of are projected at zero. The asset disposal gain appears in Exhibit I as Other Income ($14).

These amounts reflect funding decisions related to goals, strategies, and policies. Many alternatives are explored in arriving at these results, as well as those shown in Exhibits I and II. The final approved projections become a guide to all managers and for all decisions. They are supported by detailed plans, projects, budgets, and standards. The amounts are subject to modification throughout the year for changed results and new expectations. Thus the projections are a valuable and necessary tool despite the many limitations, assumptions, and difficulties in their preparation.

Several scenarios are now presented to describe the nature of the decision process for the major alternatives. Two items are held constant—$260 Funds provided by operations and $20 Net Current Assets, needed to support operations. The votes of the 11-member board are given. Descriptions are kept brief. The decisions reached rest on evaluations that are explained throughout the book.

Financing

A. Increase debt by more than $50 and use the increase to pay a larger common dividend (2 pro—9 con). Too risky for liquidity relative to debatable stockholder benefit.

B. Borrow less (than the $50 increase) and reduce the common dividend (4 pro—7 con). Improves liquidity more than needed at expense of stockholders' current benefit. (Neither degree of liquidity or dividend policy can be measured quantitatively relative to market values.)

C. Sell common stock to reduce debt and increase dividends (1 pro—10 con). Stock sale too expensive for small amounts. No need to reduce debt. Stock sale to pay larger dividend is poor financing, not beneficial to stockholders.

D. Buy common stock (treasury shares) and reduce common dividend (0 pro—11 con). Reduces company capital stock and has inequitable effect on stockholders.

E. Pay preferred dividend (11 pro—0 con).

Investing

A. Approve capital expenditure budget for $240 and the $20 for Net Current Assets (9 pro—2 con). These plans meet all criteria for investment.

B. Reduce investments in favor of slower growth and less operating risk and reduce debt to decrease financial risk (5 pro—6 con). Risk tolerable in combination as company risk, relative to growth goals and current outlook.

C. Reduce investments as in B but increase common dividend (3 pro—8 con). Favors short term over long term. Would affect company market image adversely.

D. Acceptable projects totaled $265, but $25 has been deferred for later evaluation to keep a safer liquidity position (10 pro—1 con). The extra growth attributable to the $25 deferred is not worth the added liquidity risk if the borrowing increase is raised to $75.

E. Accept the $265 project total and reduce common dividend from $30 to $5 (1 pro—10 con). This trade-off overvalues the future at an unacceptable increase in operating risk. The projected common dividend of $30 is subject to future approval based on developments, and it would not be prudent to reduce this amount now. The projected payout ratio is (Exhibit I) $30 to $80 available to common, or 37.5%, compared with the current $6 to $36, or 16.7%. The board is resolved to bring the dividends into line with industry practice (a subjective decision). The effect of dividend policy on market price remains indeterminate despite extensive analysis. Investors respond to portfolio choices on the basis of many factors—a subject for personal finance.

Factors affecting the dividend decision might include:

- Pressure from large stockholders (including board members)
- Risk attitudes toward growth and debt
- Preference for present over future payment as hedge against uncertainty (the bird-in-hand dividend now compared with future dividend possibilities)
- Thwarting of corporate raiders by reducing cash and appealing to stockholders
- Signaling of confidence in the future
- Movement toward better record to support future stock issue
- Movement in line with industry practice
- Gearing of amounts relative to inflation to protect stockholders' purchasing power

The following table summarizes votes of the board of directors on the projections, relative to amounts adopted (UP = more than, DOWN = less than amounts projected in Exhibit III):

Financing	Debt	Com. Div.	Sell Stock	Buy Stock	Invest.
A (2–9) NO	UP	UP			
B (4–7) NO	DOWN	DOWN			
C (1–10) NO	DOWN	UP	UP		
D (0–11) NO		DOWN		UP	
E (11–0) YES—pay preferred dividend of $20.					

Investing					
A (9–2) YES—approve investing $260 total.					
B (5–6) NO	DOWN				DOWN
C (3–8) NO		UP			DOWN
D (10–1) YES—defer $25 of projects.					
E (1–10) NO		DOWN			UP

Once the Projected Income Statement (Exhibit I) is accepted, the $260 funds total provided by operations follows. The board may have probability ranges for reference. At least quarterly, new projections are made to govern current decisions on common dividends, debt, and capital expenditures. Investments in net current assets follow operating requirements.

Translation from accruals to funds is essential to financial management. Equally essential is the translation from funds to cash.

CASH PLANNING

To qualify as cash, it must be on hand or available at face amount within 24 hours as legal tender. At the next remove are near-term cash resources, which may become cash in a slightly longer period and possibly at some discount. Marketable securities (immediately saleable at market) are classified as cash, by definition, and may be combined with cash on the Balance Sheet. Other securities may be marketable over a longer term and at a discount, or premium. Cash availability is further supported by items with longer periods for realization and less ready marketability. The ultimate total cash realization is achieved by liquidation. This may be voluntary by owners who want to convert asset ownership to cash to meet portfolio needs. Involuntary bankruptcy results in zero cash realization by the owners.

The many degrees and kinds of cash availability are related to cash needs, which also vary in amount and timing. A degree of uncertainty attaches to possible tax deficiency assessments (usually provided for in a disguised liability account), lawsuits, uninsured perils, warranties, endorsements. These items are known as "contingent liabilities." There may also be "contingent assets."

The probable range of cash flows in and out over time indicate the amount of cash (or cash availability) to have on hand—an asset that provides risk protection but not profit. The cash balance can be said to consist of the amount needed for handling ongoing transactions, an added sum to accommodate the expected degree of cash swings, and possibly a further balance to facilitate quick action for sudden opportunities that may emerge.

When more cash is available than needed for all planned or probable needs, it serves no purpose and should be paid out in dividends. When cash availability is threatened, defensive measures to preserve liquidity are dictated, which may be taken at some expense to profits.

Cash planning consists of the meticulous detailing of all cash sources and needs by item over time. Cash control consists of monitoring actual cash transactions, with prompt response to changed results or expectations. The degree of detail and timing depends on the individual company and the current situation.

Contingencies must be provided for

- Failure of a major customer
- Need to support a supplier
- Slow collection due to poor conditions
- Adverse tax assessment or lawsuit
- Major investment gone sour
- Uninsured casualty loss
- Opportunity for bargain purchase
- Need to defend against raiders
- Chance to buy another company
- Interruption from strikes or disasters

The degree of liquidity is a subjective judgment with lost profitability as the opportunity cost. Lack of liquidity may have a higher cost. The balance requires careful and constant evaluation.

Liquidity has become increasingly significant with inflation, high interest rates, an "overvalued" dollar, foreign competition, moves toward deregulation, fiscal and monetary policies, rapid technological change, and world tensions.

The increased attention to liquidity has led to some misleading measures such as "cash earnings per share." Cash arises from profitable investments over a period of time. Profit is an accrual measurement, translated first into funds and then into cash.

The differences between funds and cash are illustrated here:

	Balance Sheet		**Income Statement**
	Dr.	**Cr.**	
Sales	A/R $200		Sale $200
Cost	_____	Inv. $120	Cost 120
Net		CA 80	GM 80
Purchase	Inv. 145	A/P 145	
Collect	Cash 100	A/R 100	
Pay	A/P 145	Cash 140	disc + 5
Collect	Cash 90	A/R 100	disc − 10
Net		CA − 5	disc − 5
Cum		CA 75	GM 75

Funds Statement:

GM		$ 75
CA: A/R	$ 0	
Inv	25	
A/P	0	
Cash	50	75

Cash Statement:

Collect	$100	
Pay		140
Collect	90	
	190	140
Balance	$ 50	

A cash plan should include:

- Time periods—days, weeks, months, quarters
- All items detailed
- Minimum cash balance, $15
- Loan requirements to be determined

Periods	1	2	3	4	5	6
Cash receipts	$ 80	$90	$100	$110	$115	$130
Cash payments	100	90	140	125	110	80
Net	− 20	0	− 40	− 15	+ 5	+ 50
Cash balance	35	15	15	15	15	15
	+ 15	+ 15	− 25	0	20	65
Borrow + (repay −)			+ 40	+ 15	− 5	− 50
Minimum cash balance			+ 15	+ 15	+ 15	+ 15
Loan balance			$ 40	$ 55	$ 50	$ 0

This plan indicates the need now to establish a loan source for $60 to $75 to allow for cash-flow fluctuations, with the first advance to be made in about three months for a period of about three months.

PART 2

The Investing Process

Chapter 4 covers the area most critical to the future—capital expenditures—for both analysis and administration.

Chapter 5 depicts the techniques for analyzing investments in the current assets needed to support operating plans (separate from those included in capital expenditure proposals). Also covered are current asset management and sources of short-term funds.

Chapter 6 explores the arcane area of uncertainty and risk, which pervades the decision process. Some useful approaches are described, with cautionary notes on several current fallacious methods.

Chapter 7 explains bond refunding—a unique case of capital expenditure without risk—with detailed examples. Defeasance is also described, with an example of "in-substance defeasance," a relatively new technique.

Chapter 8 analyzes mergers with other companies, primarily by exchange of stocks—another form of capital expenditure.

CHAPTER 4

Capital Expenditures

THE CHALLENGE AND OPPORTUNITY

BASIC CONSIDERATIONS

The major challenge to management is to find, develop, and evaluate investment opportunities to insure growth and profitability within prudent limits of risk and liquidity. Without new investments a company continues to liquidate. Risky projects may go sour and impair profits and liquidity.

The handling of major investments—capital expenditures—is guided by company goals, strategies, and policies, supported by objectives, plans, and programs. Capital expenditure projects collectively relate to the plans and programs. Analysis of profitability, risk, and liquidity is essential but, at best, is only a guide to management judgment. Faulty or inadequate analysis can limit perception and cause costly errors.

Most strategic decisions are beyond relevant quantitative expression. Some projects are mandated by government, or contract. Many projects provide only intangible benefits. Yet it is likely that significant analysis is applicable to well over half the total projects in dollar terms and even more in total number of projects.

Capital expenditures require evaluation of:

- Fixed assets (life over one year and capitalized)
- Expenses—charges to expense as incurred
- Current assets—less related current liabilities
- Intangibles such as management time
- Use of existing facilities (opportunity cost)
- Loss of sales of existing products.

Evaluation must also include competitive response, the regulatory situation, employee reactions (morale), public relations, stockholder relations, and internal politics.

Chapter 5, "Net Current Assets," deals with investments needed to support operations, separate from the net current assets included in capital expenditure projects (covered in this chapter). Chapter 6, "Uncertainty and Risk," explores this difficult area in depth. Chapter 7, "Bond Refunding and Defeasance," describes bond refunding, which is a capital expenditure without risk, plus the recently approved method for bond retirement through defeasance. Chapter 8, "Acquiring Other Companies," concerns the capital expenditure decision relative to the acquisition of entire companies. Chapter 10, "Financial Leases," analyzes financial leases as a financing decision independent of the investment decision. Chapter 12, "Capital Structure," includes analysis of the discount rate used for determining present value in investment analysis.

Capital expenditures involve large sums for long periods and are difficult to stop or alter, once started, without high cost. Risk is necessarily high for many projects.

Each project requires full identification and exact description, including:

- Amounts of all cash flows in and out by item and by period
- Consideration of inflation for each item for each period
- Discount rate based on the current cost of funds and tax rates
- Calculation of NPV, yield, and accounting rate of return
- Risk evaluation
- Cash payback and effect on liquidity
- Intangibles, as described above, that are relevant

Examples of relevance include (1) a project for cost reduction that has a high yield based on a life exceeding that of the product line it relates to; (2) introduction of a new product will seriously impair sales of an existing product; (3) capacity expansion will require a major step-up in utility capability; (4) development of export sales will jeopardize sales to a major customer; (5) projects that overtax management time and skill; (6) projects that entail opportunity costs.

All calculations are based on projected cash flows and estimated life. Taxes must be applied correctly because of their major impact and uneven effect on different projects (expensed items, depreciated assets, assets not depreciated, and tax credits and allowances). The tax code is complex, changing, subject to differing interpretations. No attempt is made to reflect current tax practice; tax experts should participate in the tax aspects of each project.

Financial profitability analysis is based on the cash flows for the project life. Book records are kept according to accounting practice—accrual accounting. The differences between the two can be substantial. Profits must be calculated by both methods for management guidance. The problem arises because financial analysis is based on cash for the project life and financial profit determined— NPV and yield. Record keeping for accrual accounting requires regular periodic reports, necessitating time cut-offs, estimates, and assumptions. Each period includes both completed transactions and those still in progress. Also, book records are based on historical accounting and bookkeeping procedures, which are not fully consonant with financial analyses.

EXAMPLE A

Machine cost, $20,000; four-year life; straight-line (SL) depreciation; no salvage; save $9,000 per year; tax, 40%; discount rate, 10% after tax.

Cash Computation

		Books	Cash
Save		$9,000	$9,000
Depreciation	$\left(\dfrac{\$20,000}{4 \text{ years}}\right)$	5,000	
		4,000	
Tax (40%)		1,600	1,600
Net income		2,400	
Add back Depreciation		5,000	
Cash		$7,400	$7,400

The book column is needed to compute the tax liability, which is a cash flow. Net income is needed to compute accounting profit. Net income plus depreciation equals cash. The cash column is not required but clarifies the situation. If the tax is omitted, the gain is seriously overstated. If tax is computed without the deduction for depreciation, the gain is seriously understated. Savings, or gains, signify both cost reduction and revenue increase. It is essential to be clear as to whether amounts are before tax (savings or gain) or after tax.

NPV (Net Present Value)

Annual cash—above	$ 7,400
Annuity factor (f)	
for 10% and 4 years =	
PV f	$\times$ f 3.170
	PV 23,458
Cash outlay	− 20,000
	NPV $ 3,458

Note that $7,400 for 4 years is $29,600 undiscounted, or zero interest. The cash outlay of $20,000 is made currently and so is not discounted.

Tax payments are considered to be concurrent with savings because companies must make quarterly tax payments. Year time periods are used and PV factors (f) are based on the year-end. These bases are sufficiently accurate for the purpose. Most cash estimates are subject to a considerable range.

The present value calculation puts all dollars on a "now" basis. This project shows a gain of $3,458 (NPV) in "now" dollars at the 10% discount rate. The company is that much better off now, although actual realization will entail four years.

With a discount rate of 18%, we have:

Annual cash	$ 7,400
18%, 4 years PV	× f 2,690
	PV 19,906
Cash outlay	− 20,000
Negative NPV − $ 94

The firm would be worse off by $94 now at 18%.

Discount Rate

The company's current borrowing rate is 16⅔%, and the tax is 6⅔% (at a 40% tax rate) with the after tax rate 10%. The rates reflect current conditions for the company and for the capital markets, relative to a medium-term time frame—10 to 20 years. The rate should be based on company expectations for borrowing money through available channels—banks, bond issues, leases—on the best terms available and within the limits of planned capital structure. The rate should be used for discounting in all investment decisions. It should be changed whenever conditions require it. It is also the basis for measuring the leverage of debt on equity earnings.

Possible discount rate ranges can be illustrated:

Borrowing Rate	Net % After Tax Rate			
	30%	40%	50%	60%
24%	16.8	14.4	12.0	9.6
20	14.0	12.0	10.0	8.0
16	11.2	9.6	8.0	6.4
12	8.4	7.2	6.0	4.8
8	5.6	4.8	4.0	3.2

This table shows a range from 3.2% to 16.8% for the net interest cost (discount rate).

If the discount rate used is below the required rate, some projects can show a positive NPV but actually produce a negative result. With a discount rate over the required rate, some profitable projects will show negative results, and good opportunities will be missed.

As a simple example, if a merchant borrows $10,000 for a year at 18% he pays $1,800 to the lender. If the $10,000 is used to purchase goods on which $1,500 is realized, he has lost $300. With a sales gain of $2,000, he has $200 surplus cash (positive leverage). Both interest rates and profit estimates are essential to the analysis.

The discount rate is also known as the "investment rate," "hurdle rate," and "cut-off rate." The term *cost of capital* should be avoided; it is ambiguous and not relevant to the investment decision. See Chapter 12, "Capital Structure."

Yield

Yield can be found for annuities:

$$\text{Outlay} \over \text{Annual cash} \quad \frac{\$20,000}{\$\ 7,400} = \text{f } 2.703 \text{ for 4 years}$$

This f (PV factor) falls between 17% and 18% in the annuity table. To interpolate:

17%	f 2.743	f 2.743
	—	f 2.703
18%	f 2.690	—
	f 0.053	f 0.040 = f 0.755

The yield is 17.755% (17.759% by calculator). The use of 17.755% as the discount rate would produce zero NPV, by definition.

NPV is the gain in present dollars, but it must also be expressed as a percentage, or yield, for clarity of understanding and comparison with other project yields. This rate is needed for communication even though a plus NPV is a positive measure of profitability. Yields can be ranked together with the NPV dollars and other relevant factors. This step is necessary as part of the review and approval process.

This rate is sometimes called an "internal rate of return," but this is misleading and unnecessary; it is in no way internal. All cash flows enter into the cash pool and become part of cash management.

If the cash flows are not even each year, calculation must be made for each year separately, as shown later.

The discount rate should be approved by top management, revised as necessary and used throughout the organization for all investments, and both NPV and yield computed. The use of a single, pre-determined rate to calculate NPV for all investments ensures uniformity and comparability and simplifies analysis. NPV calculations always produce a correct answer, from which a correct yield is determinable. If the analysis is made initially for yield, results can be erroneous in certain situations, which are illustrated later.

The following four illustrations show the interrelationships of NPV and yield, using four years and a 10% discount rate for all—f 3.170:

#1 Outlay	$20,000	$20,000	$ 20,000	$ 20,000	SAME
Annual Cash Gain	$ 5,600	$ 7,400	$ 9,200	$ 11,000	UP
Mult. PV (f 3.170) =	$17,752	$23,458	$ 29,164	$ 34,870	
Subtract PV = NPV	−$ 2,248	$ 3,458	$ 9,164	$ 14,870	UP
Outlay/Gain = f	f 3.571	f 2.703	f 2.174	f 1.818	
Annual Yield %	4.7%	17.7%	29.8%	41.2%	UP

#2 Outlay	$18,000	$20,000	$ 22,000	$ 24,000	UP
Annual Cash Gain	$ 7,400	$ 7,400	$ 7,400	$ 7,400	SAME
Mult. PV (f 3.170) =	$23,458	$23,458	$ 23,458	$ 23,458	
Subtract PV = NPV	$ 5,458	$ 3,458	$ 1,458	−$ 542	DOWN
Outlay/Gain = f	f 2.432	f 2.703	f 2.973	f 3.243	
Annual Yield %	23.4%	17.7%	13.0%	9.0%	DOWN
#3 Outlay	$ 2,000	$20,000	$200,000	$2,000,000	UP
Annual Cash Gain	$ 740	$ 7,400	$ 74,000	$ 740,000	UP
Mult. PV (f 3.170) =	$ 2,346	$23,458	$234,586	$2,345,800	
Subtract PV = NPV	$ 346	$ 3,458	$ 34,580	$ 345,800	UP
Outlay/Gain = f	f 2.703	f 2.703	f 2.703	f 2.703	
Annual Yield %	17.7%	17.7%	17.7%	17.7%	SAME

(Constant yield with increasing NPV)

#4 Outlay	$ 2,000	$20,000	$200,000	$ 500,000	UP
Annual Cash Gain	$ 1,722	$ 7,400	$ 64,182	$ 158,820	UP
Mult. PV (f 3.170) =	$ 5,458	$23,458	$203,458	$ 503,458	
Subtract PV = NPV	$ 3,458	$ 3,458	$ 3,458	$ 3,458	SAME
Outlay/Gain = f	f 1.161	f 2.703	f 3.116	f 3.148	
Annual Yield %	77.4%	17.7%	10.8%	10.3%	DOWN

(Constant NPV with decreasing yield)

Note that in all four illustrations the second column is the same. These tables underscore the need for both NPV and yield.

Accounting Rate of Return

The accounting rate of return calculation is based on accrual accounting as practiced by the firm—bookkeeping as compared with cash is used. The only difference between cash and accrual accounting is time. For financial analysis the period is the life of the project, and all amounts are cash. A single result is reached for the entire period—no time subdivision is applicable. For accounting purposes, financial statements are prepared monthly, quarterly, and annually, and publicly owned companies issue periodic reports. Each statement date necessitates a cut-off and determination of balance sheet values for ongoing transactions and activities.

Significant differences often occur between the two approaches. The accounting treatment of a project and the rate of return must be defined so that management is aware of the impact on earnings. A major project may have a high NPV and yield but cause a loss of accounting profit in the first year or longer. The extent of the negative impact on income (and EPS) needs to be evaluated for its possible effect on market valuation.

Pressure for profits may have a negative effect on desirable investments—a case of the short run versus the long run. This dilemma may be even more acute in the evaluation of projects for divisions within the company. Current ROA may be temporarily depressed although improved for the project life.

In the example used, annual gain is $9,000 for four years, or $7,400 cash, after tax deduction of $1,600 (40% of $4,000 gain after depreciation). Note that when cash ($7,400) and depreciation ($5,000) are known, the net income ($2,400) is determinable. It is not necessary to know the gain or tax.

The accounting for each year is:

	Net Income	Asset Balance	ROA	Average Asset	Average ROA
Year 1	$2,400	$20,000	12%	$17,500	13.7%
Year 2	2,400	15,000	16	12,500	19.2
Year 3	2,400	10,000	24	7,500	32.0
Year 4	2,400	5,000	48	2,500	96.0
End of Year 4		0			

These rates compare with the financial yield of 17.755% for the project life.

The ROA increase is very rapid as the asset base declines with constant net income. In this case, the ROA for year 1 is below the project yield, for both methods of computation. In many cases, there is a loss in the first year because of expensed items and accelerated depreciation, illustrated later.

This example helps to show the possible depressing effect on profits for many new projects in a year. It also points up the relatively high rates generated with old assets, some of which may be fully depreciated. The proper understanding, handling, and reconcilement of financial analysis and accounting practice are essential to clear evaluation of proposals and the measurement of results.

The accounting rate of return for the full four years could be an average:

$$\$2,400/\$10,000 = 24\%.$$

This is not a useful computation and is misleading. It is not correct for decision-making and does not occur in accounting analysis.

The handling of depreciation and interest on debt requires careful attention.

Depreciation is recognized for accounting because of periodic reporting. Net income is $2,400 per year, or $7,400 cash less $5,000 depreciation. Total depreciation equals cost: 4 years $\times$ $5,000 = $20,000. For year 1, the rate of return is $2,400 divided by $20,000 = 12%. Financial analysis is based on the total project life, and the calculations include the total amount of depreciable assets: cost $20,000 divided by cash $7,400 = f 2.703 = 17.755% yield. The cash receipts recover the $20,000 cost and more to provide the yield and positive NPV ($3,458).

The computations omit interest on debt. The leverage effect of debt on ROE is disregarded. It applies to all operations and need not be considered in project evaluation. It relates to capital structure, not earnings on assets. With no borrowing, ROA and ROE are equal.

Restating the cash computation of Example A:

	Books		Equivalent
Save	$9,000	EBIT	$4,000
Depr.	5,000	Interest	0
	4,000	EBT	4,000
Tax	1,600	Tax	1,600
NI	2,400	NI	$2,400
Depr.	5,000		
Cash	$7,400		

Cash Payback

Cash payback expresses the number of years it takes for cash inflow to equal the outlay.

$$\frac{\text{Outlay}}{\text{Cash}} \quad \frac{\$20,000}{\$\ 7,400} = 2.703 \text{ or } 2.7 \text{ years}$$

This is a break-even equation and is in addition to NPV and yield. (The answer for annuities is the same number used for finding yield f 2.703.)

This is a measure of liquidity and is not directly related to NPV, or yield, or risk. It is part of cash planning. Cash payback examples for annuities are:

Outlay	$20,000	$20,000	$20,000	$20,000
Cash	$10,000	$ 6,000	$ 4,000	$ 2,000
Payback Years	2	$3\frac{1}{3}$	5	10

For uneven cash flows, we have:

Outlay	$20,000	$20,000	$20,000	$20,000
Cash:				
Year 1	10,000	4,000	8,000	4,000
Year 2	6,000	6,000	7,000	5,000
Year 3	4,000	10,000	6,000	6,000
Year 4	—	—	5,000	7,000
Year 5	—	—	4,000	8,000
Payback Years	3	3	$2\frac{5}{6}$	$3\frac{5}{7}$

Thus payback disregards both cash patterns within the period and cash beyond the period.

A comparison of payback and yield follows:

Outlay	$20,000	$20,000	$20,000	$20,000
Cash:				
Year 1	6,000	6,000	6,000	6,000
Year 2	6,000	6,000	6,000	6,000
Year 3	6,000	6,000	6,000	6,000
Year 4	—	6,000	6,000	6,000
Year 5	—	—	6,000	6,000
Year 6	—	—	—	6,000
Payback Years	MINUS	$3\frac{1}{3}$	$3\frac{1}{3}$	$3\frac{1}{3}$
Yield	LOSS	7.7%	15.2%	19.9%
	−2,000			

A particular use of payback is to plan the amount of down payment and installments for sales where repossession may be needed:

Price	$15,000 (includes finance charge)
20% down	3,000
Owe	$12,000

	Open Balance	Estimated Net Salvage	Margin
Pay 1	3,000	$9,000	$10,000	$1,000
Pay 2	3,000	6,000	6,600	600
Pay 3	3,000	3,000	3,300	300
Pay 4	3,000	0	100	100

Payback may be considered a guide to uncertainty. If two projects have the same yield, the one with a shorter payback may appear safer. This idea can be a trap. Long payback projects may be safe, such as for a bond refund (Chapter 7) or for machine tools of known performance capability. Short payback projects— such as for fashions, toys, novelties—may be highly risky. The evaluation of risk is presented in Chapter 6.

Cash payback should be computed for each project as a matter of information and to feed into the cash plan. In a period of severe liquidity pressure, cash payback could affect the decision.

EXAMPLE B

Most projects include outlays for items that are expensed at once, in addition to fixed assets, which are depreciated. The tax is applied to the expensed items, improving the cash flow and profitability as compared with depreciated assets. Classification of items as fixed assets or expense, often arbitrary, is made according to company accounting practice, reflecting both the tax code and GAAP.

Also, many projects require some increase in net current assets (net CA), which are not taxable. These outlays are recouped at the end of the project. Continuing with Example A (4 years, 10%), we have:

Outlay

Machine		$20,000 (depreciated)
Expense	$4,000	
less tax	1,600	2,400 (net)
Net CA		1,000 (recouped)
Total outlay		$23,400

Cash

Per Year	$ 7,400 4 years
Net CA	$ 1,000 at end of period

NPV (Net Present Value)

Total Outlay				$23,400
PV Cash:				
Per Year	$7,400 × f 3.170	$23,458		
Net CA	$1,000 × f 0.683	683	24,141	
NPV			741	

The NPV in Example A is $3,458, and this NPV of $741 is $2,717 lower (net expense $2,400 plus net CA $1,000 less recovery of $683). Project NPV may be seriously overstated without the inclusion of all relevant project expenses and required increases in net CA. For this illustration, the increased expenses and net CA are incurred at the beginning of the project.

Yield

Trial and error must be used. The yield must be over 10% because NPV is positive.

Try 12%

$7,400	×	f 3.037	=	$22,474		
1,000	×	f 0.636	=	636	$23,110 PV	
Outlay					23,400	
					−$ 290 NPV	

It is too low, and you need a lower rate.

Try 11%

$7,400	×	f 3.102	=	$22,925		
1,000	×	f 0.689	=	689	$23,614 PV	
Outlay					23,400	
					$ 214 NPV	

By interpolation we have about 11.4% compared with 17.75% in Example A. Linear interpolation is usually accurate enough; there is a bias because the tables are logarithmic.

An alternative using PV is:

12%	$23,110	$23,110
	—	23,400
11%	23,614	—
	$ 504	$ 290 = 57.5% = 11.425%

Accounting Rate of Return

Year 1	Net income $2,400	
	less expense 2,400	$ 0
Year 2	Net income	2,400
Year 3	Net income	2,400
Year 4	Net income	2,400

Fixed asset average plus net CA:

Year 1	$17,500 + $1,000 = $18,500
Year 2	12,500 + 1,000 = 13,500
Year 3	7,500 + 1,000 = 8,500
Year 4	2,500 + 1,000 = 3,500

Annual ROA on Asset Averages:

Year 1	NI $ 0	$18,500	0.0%
Year 2	NI 2,400	13,500	17.8
Year 3	NI 2,400	8,500	28.2
Year 4	NI 2,400	3,500	68.6

These rates increase sharply by year and compare with the project yield of 11.4%.

In many cases there is an actual loss in year 1:

Outlay

Machine		$20,000 (4 years)	
Expenses	$15,000		
less tax	6,000	9,000	$29,000
Annual cash gain	$11,000		
at 10% for 4 years f 3.170 =			34,870
			NPV $ 5,870

$$\text{Yield } \frac{\$29,000}{\$11,000} = \text{f } 2.636 = 19.0\%.$$

Year 1 Net income	$6,000 (cash $11,000 − depr. $5,000)
Expense—net	$9,000

		Av. Asset	ROA
Year 1 Loss	− $3,000	$17,500	− 17.1%
Year 2 Net income	6,000	12,500	48.0
Year 3 Net income	6,000	7,500	80.0
Year 4 Net income	6,000	2,500	240.0

Cash Payback

This item is taken from NPV, above:

$$\frac{\text{Outlay}}{\text{Cash}} \quad \frac{\$23,400}{\$\ 7,400} = 3.16 \text{ years}$$

or

		Cum		Cum Years
Year 1	$7,400	$ 7,400		1.00
Year 2	7,400	14,800		2.00
Year 3	7,400	22,200		3.00
Year 4	7,400	1,200	12/74 =	3.16
Year 4	1,000	—		
		$23,400		3.16

If this project had only a three-year life, we would have:

		Cum
1. $7,400		$ 7,400
2. $7,400		$14,800
3. $7,400		$22,200

Total cash is $1,200 short of the outlay.

Profitability Index

The profitability index (PI) is taken from the NPV computation in Example B:

$$\frac{\text{PV}}{\text{Outlay}} \quad \frac{\$24,141}{\$23,400} = 1.03\tfrac{1}{6} \text{ PI}$$

or

$$\frac{\text{NPV}}{\text{Outlay}} \quad \frac{\$\ \ 741}{\$23,400} = 0.03\tfrac{1}{6} \text{ PI}$$

The PI index is not needed and can be misleading. It agrees either with the NPV and provides nothing new, or it is in error. For example, timing classifications can effect PI with no change in NPV.

Period	Outlay	Cash In	Net	10% f	PV
0	$20,000	—	$20,000	1.000	−$20,000
1	15,000	$15,000	0	0.909	0
2	—	15,000	+ 15,000	0.826	12,390
3	—	15,000	+ 15,000	0.751	11,265
	$35,000	$45,000			23,655 PV
					$ 3,655 NPV

$$\frac{\$23,655}{\$20,000} = 1.183 \text{ PI}$$

Alternatively:

Period	Outlay	PV	Cash In	PV
0	$20,000	−$20,000	0	0
1	15,000	− 13,635	$15,000	$13,635
2	—	—	15,000	12,390
3	—	—	15,000	11,265
	$35,000	−$33,635	$45,000	$37,290
				− 33,635
		SAME		$ 3,655 NPV

$$\frac{\$37,290}{\$33,635} = 1.109 \text{ PI LOWER}$$

This type of error is common, particularly with the practice of deducting salvage PV from outlay.

Project size also causes errors. For example, two projects with five-year lives and 10% discount rate (f 3.791) reveal the following:

	A	B
1. Outlay	$5,000.0	$50,000
2. Cash	$1,500.0	$14,000
3. PV (Cash × f 3.791)	$5,686.5	$53,074
4. NPV (Outlay − PV)	$ 686.5	$ 3,074 (Hi)
5. PI (PV/Outlay)	1.1373 (Hi)	1.0615
6. Yield (Outlay/Cash)	$5000/$1,500	$50,000/$14,000
=	f 3.333	= f 3.571
=	15.2% (Hi) =	12.4%

A project with a higher NPV ($3,074) is always more profitable, regardless of the PI or yield. The lower NPV project has the higher PI (1.1373); thus it is an erroneous and superfluous indicator.

SALVAGE OR RESIDUAL VALUE

Estimating the net recoverable value of used assets at a future date is speculative, but it is frequently necessary to calculate project profitability. Future market conditions are difficult to forecast. Removal, reconditioning, and disposal costs could exceed market value—an outlay cost rather than recovery. The current tax code permits asset cost to be fully depreciated without recognition of salvage value. Disposals for proceeds exceeding book value are taxable according to the tax code in effect at the time.

Many projects can be dealt with as having no salvage value. A shorter life with salvage may be used in some cases, rather than a longer life at zero salvage. For example:

Outlay	$20,000 4 year life SL depr.
Cash gain	$ 6,000 discount rate 10%
NPV	$ 6,000 × f 3.170 = $19,020 PV
Outlay	20,000
Negative	− $ 980 NPV

If this project can be estimated to have $1,500 net salvage value after tax, the salvage PV is $1,500 × f 0.683 = $1,025. The NPV rises from −$980 to +$45. If the before tax amount is $2,500, this can be related to the outlay.

When a project has a negative NPV it is possible to work backwards to find the net salvage needed to bring NPV to zero. Then the probability of realizing this amount, or more, can be appraised. For instance, if a ten-year project discounted at 10% has a negative NPV of $3,855, this amount divided by the 10 year—10% factor (f 0.3855) = $10,000 after tax. If this is $20,000 before tax, it can be related to the original outlay for reasonableness.

Land is a separate case. Assume:

Outlay	
Land	$300,000
Warehouse	450,000 (15 years)
	$750,000
Cash, $90,000 (15 years = 10% discount rate) $90,000 × f 7.606 =	$684,540 PV
	−$ 65,460 NPV

This negative result is based on land having zero value in 15 years. Assuming the land is still worth its cost of $300,000 in 15 years:

Land PV	$300,000 × f 0.2394 =	$ 71,820
Cash PV	above	684,540
		756,360
Outlay		750,000
NPV		$ 6,360

Assuming an increase in land value would be speculative but assuming a lower value could be unfounded, at zero NPV, the resulting land value is:

$$\$750,000 - \$684,540 = -NPV \ \$65,460 \div f \ 0.2394 = \$273,434$$

This is a drop of $26,566 from $300,000, or 8.85%. This procedure provides a measure of the break-even value.

For another example, a truck costs $25,000, has a five-year life, and has a cash gain of $6,000 a year:

$$PV \ \$6,000 \times f \ 3.791 \ (5 \ years—10\%) = \$22,746 \ PV$$

The NPV is −$2,254 ($25,000 − $22,746) with no salvage value. The $2,254 divided by f 0.621 (5 years—10%) = $3,630 after tax, or $7,260 before tax. Thus in five years the truck resale value would have to be $7,260, or 29% of cost, to reach zero NPV.

UNEVEN CASH FLOWS

Most projects have uneven cash flows. PV calculation can be made with the prescribed discount rate and the correct NPV and yield determined. Calculators and computers perform the calculations speedily. However, the entire analysis must be fully and correctly stated to enable programming and solution. For example:

Outlays by Years		Year	Terminal Value
Land	$10,000	0	$10,000
Warehouse	45,000	1	0
Expenses (net)	18,000	1	0
Net CA	17,000	2	17,000

The gain is cash $12,000, 15 years, for years 2–16, with a discount rate of 10%. The calculations are:

Outlay		f	PV
Land	$10,000	1.000	$10,000
Whse.	45,000	.909	40,905
Expenses	18,000	.909	16,362
Net CA	17,000	0.826	14,042
Net outlay by year 2, PV at time 0			$81,309

Cash

$12,000 annuity = 15 years:

Year 16		f 7.824		
Year 1		f 0.909		
$12,000	×	f 6.915	=	$82,980
Discount for 1 year at		f 0.909	=	$75,429
PV at time 0				$ 5,880

Residual Value

Land	$10,000	year 16	f 0.218	$2,180
Net CA	17,000	year 16	f 0.218	3,706
				+ 5,886
NPV				6

PV Recap	Outlay		$81,309	
	Cash	$75,429		
	Residual	5,886	81,315	$ 6 NPV

Note that all cash flows are expressed at current (discounted) amounts because the decision is made now. The NPV at $6 is at the break-even point with a yield at 10%, the discount rate (with a tiny plus).

Cash flow timing can be clarified with a time chart:

Years	Outlays	Cash	Payback Years
0	$10,000		
1	45,000		
1	18,000	$ 0	1
2	17,000	$12,000	$\frac{1}{1}$
	$90,000	$12,000	2
		$78,000	$6\frac{1}{2}$
		12,000 =	$8\frac{1}{2}$

Using the accounting rate of return (000) we have:

Year		Net Income	Assets	ROA
1	Exp.	−$18	$10 + $45 = $55	−32.7%
2	($12 − $3)	9	$55 + $17 = $72 − $ 3 = $69	13.0
3		9	72 − 6 = 66	13.6
4		9	72 − 9 = 63	14.3
5		9	72 − 12 = 60	15.0
16		9	72 − 45 = 27	33.3

Net income is $12 cash − $3 depreciation = $9 NI. The warehouse depreciation of $3 is taken at year-end, and the balance is not averaged.

All of these measures indicate the need to evaluate the project carefully. An example with a single outlay and uneven cash gains (which occurs often) is:

Machine cost, $60,000; four years; SL depreciation; tax 40%; discount rate, 10%.

Year	Gain	Depr.	Net	Tax	NI	Cash	f	PV
1	$ 5	$15	−$10	−$ 4	−$ 6	$ 9	0.909	$ 8,181
2	15	15	0	0	—	15	0.826	12,390
3	35	15	20	+ 8	12	27	0.751	20,277
4	55	15	40	+ 16	24	39	0.683	26,637
	$110	$60	$50	$20	$30	$90		67,485
	Outlay							60,000
	NPV							$ 7,485

The yield is about 14.5%, by trial and error:

$$\text{NPV at 15\%} \quad -\$756$$
$$\text{NPV at 15\%} \quad +\$741$$

(The details are omitted.)

The cash payback is:

Year	Cash	Cum.		Years
1	$ 9	$ 9		1.00
2	15	24		2.00
3	27	51		3.00
4	(9/39)	60	($9/$39) =	.23
				3.23

The accounting rate of return is:

Year	NI	Asset Av.	ROA
1	−$ 6	$52.5	−11.4%
2	0	37.5	0.0
3	12	22.5	53.3
4	24	7.5	320.0

This profitable project is negative only in its accounting expression. This example reflects a common dilemma for management, particularly with pressure for current "performance."

The use of accelerated depreciation contributes to the lop-sided ROA pattern. If sum-of-the-year digits (SYD) is used ($60/10 = $6 for year 4):

Year	Restated Gain	SYD Depr.	NI (same as SL)	Asset Av.	ROA
1	$ 14	$24	−$10	$52.5	−19.0%
2	18	18	0	37.5	0.0
3	32	12	20	22.5	88.9
4	46	6	40	7.5	533.3
	$110	$60	$50		

The NI column agrees with the above example—using SL, so the NPV result would still be NPV $7,485. However, the gains were derived and so differ from the example and are less pronounced. This is a form of break-even analysis for gain, using SL and SYD depreciation.

Using the same gains with SYD, we have:

Year	Gain	Depr.	Net	Tax	NI	Cash	f	PV
1	$ 5	$24	−$19	−$ 7.6	−$11.4	$12.6	0.909	$11,453.4
2	15	18	− 3	− 1.2	− 1.8	16.2	0.826	13,381.2
3	35	12	+ 23	9.2	+ 13.8	25.8	0.751	19,375.8
4	55	6	+ 49	19.6	+ 29.4	35.4	0.683	24,178.3
	$110	$60	$50	$20.0	$30.0	$90.0		68,388.6

PV with SL depr.	67,485.0
Increase for SYD	903.6
NPV with SL depr.	7,485.0
NPV with SYD	$ 8,388.6

The yield is about 15.1%, compared with 14.5% with SL depreciation (details omitted).

The accounting rate of return range with SYD is greater:

Year	NI	Asset Av.	ROA with SYD	ROA with SL as above
1	−$11.4	$52.5	− 21.7%	− 11.40%
2	− 1.8	37.5	− 4.8	0.00
3	+ 13.8	22.5	+ 61.3	+ 53.39
4	+ 29.4	7.5	+ 392.0	+ 320.00

Projects with cash flows that change signs are not infrequent. The use of the discount rate provides the correct NPV, and yield can be found by trial and error. With cash sign reversals, it is possible arithmetically to have more than one yield, or none. With NPV first determined, the relevant yield is apparent. An example of sign reversal with $8,232 outlay and 9% discount is:

				PV	
Cash	Plus	Minus	9% f	Plus	Minus
Year 1	$10,000	—	0.917	$ 9,170	—
2	—	$ 1,000	.842	—	$ 842
3	10,000	—	.772	7,720	—
4	—	11,000	0.708	—	7,788
				+ 16,890	−$8,630
				− 8,630	
				8,260 PV	
	Outlay			8,232	
				$ 28 NPV	

The yield appears to be slightly higher than 9%. But by trial and error the yield is found to be 15%:

				PV	
Cash	Plus	Minus	15% f	Plus	Minus
Year 1	$10,000	—	0.870	$ 8,700	—
2	—	$ 1,000	.756	—	$ 756
3	10,000	—	.658	6,580	—
4	—	11,000	0.572	—	6,292
				15,280	−$7,048
				− 7,048	
				8,232 PV	
	Outlay		NPV	8,232	
				$ 0 NPV	

MACHINE REPLACEMENT

It is good practice to review all productive assets periodically to evaluate retention versus replacement. Machine replacements are a major portion of the projects for many companies. For example:

Purchase new machine:

   Cost, $18,000-10 years-SL depr.
   Net salvage, $2,800 in ten years.

Replace old machine (balances):

   Book value, 4,000-four years-SL depr.
   Net salvage in four years—zero
   Current market value, $6,000

Tax, 40%; discount rate, 10%.

Outlay

New machine		$18,000
Sell old machine	$6,000	
less tax:		
Sale	$6,000	
Book	4,000	
Gain	2,000	
Tax	800	5,200
Net outlay		$12,800

The gain is $3,000 for ten years:

Gain

Gain	$3,000
Depr.	1,800
	1,200
Tax	480
NI	720
Depr.	1,800
Cash	$2,520

PV $2,520 × f 6.145 = $15,485
Salvage $2,800
− tax   1,120
             1,680
×   f 0.386   = +   648
PV new machine $16,133

However, depreciation on the old machine is lost as a tax deduction:

Depr.	$1,000
Tax	$ 400
4-year f	3.170 =

	−$ 1,268
Net PV	14,865
Net outlay (above)	12,800
NPV	$ 2,065

An alternative is:

4 years (1–4)   Gain $3,000

Depr.	$1,800	
Depr.	− 1,000	800
		2,200
Tax		880
NI		1,320
Depr.		800
Cash		2,120
f		3.170
PV		$6,720

6 years (5–10)   GAIN $2,520 (above)

10 year f 6.145		
− 4 year f 3.170		
= 6 year f 2.975	=	$ 7,497 PV
Add 4 years		6,720 PV
		14,217 PV
Add salvage		648 PV
		14,865
Net outlay		12,800
		$ 2,065 NPV

LEARNING CURVE

Labor-intensive operations can be performed faster as experience is gained. Time reductions per unit can be measured for actual operations. Future performance requires projection of all factors that may relate to output. Rates of reduction per unit can be stated as learning curves, usually based on doubling quantities.

A learning curve (LC) of 100% means that there is no time saving:

Quantity	100% Av. Output	Total Output	Total Output Differences Divided by Q	Per Unit Output
1	100	100	—	—
2	100	200	100/1	100
4	100	400	200/2	100
8	100	800	400/4	100

A learning curve of 50% is not attainable:

Quantity	50% Av. Output	Total Output	Total Output Differences Divided by Q	Per Unit Output
1	100	100	—	—
2	50	100	0/1	0
4	25	100	0/2	0
8	$12\frac{1}{2}$	100	0/4	0

The schedule states that added quantities are made in zero time; this is thus an ultimate limit.

Learning curves are limited by changes in products, methods, equipment, or personnel and by external factors affecting productivity. Their ranges fall between 65% and 95% generally, with a mode of 80%.

An example of an 80% LC follows:

Quantity	80% Av. Output	Total Output	Total Output Differences Divided by Q	Per Unit Output
1	1,000.0	1,000.0	—	—
2	800.0	1,600.0	600.0/1	600.0
4	640.0	2,560.0	960.0/2	480.0
8	512.0	4,096.0	1,536.0/4	384.0
16	409.6	6,553.6	2,457.6/8	307.2

An example of a 90% LC follows:

Quantity	90% Av. Output	Total Output	Total Output Differences Divided by Q	Per Unit Output
1	1,000.0	1,000.0	—	—
2	900.0	1,800.0	800.0/1	800.0
4	810.0	3,240.0	1,440.0/2	720.0
8	729.0	5,832.0	2,592.0/4	648.0
16	656.1	10,497.6	4,665.6/8	583.2

These differences are dramatic. The per unit comparison shows:

Quantity	90%	80%	Ratio 90% to 80%
1	0.0	—	—
2	800.0	600.0	1.3333
4	720.0	480.0	1.5000
8	648.0	384.0	1.6875
16	583.2	307.2	1.8984

Learning curve projections can be vital to capital expenditure projects when relevant and to bidding on large contracts. For example a machine can be purchased for $800,000.00. It has a 10 year life and can save $80,000 a year. The discount rate is 10% (f 6.145)

PV Cash $80,000 × f 6.145 = $491,600
Outlay   800,000
NPV   −$308,400

Yield $\dfrac{\$800,000}{\$\,80,000}$ = f 10.0 =   zero

Application of the 80% curve for Q 8 at $12 (per table) increases the $80,000 cash to $156,250 ($80,000/0.512). It is assumed that the 0.512 average is reached in a few months and then levels off.

Cash $156,250 × f 6.145 = $960,156
Outlay   800,000
NPV   +$160,156

Yield $\dfrac{\$800,000}{\$156,250}$ = f 5.12 =   14.5%

Application of the 90% curve for Q 8 at 0.729 (per table) increases the $80,000 cash to $109,740 ($80,000/0.729).

Cash $109,740 × f 6.145 = $674,350
Outlay   800,000
NPV   −$125,650

Yield $\dfrac{\$800,000}{\$109,740}$ = f 7.29 =   6.2%

To Recap:

LC	NPV	Increase	Yield
100%	−$308,400	—	0.0%
90	− 125,650	$182,750	6.2
80	+ 160,156	285,806	14.5
		$468,556	

The break-even LC is close to 85% with a 10% discount rate. Clearly, LC estimation is essential and can govern the decision. Costly errors of omission and commission are possible without careful attention.

TAX FACTORS

The tax code (currently) encourages investment, principally by allowing accelerated depreciation, shorter lives, omission of salvage value, and investment tax credits. Assets are classified into defined groups. Tax laws, regulations, and interpretations are complex, technical, and constantly changing. Competent tax advice is essential to investment analyses. Accelerated depreciation is illustrated in detail in Chapter 2 under "The Interest Method for Depreciation."

Investment tax credits are direct deductions from the tax bill and so reduce the outlay by the full amount allowed. For example:

Outlay	$20,000
10% credit	2,000
	$18,000
15 years cash	$ 3,000 = f 6.0
Yield	14.5%
Without the credit:	
Outlay	$20,000
15 years cash	$ 3,000 = f 6.667
Yield	12.4%

Use of the investment credit does not reduce the depreciable amount.

The current marginal tax rate is deducted from the current borrowing rate to determine the discount rate. The tax rate should be reviewed currently, as well as the borrowing rate. For example, if the borrowing rate remains at 18% but the tax rate falls:

Borrow At	Tax Rate	Balance	Discount Rate
18%	60%	40%	7.2%
18	50	50	9.0
18	40	60	10.8

Similarly, with a constant tax rate, we have:

Borrow At	Tax Rate	Balance	Discount Rate
14.4%	50%	50%	7.2%
18.0	50	50	9.0
21.6	50	50	10.8

Thus a lower tax rate has the same effect as a higher borrowing rate on the discount rate. The high rate indicated by the tables is:

Borrow at 21.6% − 40% tax rate = Balance 60% = 12.96% Discount rate.

and the indicated low rate is:

Borrow at 14.4% − 60% tax rate = Balance 40% = 5.76% Discount rate.

The discount rate determines both NPV and yield. It should be kept current and reflect marginal borrowing and tax rates. The tax rate should (usually) be a national average of the effective rate expected to be applicable in the near future, including federal, state and local taxes, net of applicable credits.

MUTUALLY EXCLUSIVE PROJECTS

Many investment decisions involve a choice among several feasible alternatives, which can have different cash flows. Only one project can be undertaken. The one selected is included in the capital expenditure budget.

Example 1a—Equal Yields and Cash

	Life	Outlay	Cash	f	Yield
Project A	10 years	$33,550	$5,000	6.71	8%
Project B	5 years	20,000	5,000	4.00	8
	+ 5 years	+$13,550	$ 0		

The choice of A is a decision now to commit to the 8% yield five years from now, for another five years, at an extra outlay of $13,550. Choice of B leaves open the future decision and favors liquidity by the lower outlay.

Example 1b—Equal Yields and Outlays

	Life	Outlay	Cash	f	Yield
Project C	10 years	$20,000	$2,980	6.71	8%
Project D	5 years	20,000	5,000	4.00	8
	+ 5 years	$ 0	+$2,020		

D favors liquidity by the larger cash flow and defers the next decision for five years. Preference for A and C would hinge on a strong preference to lock in the 8% for the added five years. These examples are artificial but help to define the nature of the analyses.

Example 2a—Equal Lives

	Life	Outlay	Cash	f	Yield
Project E	5 years	$18,000	$5,000	3.60	12.1%
Project F	5 years	10,000	3,000	3.33	15.0
		+$ 8,000	+$2,000	4.00	8.0%

The added cost for E with a 12.1% yield is, in effect, Project F plus the difference between E and F. The extra $2,000 cash earns 8% on the extra outlay of $8,000. The choice of E is then for F plus the difference. With equal lives, E provides more cash but lower yield. The choice then hangs on the 8%. If the discount rate is 8% or less, E is favored. If the discount rate is over 8%, then F is preferred because the extra outlay would have negative NPV.

Example 2b—Equal Lives Again

	Life	Outlay	Cash	f	Yield
Project G	8 years	$24,000	$4,500	5.333	10.0%
Project H	8 years	18,000	3,200	5.625	8.6
		+$ 6,000	+$1,300	4.615	14.1%

Project G is H at 8.6% and G/H at 14.1%. With a discount rate over 10%, neither project is acceptable.

Example 2c—Equal Lives, Equal Yields

	Life	Outlay	Cash	f	Yield
Project I	8 years	$24,000	$4,500	5.333	10%
Project J	8 years	18,000	3,375	5.333	10
		+$ 6,000	+$1,125	5.333	10%

This equality could hinge on liquidity and favor J for its lower outlay. But all have equal paybacks, as well as yields.

Example 3a—Unequal Lives, Annuity Method

	Project K	Project L
Life	11 years	6 years
Cash	$ 3,500	$ 2,700
10% f	6.495	4.355
PV	$22,733	$11,759
Outlay	$19,000	$10,000
NPV	$ 3,733 HI	$ 1,759

Annuity

$$\frac{\$3,733}{f\ 6.495} = \$574.75 \text{ HI} \qquad \frac{\$1,759}{f\ 4.355} = \$403.88$$

Yield

$$\frac{\$19,000}{\$\ 3,500} = f\ 5.429 \qquad \frac{\$10,000}{\$\ 2,700} = f\ 3.704$$

$$= 14.1\% \qquad\qquad = 15.8\% \text{ HI}$$

K has a higher NPV but a lower yield. However, K provides an annuity of $575 for 11 years, and L's annuity is only $404 for 6 years. Thus K is better by $171 per annum.

The annuity method neatly and accurately distinguishes the preferable NPV by its annuity equivalent. A higher NPV can have a lower annuity and thus not be preferred. NPVs are not comparable when based on different time periods, but this discrepancy is resolved by the annuity equivalents.

Example 3b—Unequal Lives Again

	Project M	Project N
Life	15 years	8 years
NPV at 10%	$4,000 HI	$3,200
10% f	7.606	5.335
Annuity	$ 526	$ 600 HI

Details are minimized to focus on the critical factors. The higher NPV for M provides a lower annuity because it is for 15 years. The lower NPV for N, for 8 years, gives a higher annuity—$600.

Yields are not given; they do not affect the decision.

Example 4—Cost Reduction

	Project O	Project P
Life	3 years	5 years
Outlay	$60,000	$ 80,000
Annual Cash Cost	$15,000	$ 15,600
10% f	2.487	3.790
PV	$37,305	$ 59,124
PV Outlay total	$97,305	$139,124
Annuity	$39,125	$ 36,708

The viewpoint shifts to lower cost rather than higher gain. P costs more in outlay and in operating cost, for a PV total of $139,124. But the annual cost is only $36,708 for five years, compared with $39,125 (O) for three years, less by $2,417.

INTANGIBLE BENEFITS

When gains cannot be quantified, projects tend to be evaluated by adjectives. It may be constructive to derive an amount for intangible benefits by use of the known factors—outlay, life, discount rate. For example, a project is planned to improve public relations: outlay, $68,000; life, six years; discount rate, 10%; tax, 50%.

$$\frac{\$68,000}{f\ 4.355} = \$15,614, \text{ or } \$31,228 \text{ before tax.}$$

With zero NPV at 10%, the benefits should be expected to exceed $31,000 for six years. Outlay and life may also be redetermined. This method helps to focus on a hard number.

If the discount rate is 6%:

$$\frac{\$68,000}{f\ 4.917} = \$13,830, \text{ or } \$27,660 \text{ before tax.}$$

With a 15% discount rate:

$$\frac{\$68,000}{f\ 3.784} = \$17,970, \text{ or } \$35,940 \text{ before tax.}$$

Considerations of risk and liquidity also apply. The accounting effect would be higher outlay—capitalized or expensed—and no determinable gain.

CAPITAL RATIONING

All projects approved for profitability, liquidity, and risk enter into the budget, and the total for all of the proposals becomes known. Some projects may be deferred for consideration in the next budget for a number of reasons. The proposals may appear, in total, to overtax management time and skill. Some projects would then be selected for deferment to meet this limitation. Other guidelines are the projects that appear to be best able to be held up relative to operational plans. Also, short-term liquidity constraints could lead to some postponements. Management may choose to defer borrowing because of current and anticipated market conditions. A stock issue may be decided against or deferred for a better market.

Projects selected for postponement would depend on the effect of delay relative to profitability, liquidity, and risk, as well as on operational plans. Deferred projects would be included in a subsequent budget but would also have to be reworked to reflect current factors at that time. Broader considerations could apply such as changed goals and strategies, internal management conflicts, takeover developments, changing industry conditions, foreign relations, pending tax changes, technological developments, and competitive thrusts.

Thus capital rationing is a broad, complex topic that is necessarily judgmental. It is temporary, but there is an opportunity cost equal to the NPV for each project not approved. Presumably, what is gained by rationing exceeds the NPVs of the projects deferred.

ADMINISTRATION

Project Classification

All projects must be fully identified and classified by some scheme as a procedural aid. The large variety of projects and the degree of overlap make classification schemes difficult and arbitrary. Each company must develop a plan to suit its needs. A scheme might be:

Strategic—major amounts—long lives—high risk—policy questions—major impact of failure—top level approval required (quantification often not practical)

New Products—new markets—old markets

Product Improvement—new markets—old markets

Increased Capacity—higher volume—lower cost (economy of scale)

Cost Reduction—same capacity

Mandated—government or contract requirement—no choice

Communication—satellites—short wave—longlines—cellular—computer control

Computers—equipment configurations

Replacements—relatively routine upkeep

Public Relations—all external

People Relations—all internal

All projects must appear in some category or sub-classification (with no mis-cellaneous heading).

Project Definition

Each project should be fully and clearly defined as to purpose, and it should be independent: its approval would not necessitate undisclosed subsequent outlay; it is one of several mutually exclusive projects; it does not combine actions better proposed as separate projects.

The major task is to define all cash flows by time period and on an incremental basis—exactly how much cash the project requires and produces. Each item must be a specific element and be stated in terms of cash only. A project to boost sales of A might reduce sales of B, and this must be measured. Added labor requires statement of the wages, plus actual costs directly attributable to the wages, such as for cash fringe benefits. Not permissible are items such as overhead, depreciation, or allocations, which are not specific cash outlays and directly related to the project. Approval of the project should generate cash flows as planned. Disapproval should have no effect on cash.

Debatable areas include use of existing space and existing facilities, such as utility generation. Adding employees may use up available parking areas—at some time more space will have to be provided. Recognition of such costs in individual projects is pragmatic and judgmental. In any event, the situation should be described. The evaluation may have to include other relevant projects and operating plans.

A project that is scheduled to become a capital (financial) lease should be fully analyzed as a purchase and the lease alternative defined. The source of the funds is a financing (not investing) decision.

Approval and Control

Projects must be approved at the appropriate management level for inclusion in budgets and financial plans. The total capital expenditure budget is the basis for overall review and approval and evaluation for the effect on growth, prof-itability, liquidity, and risk. Some projects may be deferred, as described in ''Capital Rationing.'' Others may be rejected, or further analysis may be re-quired. The budget, as amended, is then brought into the financial plans, but this step should not constitute approval for any project to be started.

A separate quarterly (periodic) report, based on the approved budget, should be submitted for final approval to take action on the individual projects. Projects may differ from the budget submission. Again, some projects may be cancelled or deferred, or further data may be required.

Approved projects should be monitored for both timely performance and compliance with the approved outlays. Some projects, because of adverse developments, may have to be held up or abandoned.

A final report for each project should compare actual results with the proposal, including dates, outlays, and estimated life and benefits. This step closes the project control cycle and provides the basis for operational review.

Operation Review and Appraisal

When the project is completed, a decision should be made whether a later review is necessary. For many projects it is either not necessary or impractical. If a review is to be made, it should specify when, by whom, and for what factors. The data that needs to be measured should be defined as part of the existing procedures or specific provision made to obtain it. Examples of data that may require a separate procedure include: machine maintenance, material usage, scrap, set-up time, labor cost, output rates, downtime. Detailed instructions are necessary to ensure collection of the required facts.

At the time of review, all of the data should be evaluated and a report made. Possible results include:

Better performance than projected.

Performance that should be improved.

Poor performance calling for some modifications.

Bad performance with improvement not likely. Replace or abandon.

Reschedule review.

All measurements relate to the project as defined when completed. When performance ranges are made as part of risk evaluation, they should be related to the performance found. All reviews should emphasize the possibilities for constructive action based on the experience to date.

Review programs can contribute to the preparation of project proposals, in a clear and responsible manner. Performance findings can enlighten the search for better investments. Bias in the preparation of proposals may surface and help guide preparers to more industrious and responsible efforts.

CHAPTER 5

Net Current Assets

MANAGING CURRENT OPERATIONS

Investments in current assets are subject to the same criteria that guide capital expenditures (or long-term assets)—profitability, liquidity, risk. The basic choice is between paying dividends or making investments. Stock prices reflect these management decisions.

Assets are classified on a balance sheet as current if realization can be expected within one year or within the industry operating cycle if longer. Longer term receivables and inventories, as well as security investments, plant and equipment, and deferred charges, are stated separately on a balance sheet. All liabilities payable within one year are classified as "current liabilities": payables, accruals, taxes, dividends, deferred credits, loans due within one year, and the current portion of long-term debt. Non-current liabilities include all longer term loans and bonds, less portions due within one year. Deferred taxes may be current, non-current, or both.

The difference between current assets and current liabilities, called "working capital," is not shown net on a balance sheet, as a rule. The concept of working capital is not useful for financial purposes, and it is debatable in accounting. For financial analysis, all current liabilities repayable with interest are reclassified as debt. The remainder have no explicit cost and are sometimes called "spontaneous credit." These liabilities are deducted from current assets to arrive at net current assets. This balance is the amount that must be managed, and it is financed by the capital structure.

Planning and control to achieve operating goals with a minimum investment in net current assets rests on analysis of the individual components.

INVENTORIES

Investment in inventories depends on evaluation of three factors: cost of ordering (from vendors or for production in the factory); cost of carrying stock on hand; and cost incurred by being out of stock.

Purchase ordering costs include requisitioning, purchase orders, receiving, inspection, handling, accounting, and payment. Production ordering costs include requisitions, production orders, set-up costs, inspection, handling, and accounting.

Carrying costs generally are in a range from 20% to 40% of inventory cost. Included are interest, taxes, insurance, labor, space charges, loss, deterioration, obsolescence, and record keeping.

Out-of-stock costs are difficult to estimate but may be significant. For finished goods, costs involve lost orders, lost customers, customer dissatisfaction, extra costs of obtaining stock in a hurry, and impaired morale of sales force. For in-process work, there are slow-down and shut-down costs, extra costs for set-ups, added costs to obtain missing items in a hurry, and impaired labor morale. For materials and supplies, there are extra costs to expedite delivery and for production delays. Approximation of all of these costs is necessary even if difficult to make.

Analysis of changes in these activities should be based on incremental costs, not averages, according to the degree of change, its timing, and likely effect on each cost element. For example, a purchasing department with an annual cost of $250,000 and issuing 1,000 orders has an average cost of $250 per order. An increase or decrease of only one order would affect only the forms costs, perhaps $1, not $250. A change of 100 orders would require incremental analysis. The additional dollars needed to handle another 100 orders might be found to be $10,000:

		No. of Orders		Dollars		Average
Present		1,000		$250,000		$ 250
Add	(10%)	+ 100	(4%) +	10,000	(40%)	100
		1,100		$260,000		$(236+)

If orders are reduced by 100, the expense reduction might be only $8,000:

		No. of Orders		Dollars		Average
Present		1,000		$250,000		$ 250
Deduct	(10%)	− 100	(32%) −	8,000	(32%)	− 80
		900		$242,000		$(269−)

Only the incremental averages—$100 and $80 are relevant for analysis.

Variable budgets for expense control are based on planned operations, usually for one year. They may supply useful information but do not serve the purpose of incremental analysis, which is necessarily pragmatic.

The factors controlling inventory levels should get primary attention: sales forecasts, ability to meet demand changes both quickly and economically, dependable production, reliable suppliers. These needs are greatly supported by participative management, just-in-time scheduling, and zero defects. These approaches have significantly reduced costs, lowered inventory levels, improved delivery, and increased sales and profits, both here and abroad.

Certain analytic techniques may be useful within the framework of the larger considerations.

The EOQ—economic order quantity—equation balances the cost of ordering stock with the cost of carrying it in inventory.

Example 1

Quantity needed for one year $= X$

Incremental cost of one order $= C$

Incremental carrying cost as a percent of purchase price $= H$

The formula is:

$$EOQ = \sqrt{\frac{2 \times X \times C}{H}}$$

If $X = 2,700$ units; $C = \$12$; $H = \$8$ (20% of $40), then

$$EOQ \sqrt{\frac{2 \times 2,700 \times \$12}{\$8}} = \sqrt{\frac{\$64,800}{\$8}} = \sqrt{\$8,100} = 90 \text{ units}$$

Each purchase order = 90 units $\times$ $40 = $3,600. Dollar formula:

$$\sqrt{\frac{2 \times \$108,000 \times \$12}{20\%}} = \sqrt{\frac{\$2,592,000}{20\%}} = \sqrt{\$12,960,000} = \$3,600$$

$$\text{Number of orders per year} = \frac{2,700}{90} = 30$$

$$\text{Average inventory} = 90/2 = 45 \text{ (linear usage)}$$

Proof: 30 orders @ $12 = $360
          45 inventory @ $8 =   360
          Total cost $720

The formula derivation is: order cost = carrying cost.

$$\frac{X}{Q} \times C = \frac{Q}{2} \times H \text{ and } 2XC = Q^2H \text{ and } \frac{2XC}{H} = Q^2 \text{ and } \sqrt{\frac{2XC}{H}} = Q = EOQ$$

Tabular analysis shows the effect of using different order quantities:

Order quantity	2,700	900	300	150	90	60	10	2
Orders per year	1	3	9	18	30	45	270	1,350
Cost at $12	$12	$36	$108	$216	$360	$540	$3,240	$16,200
Inventory average	1,350	450	150	75	45	30	5	1
Cost at $8	$10,800	$3,600	$1,200	$600	$360	$240	$40	$8
Total Cost	$10,812	$3,636	$1,308	$816	$720	$780	$3,280	$16,208

Any order quantity over, or under, the EOQ 90 increases total cost; one cost is reduced but the other is increased even more. The extra cost is fairly small within a quantity range, as above:

$$\begin{array}{rl} EOQ & 90 = \underline{\$720} \\ Q & 150 = \underline{\$816} + \$96 \\ Q & 60 = \underline{\$780} + \$60 \end{array}$$

(A change to Q 91 or 89 changes total cost by only about 5¢—Q 91 = $720.04396.)

If the current order quantity is 100 units, total cost is:

$$\begin{array}{l} \text{Order—2,700/100} = 27 \times \$12 = \$324 \\ \text{Carry—100/2} = 50 \times \$8 = \qquad \underline{\$400} \\ \qquad\qquad\qquad\qquad\qquad\qquad\qquad \$724 \end{array}$$

For 80 units, it is:

$$\begin{array}{l} \text{Order—2,700/80} = 33\tfrac{3}{4} \times \$12 = \$405 \\ \text{Carry—80/2} = 40 \times \$8 = \qquad\quad \underline{\$320} \\ \qquad\qquad\qquad\qquad\qquad\qquad\qquad\quad \$725 \end{array}$$

Total cost is changed by only $4 to $5 for orders of 10 units more or less than EOQ. However, if the order quantity has been 300, the total cost is $1,308 (per table) or $588 over the $720 minimum. In all cases, incremental costs should be used. This was not attempted in these examples to preserve clarity. In practice, it is a difficult but necessary consideration.

Many other factors can affect the order quantity—minimum order sizes, packing containers, freight, handling, shortage of items currently available, delivery uncertainties, possible price increases.

Example 2

The effect of reducing order cost is:

$$\begin{array}{rl} X = & 1,000 \\ C = & \$40 \\ H = & \$\,2 \end{array}$$

$$EOQ = \sqrt{\frac{2 \times 1,000 \times \$40}{\$2}} = \sqrt{40,000} = 200 \text{ units}$$

$$\begin{array}{l} \text{Total cost—Order-1,000/200} = 5 \times \$40 = \$200 \\ \qquad\qquad\quad \text{Carry-200/2} = 100 \times \$2 = \quad \underline{\$200} \\ \qquad\qquad\quad \text{minimum} \qquad\qquad\qquad\qquad\qquad \$400 \end{array}$$

Assume $C = \$1.60$ (theoretical minimum)

$$EOQ = \sqrt{\frac{2 \times 1,000 \times \$1.60}{\$2}} = \sqrt{1,600} = 40 \text{ units}$$

$$\text{Total cost—Order-1,000/40} = 25 \times \$1.60 = \$40$$
$$\text{Carry-40/2} = 20 \times 2 = \underline{\$40}$$
$$\text{minimum} \qquad \$80$$

Total cost is reduced by $320 to $80.

The purpose of this illustration is to highlight the significance of order cost to total cost. Note that both order cost and carrying cost are reduced by 80%.

Example 3

EOQ refers to vendor orders. Orders for factory production are subject to the same analysis but are termed *ELS*—economic lot size.

X = Annual production—960 units

C = \$40 incremental cost of one order for production, including set-up cost.

H = Carrying cost \$12.

$$ELS = \sqrt{\frac{2 \times 960 \times \$40}{\$12}} = \sqrt{\frac{76,800}{\$12}} = \sqrt{6,400} = 80 \text{ units}$$

$$\text{Total cost—Order-960/80} = 12 \times \$40 = \$480$$
$$\text{Carry-80/2} = 40 \times \$12 = \underline{\$480}$$
$$\text{minimum} \qquad \$960$$

If the factory order quantity is 120 units, we have:

$$\text{Total cost—Order-960/120} = 8 \times \$40 = \$320$$
$$\text{Carry-120/2} = 60 \times \$12 = \underline{\$720}$$
$$\$1,040 \ (+\$80)$$

If the factory order quantity is 40 units, we have:

$$\text{Total cost—Order-960/40} = 24 \times \$40 = \$960$$
$$\text{Carry-40/2} = 20 \times \$12 = \underline{\$240}$$
$$\$1,200 \ (+\$240)$$

To find the extent of cost reduction attributable to C, assume that it is only $2.50, not $40.

$$\sqrt{\frac{2 \times 960 \times \$2.50}{\$12}} = \sqrt{400} = 20 \text{ ELS}$$

$$\text{Total cost—Order-960/20} = 48 \times \$2.50 = \$120$$
$$\text{Carry-20/2} = 10 \times \$12 = \underline{\$120}$$
$$\text{minimum} \qquad \$240$$

Total cost is reduced from $960 to $240 or $720 less.

Assume that C is cut from $40 to $22.50:

$$\sqrt{\frac{2 \times 960 \times \$22.50}{\$12}} = \sqrt{\frac{\$43,200}{\$12}} = \sqrt{3,600} = 60 \; ELS$$

Total cost—Order-960/60 = 16 × $22.50 = $360
Carry-60/2 = 30 × $12 = $360
minimum $720

This reduction is from $960 to $720, or $240 less.

This type of analysis helps to focus attention on achievable cost reductions. Set-up costs are susceptible, for example, to large reductions in many situations.

Example 4

A lower unit purchase price for a larger order quantity requires separate analysis.

In Example 1, the EOQ was 90 for 2,700 units purchased at $40, and total cost was $720 to order and carry inventory. If the vendor quotes a price of $39 for quantities of 540 units, the price saving is:

$$2,700 \times \$1 \; (\$40 - \$39) = \$2,700$$

The order cost is: 2,700/540 = 5 × $12 = $ 60
The cost to carry is: 540/2 = 270 × $8 = $2,160

	$2,220
Total cost—Example 1	720
Extra inventory cost (Q 540, cf. Q 90)	1,500
Price saving (above)	2,700
Net gain	$1,200

This attractive alternative is subject to the validity of the $8 carrying charge (20% of $40). If increased carrying costs (obsolescence, damage) are applicable and are estimated to raise the $8.00 to $12.50, then:

Order cost 2,700/540 = 5 × $12 = $ 60
Carry cost 540/2 = 270 × $12.50 = $3,375

	$3,435
Total cost—Example 1	720
Extra inventory cost	2,715
Price saving (above)	2,700
Net loss	$ 15

Example 5

Safety Stocks (SS) of finished goods guard against stockouts (SO) that may occur because of higher sales or from delivery delays. Related costs include lost order profits, extra expenses to expedite delivery, and customer goodwill.

Safety Stocks (SS) of materials, parts, tools, and supplies may be needed to preclude production delays that cause high extra costs.

The cost of carrying SS is the incremental inventory carrying cost, expressed as a percentage of dollar value per year, as used in the EOQ formula. SO costs are difficult to ascertain but approximations are useful. Some estimate must be made of possible delivery delays and sales ranges, with probabilities, to arrive at the amount of probable over or under quantities. Some dollar amount must be determined as the cost of each stock out (SO) occurrence.

The objective is to balance the SS cost with the SO cost so that total cost is minimized. A simple example for an item of finished goods is presented to illustrate the process:

Annual sales	5,000	units
Weekly sales (50 weeks)	100	units
EOQ 500 units	10	orders per year
Delivery lead time, 4 weeks	400	units
SS carrying cost per unit	$40	per year
SO cost	$200	per occurrence

The following table of SO costs is based on sales-range probabilities related to SS units (statistical methods may be used to derive probabilities):

1	2	3	4	5
				(2 × 3 × 4)
		No. of	Cost	Total
SS Units	SO Prob.	Orders	per SO	SO Cost
0	90%	10	$200	$1,800
10	65	10	200	1,300
20	40	10	200	800
30	25	10	200	500
40	15	10	200	300
50	5	10	200	100
60	0	10	200	0

Carrying costs for SS units per year are:

SS Units	Per Unit	Annual Total
0	$40	$ 0
10	40	400
20	40	800
30	40	1,200
40	40	1,600
50	40	2,000
60	40	2,400

Inventory levels are reduced when SS units are used until replenished. Correction for this factor is negligible. The combined schedules:

SS Units	Carry Cost	SO Cost	Combined Total
0	$ 0	$1,800	$1,800
10	400	1,300	1,700
20	800	800	1,600
30	1,200	500	1,700
40	1,600	300	1,900
50	2,000	100	2,100
60	2,400	0	2,400

Minimum total cost is for 20 SS units, at $1,600, with a range from 10 to 30 units for about the same total cost. Despite the use of approximation, there is a clear indication of both the need for some SS and the fallacy of going to either extreme of SS levels.

The intangible benefit of greater delivery assurance can be measured:

SS Units	SO Probability	Cost Total	Cost Increment
20	40%	$1,600	—
30	25	1,700	$100
40	15	1,900	200
50	5	2,100	200
60	0	2,400	300
			$800

This analysis points up the relatively high cost of lower SO probabilities. Also, attention should focus on improved sales forecasting and greater reliability and flexibility in meeting change of demands.

In practice, varying assumptions about SO probabilities, SO costs, and SS carrying costs can be analyzed to help approximate a viable SS level. With a very large number of inventory items, suppliers, and customers, it is an onerous task, particularly with ever-changing conditions.

In summary, financial management should encourage planning for minimum inventories. Actual inventories should be monitored against the plans. Excess, obsolete, and damaged stocks should be weeded out promptly to reduce carrying costs and realize the tax deduction. ROA can be improved by cost reduction to increase the percentage of profit to sales as well as by asset control to increase the turnover ratio to sales.

$$\text{Present ROA:} \quad \frac{\text{Sales } \$1,000}{\text{Assets } \$\ \ 200} \times \frac{\text{Profit } \$\ \ \ 40}{\text{Sales } \$1,000} = \frac{\$\ 40}{\$200}$$

$$= 5 \quad \times \quad 4.0\% = 20.0\%$$

Planned ROA: Sales $\dfrac{\$1,200}{\$\ \ 250}$ $\times$ Profit $\dfrac{\$\ \ \ \ 45}{\$1,200}$ $=$ $\dfrac{\$\ \ 45}{\$250}$

$= 4.8 \times$ $\qquad$ $3.75\% = 18.00\%$

Revised ROA: Sales $\dfrac{\$1,200}{\$\ \ 225}$ $\times$ Profit $\dfrac{\$\ \ \ \ 49.5}{\$1,200.0}$ $=$ $\dfrac{\$\ \ 49.5}{\$225.0}$

$= 5\tfrac{1}{3} \times$ $\qquad$ $4\tfrac{1}{8}\% = 22\%$

A reduction in ROA from 20 to 18% is revised to 22% by limiting the asset increase to a smaller rate than the sales increase to increase turnover, and by reducing planned costs to improve the rate of profit to sales. The revised goal calls for increasing turnover from 5× to 5⅓× and for a profit rate of 4⅛%, up from 4%.

ROA analysis should be carried into all measurable segments of operations, but in terms of clearly established responsibility centers. Inventory control should be exercised at the item level. What is known as ABC analysis may also be applicable. For instance:

A—10% of items = 70% of dollar value

B—20% of items = 20% of dollar value

C—70% of items = 10% of dollar value.

The A items get close attention, with relatively less for B and C items. The purpose is to limit inventory control expenses relative to inventory value. Other methods are available.

Inventory turnover data are useful for statistical review but are relatively superficial. All inventory control systems should be evaluated periodically, and actual performance should be audited at intervals to insure effective results.

RECEIVABLES

Credit policies, payment terms, and collection practices affect the amount of receivables from customers. Industry practices vary widely, but companies within an industry generally have similar approaches. Credit can be an effective competitive weapon but needs to be carefully evaluated.

Incremental analysis should be used to determine profitability for alternatives. The change in profit as a percent of the change in assets provides an incremental ROA, which can be compared with the discount rate. All calculations can be made before tax when the tax effect is constant. A current borrowing rate of 18% before tax is used for the following examples.

Example 1

Increase terms from 30 to 60 days:

Sales increase from $60,000 to $66,000 =	$6,000
Variable cost (VC) 70%	4,200
Variable margin (VM) 30%	1,800
Increase in credit costs	300
Profit balance	1,500
Increase in bad debts:	
$60,000 at 2% = $1,200	
$66,000 at $3\frac{1}{3}$% = 2,200	
	1,000
Incremental profit	$500

Receivables increase

	Gross	Bad Debts		Net
$60,000—30 days ($\frac{1}{12}$ of 360)	$ 5,000	− (2%)	$100 =	$ 4,900
$66,000—60 days ($\frac{1}{6}$ of 360)	11,000	− ($3\frac{1}{3}$%)	367 =	10,633
	+$ 6,000	+	$267 =	+$ 5,733
Inventory increase				517
Asset increase				$6,250
Incremental ROA 500/6,250 = 8.0%		TOO LOW		

This ROA is based on receivables of $5,733, which contain 30% VM, $1,720, and 70% VC, $4,013. Adding inventory of $517, the total is $4,530. The ROA is then $500/$4,530 = 11%.

This cost approach is consistent with capital expenditure analysis, as explained in Chapter 4, Example A. In practice, this reduction of receivables to cost is not made for operational analysis, which is based on the accounting records.

Both methods are needed for the investment decision if there is a significant difference. For example:

	Asset Increase			Profit	
	Receivables	Inventory	Total	Increase	ROA
Per Books	$10,000	$2,000	$12,000	$1,200	10%
VC 80%	8,000	2,000	10,000	1,200	12
VC 60%	6,000	2,000	8,000	1,200	15
VC 40%	4,000	2,000	6,000	1,200	20

With a discount rate over 10% and under 20%, the VC alternatives become acceptable.

Example 2

This example is based on Example 1.

Sales increase	$6,000
VC 80%	4,800
VM 20%	1,200
Increase in credit costs	300
Profit balance	900
Increase in bad debts	1,000
Incremental loss	− $ 100

The drop in VM to 20% from 30% causes a loss. The asset base is unchanged.

Example 3

This example is based on Example 2.

Sales increase	$6,000	
VC 80%	4,800	
VM 20%	1,200	
Increase in credit costs	200	(not 300)
	1,000	
Increase in bad debts	0	(not 1,000)
Incremental profit		$1,000
Incremental assets:		
Receivables	$6,000	
Inventory	666	$6,666
Incremental ROA 15%		$1,000/$6,666

The asset total of $6,666 can be reduced to cost by subtracting the 20% VM in receivables—20% of $6,000 = $1,200; $6,666 − $1,200 = $5,466. ROA $1,000/$5,466 = 18.3%. This adjustment raises the rate over the 18% borrowing rate.

Example 4

This example concerns selling to a new class of customer with a high credit risk.

New sales	$15,000
VC 60%	9,000
VM 40%	6,000
Increased credit costs	1,200
	4,800
Bad debts at 24%	3,600
Incremental profit	$ 1,200

        Incremental assets:
          Receivables—120 days ($\frac{1}{3}$ of 360)
          $15,000/3   = $5,000
          less bad debts
          $3,600/3   1,200
                                        3,800
        Inventory   1,200 $5,000
        Incremental ROA 24% $1,200/$5,000

This appears to be attractive but is highly risky. If bad debts become 30%, the added 6% on $15,000 is $900. Profits drop to $300 and ROA to about 6%. Liquidity is also affected by the build up in assets. The requirement for unusually high bad debts and credit costs, however, should not preclude a careful evaluation of attractive profit possibilities.

Example 5

Change payment terms from 45 days to 2.0% cash discount in 10 days, net 30. Sales increase by 10.0%, VM is 15.0%, a cash discount is taken on half of the sales, and bad debts at 6.0% of sales are reduced to 5.3%.

        Sales increase: $30,000 to $33,000 $3,000
        VC 85%   2,550
        VM 15%   +$450
        Credit cost increase   − 200
                                                                  +$250

        Decrease in bad debts:
          $30,000 at 6% $1,800
          33,000 at 5.3% 1,750   +$ 50
        Incremental gain   + 300
        Cash discount—2% on $16,500   − 330
        Incremental loss   −$ 30

        Receivables:
          $30,000—45 days ($\frac{1}{8}$ of 360) $3,750
          $33,000:
             16,500—10 days ($\frac{1}{36}$ of 360)   460
             16,500—30 days ($\frac{1}{12}$ of 360)   1,375
                                                            1,835
        Receivable reduction ($3,750 − $1,835)   − 1,915
        Inventory increase   +   815
        Incremental asset decrease   −$1,100

The profit reduction is not attractive, but there is also a large decrease in assets. ROA would be improved, the extent depending on the base. For example:

	Present (assumed)	Change (above)	Proposed
Profit	$ 730	−$ 30	$ 700
Assets	$7,300	−$1,100	$6,200
ROA	10%		11.3%

The change ROA ($30/$1,100) is 2.7%. A proposal to *increase* profit by $30 for an investment of $1,100, or 2.7%, would be unacceptable. The *reverse* is acceptable because the $1,100 can be put to better use. This form of ROA analysis is in reverse but no less significant. There could also be a profit gain and asset reduction.

Restating the above table with a smaller asset reduction, we have:

	Present	Change	Proposed
Profit	$ 730	−$ 30	$ 700
Assets	$7,300	−$100	$7,200
ROA	10.0%		9.7%

This is not desirable because the ROA is reduced; the change ROA is 30% ($30/$100).

Example 6

Increase sales 10% by extending the term from 36 to 72 days.

Sales increases from	$20,000	
to	22,000	
		$2,000
VC 75%		1,500
VM 25%		500
Increased credit costs		200
Profit balance		$ 300
Bad debts:		
$20,000 at 2.0%	$400	
$22,000 at 2.5%	550	
		150
Incremental profit		$ 150
Receivables:		
20,000—36 days ($\frac{1}{10}$)	$2,000	
22,000—72 days ($\frac{1}{5}$)	4,400	
Increase	2,400	
less bad debts ($40–$110)	− 70	2,330
Inventory increase		170
Assets increase		$2,500

Incremental ROA is $150/$2,500 = 6% (cf. 18%). This is a poor proposal.

In some cases, collection is lax to avoid customer resentment. ROA is adversely affected. For instance, assume receivables increase by $250:

	Now	Later	Change
Profit	$ 200	$ 200	0
Assets	$1,000	$1,250	+25%
ROA	20%	16%	

The equivalent with no changes in assets is:

	Now	Later	Change
Profit	$ 200	$ 160	−20%
Assets	$1,000	$1,000	0
ROA	20%	16%	

High interest rates put pressure on prompt collection. Interest may be charged on overdue balances to help offset the loss.

In all cases, the factors should be carefully defined and any assumptions stated. Variations in amounts, with probabilities, may need to be estimated to reveal possible profit ranges to aid risk appraisal. The effect on liquidity also may need attention.

CASH

Planning cash balances depends on the degree of forecasting accuracy that is possible. Cash is needed to handle transactions, and some precautionary balance is needed to handle unanticipated swings in cash flows in and out. Large (lumpy) payments must be provided for dividends, capital expenditures, tax payments, and loan repayments—which are largely predictable. Additional cash should be on tap for the unplanned changes, such as forecast deviations, or for unpredictable events. The total cash may be kept at a high level to provide for unexpected acquisition opportunities—distress sales, another company or a division, company stock repurchase, patent rights.

Company cash policies vary widely. Cash is part of ROA, which is reduced by higher balances, that offer higher liquidity. This trade-off is not amenable to quantitative analyses. For example:

	ROA—Cash as % of Total Assets		
Cash	$ 909 (1%)	$ 10,000 (10%)	$ 21,111 (19%)
Other	$90,000	$ 90,000	$ 90,000
Total	$90,909	$100,000	$111,111
EBT	$20,000	$ 20,000	$ 20,000
ROA	22%	20%	18%

Temporary surplus cash can be put into marketable securities to provide some return, but the gain is offset by transaction costs. For instance, $20,000 at 12% per year would yield 1% per month or $200, but this would be offset by transaction costs. Complex formulas are available to guide this decision process, but results depend on highly variable factors difficult to forecast.

Commercial banks offer well-developed methods, at a cost, for reducing collection time and for delaying payment time. There are current developments to minimize all float, however.

Cash includes cash funds kept on hand, plus bank balances not subject to withdrawal restrictions, plus marketable securities (funds available within 24 hours). Pledged cash is excluded (and should be classified as non-current). Cash availability, more importantly, includes the ability to borrow at short notice and on competitive terms. This can be provided by a line of credit or revolving credit agreement for a small commitment fee.

Cash availability also includes the possible issuance of bonds and stock, disposal of assets, cost reductions, dividend reductions, delayed capital expenditures, stretching payments on payables, and bargain sales.

High interest rates and restricted credit availability put a premium on liquidity and impair profitability.

PAYABLES

Payment terms for vendor purchases are a part of the overall negotiation and cannot be interpreted separately.

All discount terms should be observed when the gain exceeds the company's borrowing rate. Stretching the terms impairs vendor relationships unless there is advance agreement. A vendor may accept a note with interest or may be interested in an equity position.

For terms of 2% in 10 days or net for 30 days—2/10, net 30—the rate is:

$$\frac{\$ 2}{\$98} \times \frac{360 \text{ days}}{20 \text{ days}} = 2.0408\% \times 18 = 36.73\% \text{ per year}$$

Or, either pay $98 now or keep the $98 at a cost of $2 for another 20 days (day 10 to day 30). To annualize, the percent for 20 days is multiplied by 18.

For terms of 2/10, net 60:

$$\frac{\$ 2}{\$98} \times \frac{360 \text{ days}}{50 \text{ days}} = 2.0408\% \times 7.2 = 14.7\% \text{ per year}$$

Compound daily for 365 days = 14.7%/365 = 0.04027% = 15.83% annually.

$$36.73\%/365 = 0.10063\% = 44.36\% \text{ annually}$$

If the bank borrowing rate is more, the vendor should be paid at the end of 60 days. The company is, in effect, borrowing from the vendor at a rate below the bank rate.

Cash discount terms are usually at high rates to encourage collection, reduce bad debts, and improve liquidity. The company makes a similar analysis in determining credit terms for customers, as analyzed above.

Examples

Terms	Annual %		Times per Year, 360 days
2/10, Net 60 =	14.7	($2/$98 = 2.0408%)	7.2 for 50 days
2/10, Net 50 =	18.4	($2/$98 = 2.0408%)	9.0 for 40 days
2/10, Net 40 =	24.5	($2/$98 = 2.0408%)	12.0 for 30 days
2/10, Net 30 =	36.7	($2/$98 = 2.0408%)	18.0 for 20 days
3/10, Net 70 =	18.5	($3/$97 = 3.09%)	6.0 for 60 days
3/10, Net 60 =	22.2	($3/$97 = 3.09%)	7.2 for 50 days
3/10, Net 50 =	27.8	($3/$97 = 3.09%)	9.0 for 40 days
3/10, Net 40 =	37.1	($3/$97 = 3.09%)	12.0 for 30 days
5/10, Net 130 =	15.8	($5/$95 = 5.26%)	3.0 for 120 days
5/10, Net 100 =	21.0	($5/$95 = 5.26%)	4.0 for 90 days

LOANS

Short-term loans (one to five years) are provided by commercial banks. The use of debt as part of financial structure is contained in Chapter 12. The cost of short-term loans is based on a variety of terms. If $100 is received and $118 is repaid a year later, the rate is 18.00%. If the bank quotes an annual rate of 18.00%, it may be based on a year of 360 days. For 365 days, the rate is $365/360 \times 18.00\% = 18.25\%$.

A loan on a discount basis at 18.00% provides $82.00 now with $100.00 to be repaid in a year = $18.00/$82.00 = 21.95%. (If $100.00 is received now, $121.95 is due in one year: $121.95/$100 = 21.95%.)

If the loan specifies a minimum compensating balance of $10, the calculation for 18% interest is: $100 − $10 = $90 now and repay $118 = $18/$90 = 20%. (However, if the compensating balance requirement would be met in any event, the rate is $18/$100 = 18%.)

Loan balance due within one year are classified as "current" on the balance sheet for accounting purposes. For financial management, all borrowing is classified as "debt," regardless of maturity or type, to provide logical analysis of capital structure and leverage. Investment analysis relates to current assets less spontaneous credit (sources of funds without explicit cost) and to capital expenditures.

Loans secured with collateral are cheaper, but management's freedom of action relative to the pledged assets may be impaired. Longer term loans may be more expensive, depending on the term structure of interest rates, but provide greater liquidity. A shorter term loan requires renewal sooner when credit may be tight—a credit crunch. Loan terms should be carefully negotiated to avoid unacceptable restrictions on management. Lenders seek all of the protective covenants they can get to help insure collectibility. The loan conditions are more sensitive and significant than the interest cost in many cases.

A line of credit insures availability of funds when needed at pre-determined terms, for example, line of credit, $200,000; interest rate, 18.0% for funds used and 0.8% for unused balances. If no funds are drawn down, the cost of credit line is $1,600 for the year—an insurance cost. If the entire line is used, the cost is $36,000. If half of the line is used all year, it is:

$$
\begin{array}{rcl}
\$100,000 \text{ at } 18.0\% & = & \$18,000 \\
100,000 \text{ at } 0.8\% & = & \underline{800} \\
& & \$18,800
\end{array}
$$

The amount used has a cost of 18.8% ($18,800/$100,000). The balance of $100,000 not used cost $800 to insure its availability, a cost of liquidity.

OTHER SOURCES OF FUNDS

Longer term loans, bond issues, and stock offerings are analyzed in Chapter 12, "Capital Structure."

The largest and strongest companies can issue commercial paper, usually for a period of 270 days and backed up by a bank line of credit. The cost of commercial paper is slightly less than the bank prime rate as a rule.

Financial leases are a form of borrowing and are described in Chapter 10.

Receivables can be factored (sold) or used as collateral. Inventories can be hypothecated. These are specialized and relatively expensive sources of funds, applicable to particular industries.

Other assets may be sold to raise money even though operations and profits are impaired.

Products may be sold at bargain prices. Expenses can be reduced, particularly payrolls.

Customers may advance funds or purchase stock to keep a valued supplier in business.

The danger of impending insolvency puts a premium on liquidity over profit. Reevaluation of goals, strategies, and policies may be needed to foster survival and avoid merger or liquidation.

CHAPTER 6

Uncertainty and Risk

COPING WITH THE UNKNOWNS

THE APPROACH

All investment decisions rest on assumptions about the future that relate to the evaluation. Individual attitudes about the future and its uncertainty are subjective and not responsive to rationalization. Uncertainty relates to developments that cannot be anticipated and hence are not subject to evaluation. Uncertainty may occasion worry, but worry is not an aid to decision-making.

Risk, as distinguished from uncertainty, can be limited to those aspects of the future that are subject to some reasonable evaluation as to ranges of outcome and their probability of occurrence. The process is subjective but its written expression is necessary for constructive communication and evaluation. Disagreement on probable outcomes is to be expected, but their expression provides a basis for mutual understanding of the position of each person involved. Unexpressed fears can mitigate against sound decisions and hamper morale. An unexplained "no" is highly negative to a constructive atmosphere.

An investment project expressed with only one outcome rests on single amounts, or point estimates, for each factor. When the range of probable outcomes is expressed, it is possible to evaluate the chances for doing better than the point estimate—the upside potential—and for doing worse—the downside risk.

Individual perceptions of monetary gain and loss vary widely; this is known as the "utility function." Individual utilities are different for different kinds of risk, for different amounts of money, and for different odds. Individual utilities change over time and in response to changed conditions. They are not necessarily logically related (transitive). Clear management communication and consensus on investment decisions depend on explicit risk evaluation, particularly for the larger and more sensitive projects. Vertical communication is particularly important because of the significant difference in the effect of risk at different management levels. For instance, a junior engineer proposing a $100,000 methods change with a 10% loss probability has much more at stake than top management dealing with hundreds of proposals totaling millions of dollars.

To illustrate, assume that a project for $100,000 has a positive NPV at 10% and a yield of 18%. The project proposer estimates outcomes for a range of variables—outlay, gain, life—with the following probabilities:

Probability	Yield	
10%	Over 30%	
30	20–30	
35	10–20	(18%)
15	0–10	
10	Loss ($2,000)	
100%		

The 10% chance of a loss of $2,000 is acceptable in most circumstances. Few investments are made without some chance of losses, whether or not expressed. There is a 15% chance of earning less than 10%, the discount rate, or negative leverage. This is 25% cumulative. These odds would deter some managers, despite the high upside potential—a cumulative 40% chance of yields over 20%. This reaction reflects risk aversion as opposed to risk preference (as attributed to gamblers). The 35% probability of yields from 10% to 20% contains the point estimate yield of 18%, which splits the probabilities 50–50.

Discussion of this table of outcomes could lead to approval or rejection. In some cases it could lead to a reworking of the project, in detail, with a different outcome. The whole process of risk evaluation should help to clear some projects that would otherwise be dropped and to reject others that appear to be too risky. At the same time, accepted risk ranges are established for comparison with actual results.

Consider a proposal for $1 million with a positive NPV at 10% and a point estimate yield of 22%. The following risk table is prepared:

Probability	Cum.	Yield	
15%	15%	Loss ($100,000)	
15	30	0–10%	
15	45	10–20	
25	70	20–30	(22%)
30	100	Over 30	
100			

Despite the high yield of 22%, there is a 15% chance of losing as much as $100,000 and a 30% chance (cum.) of earning less than the 10% discount rate. Thus both the percents and the dollar amounts affect the risk evaluation. Again, the high upside potential does not affect the evaluation; it does not offset risk aversion.

These two examples would elicit different responses from individuals, and their evaluations could vary over time and be affected by changed circumstances. Companies and managers come to be known for their risk attitudes.

The preparation of ranges for outcomes requires exploration of all variables in the project and expression of probabilities—from zero up—for each outcome. This can be time consuming and subject to personal bias. However, it can be invaluable as a guide to management, and it needs to be carried out for only the largest and riskiest projects, perhaps only 1% or 2% of all proposals.

RISK ATTITUDES

One way to explore risk attitudes is to ask for a response to the following odds:

Choice	You Have Won the Certain Amount of	You Can Take a Chance of Winning Ten Times as Much	What Odds Do You Require to Take the Chance? (One Possible Choice Shown)
1	$100,000	$1,000,000	6–10
2	10,000	100,000	5–10
3	1,000	10,000	4–10
4	100	1,000	3–10
5	10	100	2–10
6	1	10	1–10

This table relates odds of ten to one with dollar amounts. With a certain $100,000 some people would not accept any odds (not even 9–10) to increase the total to $1 million at the risk of losing the sure $100,000. This is highly risk averse. The odds given at six chances in ten necessarily include four chances in ten of losing all. Very rich (and very poor) people might take odds of 1–10 because the loss of $100,000 is of little consequence; to the billionaire it is a small loss—some penniless persons would take the risk to become millionaires and accept the possible loss because they are inured to poverty.

At the other extreme, many would gamble the loss of $1 to gain $10; the odds indicated of 1–10 are in the same ratio. Some would take odds of 1–20, and others might require 2–10 or more, indicating a high utility for the certain $1.

The increasing odds shown for illustration reflect the greater utility of the larger amounts; thus $100,000 at 6–10 has six times the utility of $1 at 1–10 (the risk aversion is six times greater).

Utilities vary widely among people and over time and relate both to odds and total amounts.

Another example of utility is based on a series of payments, an annuity, in contrast to the one-shot gambles above.

Assume that a lottery pays the lump sum of $5,000 now, plus $100 per week for 50 weeks (another $5,000 over time). Each week the winner can accept the $100 or take one chance in ten (1–10) of getting $1,000 for that week. Each week provides an independent choice. How many weeks of receiving the $100 before exercising the 1–10 choice to get $1,000? How many weeks of receiving nothing before returning to the certain $100?

This annuity has a range from zero (50 chances of 1–10 odds with no payoff) to $50,000 (50 chances of 1–10 odds that all pay off). The odds are very small for either extreme. The sure result of getting 50 payments of $100 each, for a $5,000 total, can be beaten only by taking odds of 1–10. With the $100 coming in week after week, most people at some time would opt for the 1–10 odds—for one week or more. Half would gain and half would lose (statistically).

This example helps to bring out the point that with increasing wealth, the utility of money decreases.

The following three examples apply risk analysis to an investment proposal, restricting the variable to project life first, then to outlay amount, and finally to cash gain.

Project—point estimate (discount rate (10%)

Outlay $100,000—Cash gain $20,000—Life 8 years

Yield $\dfrac{\$100,000}{\$\ 20,000}$ = f 5.0 = 11.8%—8 years

Example 1—Variable Project Life

Outlay and cash gain are accepted, but project life is estimated to fall in a range of four to ten years.

Life	(f 5.0) Yield		Probability	Cum.
10	15.1%		0.1	0.1
9	13.7		.2	.3
8	11.8		.3	.6
7	9.2		.1	.7
6	5.5		.1	.8
5	0.0		.1	.9
4	− 8.4	(LOSS $20,000)	0.1	1.0
Project 8	11.8%		1.0	

The yield range is from −8.4% to +15.1%, compared with the 11.8% yield submitted. The table can be called a risk profile.

With a discount rate of 10%, this project is not attractive for most managers— there is about a 50% chance of a yield below 10%, including a possible large loss. Risk aversion is not usually overcome by the higher yields for longer life. The project might be reworked for lower outlay or higher gain. If the estimate of life below seven years is reduced to zero probability (P), and the P 0.3 reallocated, the project becomes attractive. Also, if the discount rate is 5%, rather than 10%, the project becomes more acceptable. A major purpose of the risk profile is to stimulate communication and improve evaluation.

Example 2—Variable Outlay

Life and cash gain are accepted, but the outlay is estimated to range as follows:

Outlay	Cash Gain on $20,000	Yield	Probability	Cum.
$ 86,880	f 4.344	16.0%	0.1	0.1
92,780	4.639	14.0	.2	.3
99,360	4.968	12.0	.2	.5
106,600	5.330	10.0	.2	.7
114,940	5.747	8.0	.1	.8
124,200	6.210	6.0	.1	.9
134,660	6.733	4.0	0.1	1.0
Project $100,000	f 5.000	11.8%	1.0	

Again, the probability is about 50% that yield will fall below the 10% discount rate, but the minimum yield is 4%. This risk profile would be acceptable to some managers.

An important factor in risk analysis, not shown by the examples, is the size of the project relative to total operations. If this example is a large part of the total operations, many would not want to take the risk. If it is a small part of the total, and one of many proposals, it is less threatening.

Example 3—Variable Cash Gain

Outlay and life are accepted. The estimated cash gain range is:

Cash Gain	Outlay $100,000	Yield	Probability	Cum.
$26,060	f 3.837	20.0%	0.1	0.1
24,525	4.078	18.0	.1	.2
23,020	4.344	16.0	.1	.3
21,560	4.639	14.0	.2	.5
20,130	4.968	12.0	.2	.7
18,745	5.335	10.0	.2	.9
17,400	5.747	8.0	.1	1.0
Project $20,000	f 5.000	11.8%	1.0	

With a 10% discount rate, this profile is favorable. There are seven outcomes in each example. If all three are combined, total outcomes are $7 \times 7 \times 7 = 343$. This is easy to program on a computer but too cumbersome to handle manually.

Several combinations can be picked out:

	Most Profitable	Least Profitable	Median Point
Life	10 (P 0.1)	4 (P 0.1)	7 (P 0.1)
Outlay	$86,880 (P 0.1)	$134,660 (P 0.1)	$106,600 (P 0.2)

	Most Profitable	Least Profitable	Median Point
Gain	$26,060 (P 0.1)	$ 17,400 (P 0.1)	$ 21,560 (P 0.2)
	f 3.334	f 7.739	f 4.944
Yield	+27.3% (P 0.001)	−22.0% (P 0.001)	+9.53% (P 0.004)

Outlay	$134,660
Gain	− 69,600 = 4 × $17,400
LOSS	=$ 65,060

Each of these 3 out of 343 outcomes has a very small probability—one in a thousand for the most and least extremes.

A consistent method for summarizing the outcomes for projects is needed to facilitate comprehension and comparisons.

RISK PROFILES AND EVALUATION

A predetermined set of yield ranges is needed so that all projects can be summarized in comparative form. A set of five yield ranges is convenient, starting with a loss range, followed by three equal ranges, with a fifth range for the excess.

The following tables illustrate ranges for discount rates of 5% and 10%:

Yield Ranges	Yield Ranges
Loss	Loss
0–5 %	0–10%
5–10	10–20
10–15	20–30
Over 15	Over 30

Thus two ranges are below the discount rate, and three are above it. The top range needs no subdivision. Optional supporting detail includes the number and amount of the projects in each range, the maximum loss and its probability, the maximum yield and its probability, and a list of all projects.

In practice, relatively few projects would need full risk analysis. It would, however, be constructive to require proposers to submit a tentative risk profile, at least for certain specified classes and amounts of proposals. Larger and riskier projects should have an independent risk appraisal.

It is also highly advisable to establish an acceptable level of loss probability— say 10%—and a maximum percent for yields below the discount rate—say 25% (including the loss rate, if any) as a basis for project submission for approval. Projects with over 25% probability below the discount rate, or over 10% loss, would not be submitted. Qualified projects for submission would, however, be subject to review and approval.

The purpose of these instructions is to encourage the development of projects and to avoid premature abandonment. The ability to bear risk is least at the lowest organization levels. At higher levels, statistical benefits can be assessed (the law of large numbers). A single project with a 10% chance of loss is a high risk, but for thousands of projects the risk becomes minimal. Also, for performance evaluation, actual results can be compared with the risk profile. Poor results may be within the expected range, as well as above average results. This comparison should help to avoid overreaction to either superlative or bad results.

Project preparation can be greatly aided by designating people in each organization unit to provide financial and technical assistance to all project developers.

PROJECTS IN TOTAL

Opportunities for profitable investment are limited externally by competition, by regulation, and by the law of diminishing returns. Internally, proposals should be encouraged and employee creativity fostered through a constructive atmosphere.

Investment opportunities with lower yields outweigh those with higher yields by a wide margin. The approximate statistical relationship for a large number of proposals is:

Highest yield	10% of total
Next lower	20% of total
Next lower	30% of total
Lowest	40% of total
	100%

Assuming a 5% discount rate and approved projects for $100,000, the following table can be developed:

Yield Range	Total Dollars	Range Average	Gain	Cum. Gain	Cum. Dollars	Cum. Percent
Over 20%	10,000	22%	$ 2,200	$ 2,200	10,000	22
15–20	20,000	17	3,400	5,600	30,000	$18\frac{2}{3}$
10–15	30,000	12	3,600	9,200	60,000	$15\frac{1}{3}$
5–10	40,000	7	2,800	12,000	100,000	12
	100,000	(12)	$12,000			

The 5.0% discount rate qualifies projects for $100,000 with gains of $12,000, for a weighted average return of 12.0%. The skew of the dollars in the yield range is reflected in the range average, for example, 7.0% for the 5.0–10.0% range (not 7.5%). The ROA of 12.0% would translate into a higher ROE depending on the degree of leverage—on average perhaps 15.0% to 18.0% ROE.

If the discount rate is 20%, total investment is limited to $10,000 with a 22%

ROA. This level of outlay could limit growth to zero, more or less, depending on the company, with a negative impact on stock price. With a 15% discount rate, total outlay is $30,000, with ROA of 18⅔%. Growth would be low, probably well under industry performance. With a 10% discount rate, the total outlay is $60,000 with 15⅓% ROA, which could also be below the industry level. The 5% discount rate provides full investment in terms of meeting company goals. This subject and the effect of growth on stock market evaluation are explored in Chapter 12.

If the current net borrowing rate is 10%, the schedule is:

Yield Range	Total Dollars	Range Average	Gain	Cum. Gain	Cum. Dollars	Cum. Percent
Over 20%	10,000	22%	$2,200	$2,200	10,000	22
15–20	20,000	17	3,400	5,600	30,000	18⅓
10–15	30,000	12	3,600	9,200	60,000	15⅓
	60,000	(15⅓)	$9,200			

This table is simply the first three lines of the first table based on 5%. Thus if the discount rate is 10%, total investment is reduced by 40%—to $60,000. At a 15% discount rate, only $30,000 would be approved, further hampering growth. Higher interest rates have a highly negative effect on investment levels for the company and the economy.

These tables help to underscore the critical significance of using the relevant discount rate and using incremental analysis. Overall results reflect averages for all decisions, but the averages are not relevant for decision-making.

Project performance may be better or worse than the proposal yield but, in most all cases, would fall within the risk profile (when prepared). For a large number of projects the better and worse results would average out and should be close to the projected average yield.

INFLATION

High and volatile interest rates, which hamper the investment process, reflect changing expectations of price changes, or the inflation rate (and other factors such as risk and liquidity preference).

The investment decision rests on projected cash flows that are subject to some degree of estimate, as reflected in a risk profile. If current prices are used throughout the project period, the implicit assumption is that there will be no inflation. Also, price changes for individual items necessarily may be separately forecast, independent of the inflationary effect.

Each specific element of revenue and expense must be considered separately for each future period. The amounts used reflect expected ranges due to operations, specific price changes, and the effect of inflation, and a probability must be assigned to each outcome. Thus all of these factors are reflected in the risk profile.

Company guidelines should specify rates of inflation by periods to ensure uniformity of handling, along with acceptable risk levels and the current discount rate. The current discount rate should not be altered for inflation, even though it comprises (analytically) risk, inflation, and basic (real) interest rate factors. See Appendix.

Projects have a great variety of content relative to individual expenses, types of revenues, and life. It may be essential to evaluate closely the possible differing effects on items such as service revenue, rentals, product sales by industry, labor costs, fringe benefits, salary levels, materials, freight, taxes, and utilities.

If revenues and costs are projected to increase annually by the same percentage for a given project, the margin percent is constant; the increasing dollar margins boost the yield on the original investment. In some cases, cost increases will need to be projected without a corresponding revenue rise.

Exploration of possible developments and their likelihood is at the heart of the risk profile approach. Anticipating the effect of inflation is another factor in an already difficult process.

PROJECT EVALUATION

Project A

$$\text{Outlay} = \frac{\$24,000}{\text{Cash Gain } \$4,500} = \text{f } 5.333$$

Life, 8 years. Yield 10%

The project has been accepted subject to risk evaluation: The outlay is considered certain; probability of 1 = P 1.0
Cash gain is estimated:

$3,000	P 0.2
4,500	P .7
6,000	P .1
	1.0

Life is estimated:

7 years	P 0.3
8 years	P .6
9 years	P .1
	1.0

A table of possible yield outcomes and probabilities follows:

Cost, $24,000. Cash gain, $3,000 (P 0.2) f 8.0:

	P
Life 7 years P 0.3 = Loss $3,000 (7 × $3,000 = $21,000)	0.06
8 P 0.6 = 0 (8 × $3,000 = $24,000)	.12
9 P 0.1 = 2.4%	.02
	0.20

Cost, $24,000. Cash gain, $4,500 (P 0.7) f 5.333:

Life 7 years P 0.3 = 7.3%	0.21
8 P .6 = 10.0%	.42
9 P .1 = 12.0%	.07
	0.70

Cost, $24,000. Cash gain, $6,000 (P 0.1) f 4.000:

Life 7 years P 0.3 = 16.4%	0.03
8 P 0.6 = 18.6%	.06
9 P 0.1 = 20.2%	.01
	0.10

These outcomes are listed:

Yield %	P
Loss	0.06
0.0%	.12
2.4	.02
7.3	.21
10.0	.42
12.0	.07
16.4	.03
18.6	.06
20.2	0.01
	1.00

This list can be summarized in a risk profile:

Yield	P	Cum.
Loss	0.06	0.06
0% to 5%	.14	.20
5 to 10	.21	.41
10 to 15	.49	.90
15 plus	0.10	1.00
	1.00	

This simple example with nine outcomes illustrates the process of risk estimation (including inflation). The total number of outcomes could be very high, but computer runs are easy. The standardized risk profile summary provides a comprehensible basis for evaluation and comparison of all projects.

For this example, if the discount rate is 5% (yield, 10% in project proposal), there is a 20% chance of a lower yield, including a 6% chance of loss. Individuals would respond differently to these odds, but a company could set guideline limits on the acceptable probability below discount rate. For example, the 0.20 probability of yield below the discount rate could be acceptable but not a loss rate over, say, 0.05 probability. The high chances for much greater yields would not ordinarily affect the evaluation because of risk aversion.

With a discount rate of 10%, the odds are unfavorable, with a 41% chance of a lower yield. The project might be rejected or returned for further analysis. For a large number of projects the outcome should be close to the estimates, and risk ranges would tend to cancel out. For example, many projects with 10% yields, and acceptable risk profiles, would produce 10% average results, as a statistical probability.

Project B

$$\frac{\text{Outlay}}{\text{Cash Gain}} \quad \frac{\$50,000}{\$10,000} = \text{f } 5.0$$

Life, 8 years. Yield, 11.8%. (See Table of Risk Estimates.*)

Table of Risk Estimates ($000)

Outlay	P	f	Yield	Cash gain, $10,000	P 1.0
$70	0.1	7.0	3.1%	Life, 8 years	P 1.0
60	.3	6.0	6.8		
*50	.5	5.0	11.8*		
40	0.1	4.0	18.6		
	1.0				

Cash Gain	P	f	Yield	Outlay, $50,000	P 1.0
$ 8	0.2	6.25	5.8%	Life, 8 years	P 1.0
*10	.3	5.00	11.8*		
12	.3	4.17	17.3		
14	0.2	3.57	22.5		
	1.0				

Life	P	f	Yield	Outlay, $50,000	P 1.0
6 years	0.1	5.0	5.5%	Cash gain, $10,000	P 1.0
*8	.3	5.0	11.8*		
10	.4	5.0	15.1		
12	0.2	5.0	16.4		
	1.0				

This table has 64 outcomes (4 × 4 × 4), of which only 12 are given. For instance, the worst outcome is:

Outlay $70   (P 0.1)
Cash gain $ 8   (P 0.2)
Life   6 years   (P 0.1)
= f 8.75 Yield minus (9.8%)
Loss = 6 years × $8 = $48 − $70 = $22,000 P 0.002

The best outcome is:

Outlay $40   (P 0.1)
Cash Gain $14   (P 0.2)
Life   12 years   (P 0.2)
= f 2.857 Yield 33.9% P 0.004

The project proposal is:

Outlay $50   (P 0.5)
Cash gain $10   (P 0.3)
Life   8 years   (P 0.3)
= f 5.0 Yield 11.8% P 0.045

Thus the point estimate—the project as submitted—has a 4.5% probability.

Translation of the 64 outcomes into a full risk profile would be needed to evaluate risk.

GUIDELINES

1. The discount rate used to determine NPV and yield must be a risk-free rate. Use of a higher rate distorts present values by including a risk element in the discounted dollars. More distant cash flows are increasingly biased. The effect is erratic among projects because of varying time periods and cash flow amounts. Projects differ greatly in outlays, in size and timing of cash flows, in life, and in recovery values. The nature and degree of risk vary greatly among projects. Risk is actually skewed, as shown by the examples. Only a risk-free rate provides a logical and consistent basis for risk evaluation.

2. The relevant risk-free rate in the financial markets is the U.S. Treasury ɔond rate, for a selected maturity consonant with project life. This is a pure rate,

but it would produce yields below the company borrowing rate, with negative leverage. The practical alternative is the company borrowing rate, less tax. With treasuries at 12% and company borrowing rates at 14% to 16%, the difference is 2% to 4%, reduced by tax to only 1% to 2%. Hence a rate of 7% or 8% would be used rather than the 6% rate related to the Treasury bonds. These rate differentials are variable over time and among companies but are small relative to the risk ranges applicable to most projects. Also, relatively few projects are subject to risk evaluation, so it is important for all proposals to show NPV and yield based on the company borrowing rate, net. The discount rate should be kept current and changed when there is a difference of, say, 1% or more.

The following is an illustration of the effect of rates on project NPV:

		Risk Free 6%	Company 7%	Company 8%
	10 year f =	f 7.360	f 7.024	f 6.710
A	PV cash gain	$7,360	$7,024	$6,710
	Outlay	7,360	7,360	7,360
	NPV	$ 0	-$ 336	-$ 650

Discount Rates

Use of the 6% rate would result in negative NPV for company rates of 7% and 8%.

B	PV cash gain	$7,360	$7,024	$6,710
	Outlay	7,024	7,024	7,024
		+$ 336	$ 0	-$ 314

Use of the 7% rate would produce a negative NPV for a company rate of 8%.

C	PV cash gain	$7,360	$7,024	$6,710
	Outlay	6,710	6,710	6,710
		+$ 650	+$ 314	$ 0

If the company rate is 8%, the lower rates show spurious gains.

3. Risk estimates can be broad and still be useful. Dollar ranges should be established for outlays and gain—perhaps at 10% intervals. Life estimates should be in full years. Probabilities should be expressed at intervals of 10% (P 0.1) minimum. The examples of risk analysis given illustrate the practicality of this approach. Initial risk estimates should be provided by project proposers. Risk profile categories should be standardized. Mathematical models are inapplicable because of the tentative nature of risk estimates and their inherent skew.

4. Project risk may be related to other proposals, such as introducing two new products into the same market, or establishing new vendors from the same area, or creating new production facilities in the same location. The risk relationships among all proposals need careful attention. It could be reflected in the

risk profiles but is primarily a judgmental choice. Similarly, risk may be affected by the relationships of proposals to existing operations. These situations are not readily measurable by quantitative methods.

Operating risk is largely dependent on the particular industry segment. Added investment in a given segment is necessarily in the same risk environment. Entering into new segments for diversification is a risk-reducing effort that calls for careful evaluation that is highly judgmental. Portfolio analysis of risk is applicable but difficult to apply by quantitative analysis.

5. A major challenge to management is to find investment proposals that serve company goals, strategies, and policies, within acceptable limits of profitability, risk, and liquidity. All employees (the best source) should be encouraged to seek out proposals. This process is aided by setting limits of risk acceptance to preclude premature rejection: for example, losses up to probabilities of 5% to 10% and yields below the discount rate up to probabilities of 20% to 30%. Many of such proposals may be acceptable. Any rejected proposal should be explained to preserve communication and morale.

6. Excessive hedging at each review level, for the sake of conservation, can be damaging. The arbitrary reduction of gains, or project life, or increase in outlay, would reduce the expected yield. Such estimates should be expressed in the risk profile.

7. Each organization unit, or major location, should designate people to direct the effort for developing proposals and to provide technical, financial, and procedural guidance.

8. The review process should include independent technical evaluation when applicable.

9. The internal auditors should monitor both the system and its effectiveness.

10. Approved projects should be monitored for timely performance to insure accomplishment of operating plans.

11. On completion, projects should be restated for actual outlays and current estimates of gains and life. This closes out the proposal stage and establishes the basis for performance evaluation, as described in Chapter 4.

QUESTIONABLE ALTERNATIVES

Payback Period

Shorter payback periods reduce uncertainty, but there is no correlation with the degree of risk. Payback relates to liquidity—cash out, cash in. The degree of risk relates to the nature of the project. Payback calculations are given in Chapter 4.

Short paybacks can be very risky—toys and games, personal computers, electric knives, fashions, CB radios. Long payback periods may be relatively

safe, such as for equipment with known performance ratings. A special case is
bond refunding, which is virtually risk free and generally has a long payback
period. See Chapter 7.

Some years ago, assets were classified into relevant payback periods to guide
decisions, before the development of profitability analysis.

Risk evaluation is best done with a risk profile that allows for the measurement
of all variables. Risk guided by payback can encourage acceptance of overly
risky projects and the rejection of safer and desirable projects.

Standard Deviation

This statistical method relates to a normal distribution of outcomes based on a
large number of repetitive events. These conditions do not apply to investment
proposals, which are unique and skewed as to risk.

The following example starts with the proposed risk profile and then introduces the standard deviation.

$$\frac{\text{Outlay}}{\text{Cash gain}} \quad \frac{\$10,000}{\$ 2,638} = f\ 3.791$$

Life, 5 years. Yield, 10%

Discount rate, 5% (PV $11,421)

The risk analysis is:

Outlay   P 1.0
Life   P 1.0

The risk profile is:

Cash Gain	f ($10,000)	Yield (5 years)	P	Cum.
$2,000	5.000	0%	0.1	0.1
2,310	4.329	5	.1	.2
2,638	3.791	10	.3	.5
2,983	3.352	15	.3	.8
3,343	2.991	20	0.2	1.0

There is a 10% chance for no gain and 20% chance of a yield under 5%—the
discount rate. Each manager can readily interpret this according to his own risk
aversion. Preferably, the company has pre-established limits that the profile falls
within. There is a 30% chance of yields from 5% to 10%, with higher yields at

50% odds—the upside potential. This project would be acceptable in most situations.

The standard deviation computation is:

Yield (%)	P	Extension	Yield less mean	Difference Squared	P Extension
0	0.1	0.0	−12	144	14.4
5	.1	0.5	− 7	49	4.9
10	.3	3.0	− 2	4	1.2
15	.3	4.5	+ 3	9	2.7
20	0.2	4.0	+ 8	64	12.8
	Mean	12.0			36.0 Variance

Standard deviation $\sqrt{36} = 6$

Standard Deviations	Yield Range from mean	Statistical Probability
1 ± 6	6% to 18%	68.3%
2 ± 12	0 to 24	95.4
3 ± 18	−6 to 30	99.7

The project yield of 10% (spot estimate) becomes 12% with the risk estimate.

Thus there is a 68% chance that the yield will fall between 6% and 18%. These extra calculations produce broad ranges and obscure the specificity of the risk profile. The critical distinction between downside risk and upside potential is lost.

The coefficient of variation (COV) is used to compare projects—in this case 6/M12 = 50%—for comparison with other project COVs. But it is not evident whether both should be rejected or both should be accepted, or one accepted or rejected and not the other.

Risk Classes

Projects may be grouped into risk classes such as high, average, and low—a wholly arbitrary procedure resting on subjective attitudes. Low-risk projects are discounted at the discount rate (net borrowing rate). The average and high-risk classes are discounted at higher rates, using some arbitrary differential. The low-risk projects still require risk evaluation, including the risk profile when indicated. The higher risk classes discounted at the higher rates will cause rejection of some acceptable projects and acceptance of some overly risky projects. The result will be higher, rather than lower, risk—the opposite of the intended effect. Use of discount rates higher than the basic discount rate introduces an unknown degree of bias into the results, as previously explained. For example:

$$\frac{\text{Outlay}}{\text{Cash gain}} \quad \frac{\$20,000}{\$\ 4,458} = f\ 4.486$$

Life, 6 years. Yield, 9.0%

The risk analysis is (Outlay P 1.0. Life P 1.0):

Cash	f	Yield	P	Cum.
$3,333	6.000	0%	0.1	0.1
3,940	5.076	5	1	.2
4,592	4.355	10	.3	.5
5,285	3.784	15	.3	.8
6,013	3.326	20	0.2	1.0

If the discount rate is 5%:

Cash $4,458 × f 5.076 = $22,629 PV
Outlay   − 20,000
                       + $ 2,629 NPV

NPV is positive and risk is acceptable based on the risk profile.
   If the rate used is 10%:

Cash $4,458 × f 4.355 = $19,415 PV
Outlay   − 20,000
                       − $ 585 NPV

This project does not now earn enough for its risk class—arbitrarily discounted at 10%. But examination of the risk profile shows cash of $4,592 for a yield of 10%.
   If the rate used is 15%:

Cash $4,458 × f 3.784 = $16,889 PV
Outlay   − 20,000
                       − $ 3,111 NPV

This result is seriously short of the arbitrary requirement for this risk class. The risk profile shows $5,285 cash for a yield of 15%.

Portfolio Effect

   The CAPM (Capital Asset Pricing Model) described in Chapter 9 can be used in the valuation of securities by relating company risk to market risk to determine yield. This usage restricts the term *capital assets* to securities. It is not applicable to asset investment decisions where the need is to relate project risk to the risk of all operating investments, plus proposed projects. The intent is to find the effect of a project in reducing (or increasing) operating risk. For securities, the method is known as ''portfolio analysis.''

Diversification of assets is made to spread risk, but the effect is not readily subject to quantitative analysis.

Other Quantitative Methods

Sophisticated techniques have been developed for use in particular circumstances. They require a high degree of skill and are expensive and time consuming. The results can be no better than the input. Examples are simulation, decision trees, Monte Carlo, dynamic programming, and game theory.

CHAPTER 7

Bond Refunding and Defeasance

SCALING DOWN INTEREST COSTS

BOND REFUNDING

Capital Expenditure Analysis

A bond issue with a call provision enables the issuer to call in (buy back) the bonds at prescribed dates and at specified premiums over face value. This privilege reduces its appeal to the financial markets; callable bonds require a slightly higher interest rate than straight (regular) bonds, which are not callable.

When market interest rates fall below the bond coupon rate (contract rate payable in cash for the life of the bond), the bonds may be called and replaced with new bonds to be sold at the current (lower) interest rate. The investment required to accomplish this refunding, and the consequent interest savings, can be analyzed for profitability in the same manner as described for capital expenditures in Chapter 4. Bond refunding is a capital expenditure decision.

The discount rate used to determine profitability is the interest rate for the new bonds, net of tax, the same rate prescribed for all capital expenditures. Liquidity is improved by reduction in interest cost. Risk analysis is not needed because the decision is risk free for all practical purposes. The call premium is known, and the expenses of refunding are subject to close estimation.

The refunding is made if the lower interest cost provides a positive NPV. If market rates rise sufficiently to cause the NPV to become negative, the refunding is delayed. If the market rate falls, the refunding becomes more profitable. However, a refunding based on a positive NPV should not be deferred in the hope of a lower interest rate. The known gain should be taken rather than speculate on the unpredictable market changes. The direction, timing, and degree of changes in rates are not reliably predictable.

The refunding may be slated for issue a month or so before the call date of the outstanding issue to allow time flexibility in the final issue date relative to shifting market conditions. Any duplicate interest cost arising from a time overlap is part of the investment outlay. The temporary excess can be invested in marketable securities, so the net cost is relatively small.

The refunding analysis is also based on the number of years remaining to maturity. In practice, the new issue may be, and usually is, for a longer period. This is a separate financing decision, based on financial planning. For example, 30 year bonds issued 18 years ago have 12 years before maturity. The new bonds could be issued for 12 years, or for 15 or 20 years, or longer. The added time does not enter into the analysis, which is limited to 12 years, the remaining life of the bonds to be called.

The analysis is also based on the total face value of the outstanding bonds. The new issue may be for a larger amount and frequently is. The extra amount is excluded from the analysis; it is an independent decision based on financial planning.

Both factors—timing and amount—would relate to planned capital structure and include consideration of security flotation costs.

Example of a Profitable Call

Bonds Outstanding

Face value, $45 million. Call premium, 10%—$4,500,000 (I)

Interest rate, $16\frac{2}{3}$% (II) annually.

30-year maturity—20 years remaining (III)

Deferred issue expense—$150,000 current balance (I)

New Bonds

Face value, $45 million (for analysis)

20-year maturity (for analysis) (III)

Interest rate, 15% (II) annually (current market)

New issue expense, $450,000 (I)

Other Data

Tax rate, 40%; discount rate, 9% (15%–6%)

Duplicate interest expense:

$45 million at $16\frac{2}{3}$% = $7\frac{1}{2}$ million per year, and $625,000 for one month. Income from marketable securities at 12% = 1% of $45 million = $450,000. Net $175,000 (I)

Analysis Schedule (000 Omitted)

I. Outlay (cash investment):

Call premium = 10%	$4,500		
New issue expense	450		
Duplicate interest net	175		$5,125
less tax savings (currently deductible):			
Call premium	$4,500		
Old issue expense	150		
Duplicate interest net	175	$4,825 at 40%	1,930
			$3,195 A

II. Annual interest saving:

$16\frac{2}{3}$% = 15% = $1\frac{2}{3}$%		$ 450
× $45,000 = $750		
less 40% tax	$300	

III. Tax savings on expenses:

New issue	$450	
Old issue	150	$300
Per year (divided by 20 [III]) =		15
Tax saved at 40%		6
Net annual gain		$456 B

IV. Profitability:

NPV $456 × f 9.129 (9% − 20 years)	$4,163 PV
Outlay	3,195 A
Gain in present dollars at 9% =	$ 968 NPV

$$\text{Yield} \quad \frac{\text{A } \$3,195}{\text{B } \$\ \ 456} = \text{f } 7.0066 = 13.043\% \text{ net}$$

or 21.74% before tax (cf. 15%)

V. Liquidity

Cash payback

$$\frac{\text{Net outlay}}{\text{Net annual gain}} \quad \frac{\$3,195 \text{ A}}{\$\ \ 456 \text{ B}} = 7.0 \text{ years}$$

This is a relatively long period but for a risk-free project.

EBIT (Earnings Before Interest and Tax)—Times Interest Earned

Assume EBIT	$50,000	$40,000	$30,000	$20,000
Interest at 16⅔%	$ 7,500	$ 7,500	$ 7,500	$ 7,500
Times interest earned	6⅔	5⅓	4.0	2⅔
Interest at 15%	$6,750	$ 6,750	$ 6,750	$ 6,750
Times interest earned	7.41	5.93	4.44	2.96

Liquidity is improved by the reduced interest, but the extent depends on the EBIT, which is illustrated for clarification.

Capital Structure: The D/E (Debt/Equity) ratio is not affected for analysis because of the assumption of equal amounts and maturities for both debt issues.

Net Outlay: The required $3,195 A is a capital expenditure proposal that must be approved and funded, together with all other projects. In a period of financial stringency, the refunding proposal would have high priority for profitability (high) and risk (low), but the slow payback could be a negative consideration.

VI. Accounting Treatment

The accounting effect, as for all capital expenditures, must be separately determined to ascertain the impact on ROA (Return on Assets), ROE (Return on Equity), and EPS (Earnings per Share).

Balance Sheet: Deferred charges—add $450 for the new issue and deduct $150 charged to expense; net increase, $300 (20-year amortization).

Income Statement

One time charge:			
Call premium	$4,500		
Duplicate interest	175		
Old issue expense	150	$4,825	
less 40% tax		1,930	$2,895 DR
Annual saving:			
Interest (see II)		$ 450	
less: amortization of new			
issue expense net of old			
issue expense—$450 less			
$150 = $300 ÷ 20 = 15 ×			
60%		− 9	$ 441 CR

These accounting amounts are reconciled with the financial analysis as follows:

Proof (no Discounting)

		Total		
Save $441 for 20 years		$8,820		
One time charge		− 2,895	+	$5,925
Financial basis:				
Save $456 for 20 years	=	$9,120		
Net outlay		− 3,195	+	$5,925

ROA is not needed and is inappropriate because refunding is a financing decision. The Balance Sheet debit to assets is $300, as above, and the annual saving is $441. There is also a one-time charge of $2,895. It would be prudent to assess the effect on net income, ROE, and EPS for the first year because of the first year charge—$2,895—offset by any part of the $441 annual saving falling within the year. The quarterly effect would also be of concern if statements are published.

The new bonds are issued at 15%, but it was not stated whether or not the issue is callable. This is a separate decision relative to the future. Whichever conclusion is reached, the appropriate rate is used for analysis. Thus if 15% reflects callable bonds, the lower rate applicable to straight bonds is not relevant.

The Individual Bondholder

If $10,000 face value bonds are purchased at $16\frac{2}{3}$%, 20 year maturity, for $10,000, the CY (current yield) is $16\frac{2}{3}$% and the YTM (yield to maturity) is

$16\frac{2}{3}\%$. If the market rate for these bonds drops to 15%, the bond price rises (I = interest):

	Contract	15%, 20 Yrs.	PV
P	$10,000	f .061	$ 610
I	1,667	f 6.259	10,434
		(YTM 15.0%)	$11,044 (CY 15.1%)

With a 10% call premium, the value is limited to $11,000 or $44 less. This theoretical market loss measures the sacrifice attaching to the incremental interest received over the market rate for straight bonds at the time of issue.

If the bonds were purchased 10 years ago for $10,000 (face value) and the bonds are called at $11,000, the realized yield is over $16\frac{2}{3}\%$:

	Contract	Try 17%, 10 yrs.	PV
P	$11,000	f 0.208	$ 2,288.00
I	1,667	f 4.659	7,766.55
			10,054.55
			$10,000.00 = 17.1%

The $11,000 reinvested at 15% (market rate) provides $1,650 interest annually, compared with $1,667, a decrease of $17.

If the bonds are not called, because interest rates do not drop enough to make it profitable, the bondholder receives the premium for the life of the bonds—his risk has been rewarded. The company has the extra cost for the privilege of possible recall—an unrewarded risk viewed retrospectively.

Analysis of a Call With Negative Results

Bonds Outstanding

Face value, $50,000; call premium, 7%

Interest rate, 15% (semi-annual, 7.5%)

10 years to maturity (20 payment periods)

Deferred issue expense, $300 balance

New Bonds

Face value, $50,000; 10-year maturity

Interest rate, 14% (semi-annual, 7%)

New issue expense, $500

Other Data

Tax rate, 50.0%; discount rate, 3.5% (semi-annual) ($14.0\%/2 = 7.0 \times 50.0\%$)
No duplicate interest expense

Analysis Schedule

I. Outlay:

Call premium, 7%	$3,500		
New issue expense	500	$4,000	
less tax savings:			
call premium	$3,500		
old issue expense	300	$3,800	
at 50%		1,900	
Net outlay			$2,100 A

II. Interest Saving:

15% − 14% = 1% = $500 per year
6 months = $250 less tax $125 = $ 125

III. Tax saving on expense:

New issue $500 less old issue $300 = $200/20 periods =
  $10 at 50% = $ 5
Net savings per period $ 130 B

IV. Profitability:

Net savings $130 × f 14.212 (3.5%, 20		
periods)	$1,848 PV	
Net outlay	2,100	
Negative	−$ 252 NPV	
Yield A $2,100 = f 16.154 = 2.125% 6 months after tax		
B $ 130 4.25% year after tax		
8.50% year before tax		

This proposal earns $252 less in present dollars than the required outlay. The yield before tax computes to 8.5% compared with the required rate of 14.0% (annualized basis).

Break-even calculations may be useful. For example, a call premium of 6% (not 7%) reduces the amount by $500, or $250 net. The −$252 NPV is then negative by only $2.

A break-even interest-rate calculation requires trial and error because both interest savings and the discount rate are changed. A break-even rate of 13.8628% was found, or 6.9314% for six months and 3.4657% after tax.

The interest saving is 15.0% less 13.8628% = 1.1372% times $50,000.00 = $568.60 per year, or $284.30 for six months and $142.15 after tax. Add back $5 tax saving on expense to obtain $147.15 compared with $130, calculated in II and III above.

By calculator, $147.30 at 3.4657% for 20 periods equals $2099.9993. The exact rate is 3.4656962%, or 13.8627848%, annually before tax. Advance determination of the break even interest rate for outstanding bond issues provides a signal for falling market rates.

DEFEASANCE

Defeasance is the legal satisfaction of debt before maturity by meeting specified escrow requirements. "In substance" defeasance is a relatively new technique given official accounting approval recently but subject to strict regulations that are evolving, subject to interpretation, and debatable. The treatment here is necessarily somewhat tentative.

The procedure calls for the purchase of risk-free securities, that is, Treasury notes or bonds, and placing them in an irrevocable trust. These trust funds are used to pay the interest on an outstanding bond issue of the company, as it becomes due, and to redeem the bonds at face value at maturity. Accordingly, the securities in trust must match the company bond requirements in timing and amounts.

The company bonds are then removed from the balance sheet. The gain is recorded as though the bonds had been paid in full—called "in-substance defeasance." A footnote to the financial statements is required. Gain arises to the extent that the acquisition cost of the securities (risk-free) is exceeded by the face value (book value) of the outstanding company bonds. The purchased securities must have interest payments, face value, and maturities equal to that of the company bonds but sell at a discount from face value because the current market rate is higher.

Example

Assume company bonds outstanding, $50,000; coupon rate, 8%; due in 20 years; not callable. The company has just received a tax-free damage award for $35,000 and has no attractive investment proposal on tap. Marketable securities offer a short-term, low-yield expedient. Purchasing the company bonds on the open market would be slow and expensive. The remaining alternatives are payment of an extra dividend or in-substance defeasance.

Treasury bonds at $50,000 face amount paying 8% interest, maturing in 20 years, are available at $35,000. The YTM is 12%:

	Contract	12%, 20 Years	PV
P	$50,000	f 0.103667	$ 5,183.35
I	4,000	f 7.469444	29,877.77
			$35,061.12
			$35,000.00, slightly over 12%

A gain of $15,000 arises from purchase of the Treasury bonds placed in trust and removal of the company bonds from the books. With 40% tax (or $6,000) the net gain is $9,000. This is reported as an extraordinary gain (unusual and infrequent) of $9,000 net, along with the damage award for $35,000 (no tax).

Financial Analysis

Balance Sheet	Before	After	Change
Net Assets	$200,000	$194,000	−$ 6,000 tax on $15,000
Debt:			
Banks (16⅔%)	30,000	30,000	0
Bonds (8%)	50,000	0	−$50,000 in trust
	$ 80,000	$ 30,000	
Equity (10,000 shares):			
	$120,000	$120,000	
		35,000	damage award
		9,000	defeasance gain—net
		$164,000	+$44,000 gain
Capital	$200,000	$194,000	−$ 6,000 net

The $44,000 is shown directly in the equity section rather than through the Income Statement for this illustration.

Income Statement	Before	After	Change
EBIT (Earnings Before Interest and Tax)	$ 39,000	$ 39,000	
Interest			
Banks	5,000	5,000	
Bonds	4,000	0	
	$ 9,000	$ 5,000	+$4,000
EBT (Earnings Before Tax)	30,000	34,000	
Tax 40%	12,000	13,600	− 1,600
EAT (Earnings After Tax)	$ 18,000	$ 20,400	+$2,400

Income Statement	Before	After	Change	
D/E ratio	$80/$120	$30/$164		
	67%	18.3%	DOWN	Favorable
Interest coverage	$39/$9	$39/$5		
	4.3	7.8	UP	Favorable
ROE	$18/$120	$20.4/$164.0		
	15.00%	12.4%	DOWN	(less leverage)
ROA: EBIT	$ 39,000			
Tax	15,600			
Net	23,400	23,400		
Net assets	$200,000	$194,000		
	11.79%	12.06%	UP	
Equity	$120,000	$164,000		
	10,000 shs.	10,000 shs.		
	$ 12.00	$ 16.40	UP	
EPS: EAT	$ 18,000	$ 20,400		
	10,000 shs.	10,000 shs.		
	$ 1.80	$ 2.04	UP	

In the year the gain is recorded, we have:

EAT	$20,400	EPS	$2.04
Gain	44,000	EPS	4.40
Net Income	$64,400	EPS	$6.44

Liquidity is improved, but ROE is substantially reduced (15.00% to 12.4%). EPS and book value are up substantially. ROA improves slightly. The EAT gain of $2,400 is 5.45% of the $44,000 increase in equity, reducing ROE from 15.00% to 12.4%.

In cash terms the investment of $35,000 now saves $2,400 a year for 20 years plus $9,000 at the end of 20 years—a yield of 4.48% after tax, or 7.47% before tax. This compares unfavorably with the current 12.00% rate for Treasury bonds—a high price to pay for the one-time gain of $9,000 on paper in the current year.

The alternative of paying out the $35,000 as an extra dividend leaves the company financial position unchanged. The stockholders would collectively be subject to income tax and reinvestment expense. This could be $11,000 (as a guess) or 31.4%, leaving $24,000 net gain. The same net gain could theoretically be achieved without the dividend by an increase in stock market value arising from retention of the $35,000 for use in defeasance as described.

If the price per share before defeasance was $18 it could rise to $21 after defeasance because of higher EPS and ROA, plus improved liquidity. The change in P/E would be: $18.00/$1.80 = 10 to $21.00/$2.04 = 10.3.

With 10,000 shares, the total increase in market value is $30,000. Allowing 20% tax, the net is $24,000, thus providing equivalent value to the stockholders.

The effect of the defeasance choice on market value is speculative—a large one-time gain, a small annual gain, better liquidity, lower ROE. The effect of the dividend payment is also speculative. The market response might be neutral to both alternatives. But management must consider the possibilities in making a decision.

CHAPTER 8

Acquiring Other Companies

MERGERS FOR GROWTH AND DIVERSIFICATION

THE INVESTMENT OPPORTUNITY

Productive assets are acquired by purchase from suppliers, by construction, or by the acquisition of another company, in whole or in part. Payment is by cash, or by the issuance of company stock or other securities.

Acquisition of another company by exchange of stock is a complex and highly publicized subject. The acquired company may be dissolved or continued as a subsidiary, either wholly or partially owned. Accounting is made by the purchase method, unless all conditions for a pooling of interest are met, when that method is mandated. The accounting, legal, and tax considerations are highly technical, complex, and subject to interpretation. They are often of paramount concern but are not dealt with here.

The financial goals of mergers are primarily growth and diversification. The merger decision falls broadly into the category of capital expenditures, but each one must be handled individually. Merger by exchange of stock involves both assets and capital structure on a consolidated basis.

Products and markets may be acquired more effectively by purchase of another company as compared with internal efforts, in terms of time, cost, and risk. Book values (historical cost) are often well below current replacement cost. An acquiring company may profitably pay a market price, and the acquired company may realize an immediate gain beyond what it could hope to realize by continued independent operation. The true economic benefit rests solely on creating a larger merged profit than that of the companies continuing alone—synergy.

The ratio of the stock issued by the purchaser for the stock of the selling company is a matter of negotiation. Major factors are current market price for each stock (or fair value), projected company earnings on a separate basis, the gain (synergy) to be expected by merger, and the market value of the stock after merger. Merger terms and synergy prospects that are well regarded by the market can boost the stock price to the benefit of both parties. Projecting market reaction is a principal factor in negotiation. Clearly, the handling of mergers calls for extensive experience and many technical skills.

The illustrations given are limited to the successive exploration of the effect of several stock exchange ratios, various P/E ratios, and synergy gains. The various outcomes for the two parties demonstrate the ranges that are the bases for negotiation—essentially splitting the projected gains. An overeager acquirer may pay too much and preclude adequate profitability. If this is the market judgment, the stock price falls. An unrealistic seller may hold out for too much and lose a good deal.

The total market gain is $30,000 on $60,000, or 50%. Co. X stock gains $22,000 on $50,000, or 44%. Co. Y stock gains $8,000 on $10,000, or 80%. There is no gain in net income (no synergy), but $400 shifts from Co. Y or Co. X.

If this plan is not acceptable to Co. Y, more shares must be offered by Co. X.

ILLUSTRATION A—MERGED P/E 30

A-1. Stock Exchange Ratio 1 for 4 Shares

	Co. X	Co. Y	Merged	
Net income	$ 2,000	$ 1,000	$ 3,000.00	No gain
No. of shares	1,000	1,000	1,250.00	1 for 4
EPS	$ 2	$ 1	$ 2.40	$3,000.00/1,250 shs.
Market price	$ 50	$ 10	$ 72.00	P/E 30 (× $2.40)
P/E ratio	25	10	30	Assumed
Market total	$50,000	$10,000	$90,000.00	Gain $30,000.00
Yield	4%	10%	$3\frac{1}{3}\%$	

The result is:

Stock	1,000 shs.	250 shs.	1,250 shs.
	at $72	at $72	at $72
	=$72,000	=$18,000	=$90,000
Gain	+ 22,000	+ 8,000	+ 30,000
Net income ($2.40)	$ 2,400	$ 600	$ 3,000
Gain	+$ 400	−$ 400	$ 0

A-2. Stock Exchange Ratio 1 for 2 Shares

	Co. X	Co. Y	Merged	
Net income	$ 2,000	$ 1,000	$ 3,000.00	No gain
No. of shares	1,000	1,000	1,500.00	1 for 2
EPS	$ 2	$ 1	$ 2.00	$3,000.00/1,500 shs.
Market price	$ 50	$ 10	$ 60.00	P/E 30 (× $2)
P/E ratio	25	10	30	Assumed
Market total	$50,000	$10,000	$90,000.00	Gain $30,000.00
Yield	4%	10%	$3\frac{1}{3}\%$	

The result is:

Stock	1,000 shs.	500 shs.	1,500 shs.
	at $60	at $60	at $60
	=$60,000	=$30,000	=$90,000
Gain	+ 10,000	+ 20,000	+ 30,000
Net income ($200)	$ 2,000	$ 1,000	$ 3,000
Gain	$ 0	$ 0	$ 0

The total market gain is $30,000 on $60,000, or 50%. Co. X stock gains $10,000 on 50,000, or 20%. Co. Y stock gains $20,000 on $10,000, or 200%. Net income remains unchanged. The net change from A-1 is $12,000 in market value from Co. X to Co. Y and elimination of the $400 net income transfer to Co. X.

For Co. Y to gain in net income, a still better exchange ratio is required.

A-3. Stock Exchange Ratio 1 for 1 Shares

	Co. X	Co. Y	Merged
Net income	$ 2,000	$ 1,000	$ 3,000.00 No gain
No. of shares	1,000	1,000	2,000.00 1 for 1
EPS	$ 2	$ 1	$ 1.50 $3,000.00/2,000 shs.
Market price	$ 50	$ 10	$ 45.00 P/E 30 (× $1.50)
P/E ratio	25	10	30 Assumed
Market total	$50,000	$10,000	$90,000.00 Gain $30,000.00
Yield	4%	10%	3⅓%

The result is:

Stock	1,000 shs.	1,000 shs.	2,000 shs.
	at $45	at $45	at $45

	=$45,000	=$45,000	=$90,000
Gain	− 5,000	+ 35,000	+ 30,000
Net income ($1.50)	$ 1,500	$ 1,500	$ 3,000
Gain	−$ 500	+$ 500	$ 0

The total market gain remains at $30,000, or 50%, but Co. X loses 10% and Co. Y gains 350%. Also, Co. X loses 25% of its net income while Co. Y gains 50%. The following table recaps Merged P/E 30:

	Share Exchange Rate		Market Gain $30,000		Net Income Gain -0-		P/E 30
	Co. X	Co. Y	Co. X	Co. Y	Co. X	Co. Y	Market Price
A-1	1 for	4	+$22	+$ 8	+$400	−$400	$72
A-2	1 for	2	+ 10	+ 20	0	0	60
A-3	1 for	1	− 5	+ 35	− 500	+ 500	45

A deal within these broad ranges would hinge on the future projections and relative strength of the negotiators. In practice, equity and income relationships can be refined by the use of bonds, preferred, convertibles, options, or warrants.

ILLUSTRATION B—STOCK EXCHANGE RATIO 1 FOR 4 SHARES

B-1. P/E 18

	Co. X	Co. Y	Merged	
Net income	$ 2,000	$ 1,000	$ 3,000.00	No gain
No. of shares	1,000	1,000	1,250.00	1 for 4
EPS	$ 2	$ 1	$ 2.40	$3,000.00/1,250.00 shs.
Market price	$ 50	$ 10	$ 43.20	P/E 18 (× $2.40)
P/E ratio	25	10	18	Assumed
Market total	$50,000	$10,000	$54,000.00	Loss $6,000.00
Yield	4.00%	10.00%	5.55%	

The result is:

	Co. X	Co. Y	Merged
Stock	1,000 shs.	250 shs.	1,250 shs.
	at $43.20	at $43.20	at $43.20
	=$43,200	=$10,800	=$54,000
Gain	− 6,800	+ 800	− 6,000
Net income ($2.40)	$ 2,400	$ 600	$ 3,000
Gain	+$ 400	−$ 400	$ 0

This low P/E reduces the total market value of $60,000 by 10%, but with a small gain for Co. Y, which loses $400 net income to Co. X.

B-2. P/E 22

	Co. X	Co. Y	Merged	
Net income	$ 2,000	$ 1,000	$ 3,000.00	No gain
No. of shares	1,000	1,000	1,250.00	1 for 4
EPS	$ 2	$ 1	$ 2.40	$3,000.00/1,250.00 shs.
Market price	$ 50	$ 10	$ 52.80	P/E 22.00 (× $2.40)
P/E ratio	25	10	22	Assumed
Market total	$50,000	$10,000	$66,000.00	Gain $6,000.00
Yield	4.00%	10.00%	4.55%	

Result:

	Co. X	Co. Y	Merged
Stock	1,000 shs.	250 shs.	1,250 shs.
	at $52.80	at $52.80	at $52.80
	=$52,800	=$13,200	=$66,000
Gain	+ 2,800	+ 3,200	+ 6,000
Net income ($2.40)	$ 2,400	$ 600	$ 3,000
Gain	+$ 400	−$ 400	$ 0

P/E 22 raises the price to $52.80 for a 10% gain in market value. Co. X gains $2,800 on $50,000 (5.6%) and Co. Y gains $3,200 on $10,000 (32.0%). Co. X continues to gain $400 net income at the expense of Co. Y because the stock split and EPS are unchanged.

B-3. P/E 26

	Co. X	Co. Y	Merged
Net income	$ 2,000	$ 1,000	$ 3,000.00 No gain
No. of shares	1,000	1,000	1,250.00 1 for 4
EPS	$ 2	$ 1	$ 2.40 $3,000.00/1,250 shs.
Market price	$ 50	$ 10	$ 62.40 P/E 26 (× $2.40)
P/E ratio	25	10	26 Assumed
Market total	$50,000	$10,000	$78,000.00 Gain $18,000.00
Yield	4.00%	10.00%	3.85%

The result is:

Stock	1,000 shs.	250 shs.	1,250 shs.
	at $62.40	at $62.40	at $62.40
	=$62,400	=$15,600	=$78,000
Gain	+ 12,400	+ 5,600	+ 18,000
Net income ($2.40)	$ 2,400	$ 600	$ 3,000
Gain	+$ 400	−$ 400	$ 0

The total market value gain of $18,000, or 30.0%, now gives Co. X $12,400 on $50,000 (24.8%), and Co. Y gets $5,600 on $10,000 (56.0%).

The following example is identical to A-1 (Stock Exchange Ratio 1 for 4 Shares):

B-4. Merged P/E 30

	P/E	Market Gain			Net Income Gain -0-		
		Co. X	Co. Y	Total	Co. X	Co. Y	Market Price
B-1	18	−$ 6,800	+$ 800 =	−$ 6,000	+$400	−$400	$43.20
B-2	22	+ 2,800	+ 3,200 =	+ 6,000	+ 400	− 400	52.80
B-3	26	+ 12,400	+ 5,600 =	+ 18,000	+ 400	− 400	62.40
B-4	30	+ 22,000	+ 8,000 =	+ 30,000	+ 400	− 400	72.00

In example A, negotiations hinge on the stock exchange rate, with the merged P/E given (30). In example B, with the stock exchange rate held at 1 for 4, the variable is the stock price after merger, which in turn provides a new P/E. In practice, both variables are present, together with some gain by synergy.

ILLUSTRATION C—NET INCOME GAIN, $2,000

	Co. X	Co. Y	Merged	
Net income	$ 2,000	$ 1,000	$ 5,000	Gain $2,000
No. of shares	1,000	1,000	?	
EPS	$ 2	$ 1	?	
Market price	$ 50	$ 10	?	
P/E ratio	25	10	20	Assumed
Market total	$50,000	$10,000	$100,000	Gain $40,000
Yield	4%	10%	5%	

The P/E 20 provides a new market value of $100,000. Negotiation hinges on the stock exchange ratio to determine the division of the gains in income and market value.

C-1. Stock Exchange Ratio 1 for 9

	Co. X	Co. Y	Merged	
No. of shares	1,000	1,000	1,111⅑	1 for 9
EPS	$ 2	$ 1	$ 4.50	$5,000/1,111⅑ shs.
Market price	$50	$10	$90.00	P/E 20 (× $4.50)

The result is:

	Co. X	Co. Y	Merged
Stock	1,000 shs.	111⅑ shs.	1,111⅑ shs.
	at $90	at $90	at $90
	=$90,000	=$10,000	=$100,000
Gain	+ 40,000	0	+ 40,000
Net income ($4.50)	$ 4,500	$ 500	$ 5,000
Gain	+$ 2,500	−$ 500	+$ 2,000

C-2. Stock Exchange Ratio 1 for 4

	Co. X	Co. Y	Merged	
No. of shares	1,000	1,000	1,250	1 for 4
EPS	$ 2	$ 1	$ 4	$5,000.00/1,250.00 shs.
Market price	$50	$10	$80	P/E 20 (× $4)

The result is:

	Co. X	Co. Y	Merged
Stock	1,000 shs.	250 shs. at	1,250 shs.
	at $80	$80	at $80
	=$80,000	=$20,000	=$100,000
Gain	+ 30,000	+ 10,000	+ 40,000
Net income ($4)	$ 4,000	$ 1,000	$ 5,000
Gain	+$ 2,000	$ 0	+$ 2,000

C-3. Stock Exchange Ratio 1 for 2⅓

	Co. X	Co. Y	Merged
No. of shares	1,000	1,000	1,428.00 1 for 2⅓
EPS	$ 2	$ 1	$ 3.50 $5,000.00/1,428.00 shs.
Market price	$50	$10	$70.00 P/E 20 (× $3.50)

The result is:

Stock	1,000 shs.	428+ shs.	1,428+ shs.
	at $70	at $70	at $70
	=$70,000	=$30,000	=$100,000
Gain	+ 20,000	+ 20,000	+ 40,000
Net income ($3.50)	$ 3,500	$ 1,500	$ 5,000
Gain	+$ 1,500	+$ 500	+$ 2,000

C-4. Stock Exchange Ratio 1 for 1

	Co. X	Co. Y	Merged
No. of shares	1,000	1,000	2,000.00 1 for 1
EPS	$ 2	$ 1	$ 2.50 $5,000.00/2,000 shs.
Market price	$50	$10	$50.00 P/E 20 (× $2.50)

The result is:

Stock	1,000 shs.	1,000 shs.	2,000 shs.
	at $50	at $50	at $50
	=$50,000	=$50,000	=$100,000
Gain	0	+ 40,000	+ 40,000
Net income ($2.50)	$ 2,500	$ 2,500	$ 5,000
Gain	+$ 500	+$ 1,500	+$ 2,000

The following table recaps Net Income gain of $2,000:

	Stock Exchange Ratio	Market Gain $40,000		Net Income Gain + $2,000		P/E 20 Market Price
		Co. X	Co. Y	Co. X	Co. Y	
C-1	1 for 9	+$40	$ 0	+$2,500	−$ 500	$90
C-2	1 for 4	+ 30	+ 10	+ 2,000	0	80
C-3	1 for 2⅓	+ 20	+ 20	+ 1,500	+ 500	70
C-4	1 for 1	0	+ 40	+ 500	+ 1,500	50

ILLUSTRATION D—NET INCOME GAIN, $1,000

This example includes Stock Exchange Ratio 1 for 4 shares and Merged P/E 20.

	Co. X	Co. Y	Merged	
Net income	$ 2,000	$ 1,000	$ 4,000.00	Gain $1,000.00
No. of shares	1,000	1,000	1,250.00	1 for 4
EPS	$ 2	$ 1	$ 3.20	$4,000.00/1,250.00 shs.
Market price	$ 50	$ 10	$ 64.00	P/E 20 (× $3.20)
P/E ratio	25	10	20	Assumed
Market total	$50,000	$10,000	$80,000.00	Gain $20,000.00
Yield	4%	10%	5%	

The result is:

Stock	1,000 shs.	250 shs.	1,250 shs.
	at $64	at $64	at $64
	=$64,000	=$16,000	=$80,000
Gain	+ 14,000	+ 6,000	+ 20,000
Net income ($3.20)	$ 3,200	$ 800	$ 4,000
Gain	+$ 1,200	−$ 200	+$ 1,000

SUMMARY—STOCK EXCHANGE RATIO 1 FOR 4 SHARES

P/E 20	Market Gain (000)		Net Income		Merged Market Price
	Co. X	Co. Y	Co. X	Co. Y	
NI gain, $1,000 (see D)	+$14	+$ 6	+$1,200	−$200	$64
NI gain, $2,000 (see C-2)	+ 30	+ 10	+ 2,000	0	80
NI gain, $3,000 (not shown)	+ 46	+ 14	+ 2,800	+ 200	96
No Income Gain					
P/E 30 (see A-1)	+$22.0	+$8.0	+$ 400	−$400	$72.00
P/E 26 (see B-3)	+ 12.4	+ 5.6	+ 400	− 400	62.40

This summary, based solely on the 1 to 4 exchange ratio, helps to illustrate the many possible interrelationships covering the variables presented.

One reasonable deal would be:

	Co. X	Co. Y	Merged	
Net income	$ 2,000	$ 1,000	$ 5,000.00	Gain $2,000.00
No. of shares	1,000	1,000	1,333⅓	1 for 3

	Co. X	Co. Y	Merged	
EPS	$ 2	$ 1	$ 3.75	$5,000.00/1,333⅓ shs.
Market price	$ 50	$ 10	$ 67.50	P/E 18 (× $3.75)
P/E ratio	25	10	18	Assumed
Market total	$50,000	$10,000	$90,000.00	Gain $30,000.00
Yield	4%	10%	5.5%	

The result is:

Stock	1,000 shs.	333⅓ shs.	1,333⅓ shs.		
	at $67.50	at $67.50	at $67.50		
	=$67,500	=$22,500	=$90,000		
Gain	+ 17,500	+ 12,500	+ 30,000		
Net income ($3.75)	$ 3,750	$ 1,250	$ 5,000		
Gain	+$ 1,750	+$ 250	+$ 2,000		
Stock value increase:		Co. X 35.0%		Co. Y 125%	Total 50%
Net income increase:		Co. X 87.5%		Co. Y 25%	Total 67%

At this stage, the use of preferred stock, bonds, convertibles, warrants, or cash may be negotiated to resolve differences.

CAPITAL EXPENDITURE ANALYSIS

The outlay to acquire another company is a capital expenditure. The outlay can consist of some combination of cash, stock, or other securities. The outlay amount is the market value of the cash and securities paid or the fair market value of the net assets acquired, if less. If the amount paid is greater than the fair market value of the net assets acquired, the difference is goodwill to be amortized over 40 years or less. (In a pooling of interest only book values are recorded so no goodwill can be recognized.)

The net cash gain to the acquirer must be estimated over a period of time and discounted at the discount rate to determine NPV and yield.

The risk element is relatively high because of variability in the possible cash gains and the future period. Risk analysis is critical to the purchase evaluation.

Liquidity must also be considered, particularly when the merged entity has new fixed obligations for interest or preferred dividends.

An example of profitability and risk analysis is:

$$\frac{\text{Cash outlay}}{\text{Cash gain}} \quad \frac{\$100,000}{\$\ 12,500} = f\ 8.0$$

$$\frac{\text{Cash gain}}{\text{Cash outlay}} \quad \frac{\$\ 12,500}{\$100,000} = 12.5\%\ \text{(perpetuity)}$$

Estimated Life	Yield	P	Yield Extensions
10 years	4.3%	0.1	0.43%
15	9.1	.2	1.82
20	10.9	.3	3.27
25	11.7	.3	3.51
30	12.1	0.1	1.21
		1.0	10.24%

If the company's current discount rate is 10.0%, the weighted average return is slightly higher at 10.24%. Below 17 years at 10% yield, the odds are 50–50, a long shot. With a 5.0% discount rate, the odds are good. But estimating the life of cash gains, particularly past 10 years, is necessarily speculative. For a perpetuity the yield is 12.5%, little more than the 12.1% for 30 years.

If a 15-year life is used for the analysis, cash gains can be estimated:

Estimated Cash Gain	(100,000)	Yield	P	Yield Extensions
$10,000	f 10.00	5.6%	0.1	0.56%
12,500	8.00	9.1	.2	1.82
15,000	$6\frac{2}{3}$	12.4	.3	3.72
17,500	5.71+	15.5	.3	4.65
20,000	5.00	18.4	0.1	1.84
			1.0	12.59%

With a 10% discount rate, the odds remain long—a cash gain of $13,150 splits the odds evenly.

In some cases, the total outlay may not be fully determinable at once because of the possible effect of future developments. A range of possible events and their probabilities would be needed.

Many mergers are strategic and difficult to quantify. Some estimates of probable results must, however, be made, whether or not expressed. The records show many ill-conceived mergers and outlays too high to become profitable. The analysis of disinvestment, or spin-off of unpromising operations (or companies), is part of capital expenditure analysis.

The effect on liquidity can be explored by comparing the present capital structure with that after merger (consolidated) and the effect of fixed charges.

For example, assume the following:

	Present	Estimated Merged Coverage Future				
Gain	$48	$48.0	56.0	64.0	72.0	80.0
Fixed charges	$ 6	$ 8.0	8.0	8.0	8.0	8.0

	Present	Estimated Merged Coverage Future				
Coverage ratio	8	6	7	8	9	10
Probability		0.1	0.2	0.3	0.2	0.2

This table raises the question of some liquidity impairment, which should be weighed in evaluating the proposed merger.

Questions of risk, profitability, and liquidity would condition the offer and negotiations and help to set acceptable limits and conditions.

A merger valuation may hinge on projected earnings growth. For example, if the merger indicates a gain of $1,000 a year for an outlay of $20,000, the return would be 5% as a perpetuity. If 10% earnings growth is assumed; we have:

Within Years	f	at $1,000	Yield
5 years	f 1.610	$1,610	8.05%
10 years	f 2.594	2,594	12.97
15 years	f 4.177	4,177	20.88
20 years	f 6.728	6,728	33.64

By year, for 5 years at 10%, we have:

	Gain 10%	Yield on $20,000
Start	$1,000	5.00%
Year 1	1,100	5.50
2	1,210	6.05
3	1,331	6.66
4	1,464	7.32
5	1,610	8.05
Total	$7,715/6	
Average =	$1,286 =	6.43%

This calculation assumes that all gain is paid out in dividends so that the outlay of $20,000 remains unchanged.

With all gains retained, the outlay base increases, and yield gains more slowly:

	10% Gain	Outlay	Yield (%)
Start	$1,000	$20,000	5.00
Year 1	1,100	21,100	5.21
2	1,210	22,310	5.42
3	1,331	23,641	5.63
4	1,464	25,105	5.83
5	1,610	26,715	6.03

With the $1,000 gain held constant and no dividends, yield declines:

	Gain	Outlay	Yield (%)
Start	$1,000	$20,000	5.00
Year 1	1,000	21,000	4.76
2	1,000	22,000	4.55
3	1,000	23,000	4.35
4	1,000	24,000	4.17
5	1,000	25,000	4.00

With the $1,000 gain paid out, the outlay remains $20,000 and the yield 5%. With earnings growth at 10% and all retained, EPS also increases 10% but yield is unchanged:

	Equity	Yield (%)	1,000 Shares EPS
Start	$10,000		
NI	1,000	10	$1.000
	11,000		
NI	1,100	10	1.100
	12,100		
NI	1,210	10	1.210
	13,310		
NI	1,331	10	1.331
	14,641		
NI	1,464	10	1.464
	16,105		

If all NI is paid out, equity does not increase, and yield and EPS rise in parallel.

Finally, the annual rate of gain may accelerate, increasing yields, but EPS increases at a faster rate:

	Equity	Yield (%)	1,000 shares EPS	Rate of Increase
Start	$10,000			
NI 10%	1,000	10	$1.00	—
	11,000			
NI 12%	1,320	12	1.32	32.0%
	12,320			
NI 14%	1,725	14	1.725	30.7
	14,045			
NI 16%	2,247	16	2.247	30.3
	16,292			

3-Year Period: (10% − 16%) = 60% ($1.000 − $2.247) = 125%

Thus for the three-year period, the EPS increase is double that for yield (125% to 60%).

These examples are designed to illuminate the kinds of analyses that are relevant in the evaluation of another company.

PART 3

The Financing Process

Chapter 9 describes the principal types of securities and how they are designed to meet the needs of both issuers and buyers. The nature of risk and two conventional valuation models are presented.

Chapter 10 analyzes financial leases as an alternative borrowing method. Also, the effect of alternate payment terms for several markets is explored.

Chapter 11 deals with a variety of claims on common stock issued by companies—convertibles, warrants, stock rights. Also, call and put options issued by public exchanges and traded by individuals are analyzed.

Chapter 12 examines the composition of the capital structure—the effect of capital sources in terms of cost, control, liquidity, and risk. Total financial capital must equal total operating capital (assets). The critical connecting link—the investment discount rate—is evaluated.

Chapter 13 illustrates foreign currency exchange relationships with alternative techniques for covering individual forward exchange contracts. Futures contracts and hedging are described without examples.

CHAPTER 9

Securities Valuation

WHAT THE CUSTOMERS WANT

BUYERS AND ISSUERS

The valuation of securities—principally stocks and bonds—is the province of personal finance. Individuals and financial institutions make decisions on all financial assets in relation to expectations, individual utility functions, and portfolio theory. Evaluation includes factors such as profitability, risk, liquidity, control, marketability, taxes, and inflation.

The financial manager designs security offerings for the market just as products and services are market oriented. The objective is to raise the requisite funds in the best obtainable combination of cost, risk, liquidity, and control. Overall company performance depends on both asset utilization and fund terms. Financing and investing are closely interdependent.

Both investors and security issuers evaluate:

Cash flows—amount and timing

Risk of cash flow variation—degree and probability

Interest (discount) rates over time

Dividends and market prices

Control—change in stock ownership, raiding possibilities, restrictions imposed by default

Marketability—conditions affecting sale and resale

Liquidity—effect on cash position

Costs—sale/purchase/resale

The following security types are analyzed:

Bonds—fixed income, perpetuities, callable, discount (zero coupon); but not income bonds, serial bonds, sinking fund bonds

Preferred Stock—fixed dividend and cumulative; but not non-cumulative or participating

Common Stock—voting, single class; but not other special classes of stock with limited dividend or voting participation

In Chapter 11, "Claims on Common Stock," various hybrids of the above securities are analyzed.

BONDS

Calculations are limited to three decimals for simplicity. The Appendix contains the present value tables and detailed explanations and illustrations.

Fixed Income (Straight Bonds)

A bond selling at its face value has a yield equal to the coupon rate—both yield to maturity (YTM) and current yield (CY).

Example 1. Bond Selling at Face Value

Assume face value, $10,000; market price, $10,000; coupon, 10% interest; and five-year maturity.

	Contract	5 years f 10%	PV
Principal (P)	$10,000	f 0.621	$ 6,210
Interest (I)	1,000	f 3.791	3,791
			$10,001 ($10,000)

YTM 10%. CY 10% ($1,000/$10,000).

With the same bond due in 30 years, we have:

	Contract	30 years f 10%	PV
P	$10,000	f 0.057	$ 570
I	1,000	f 9.427	9,427
			$ 9,997 ($10,000)

YTM 10%. CY 10% ($1,000/$10,000).

Note that interest is $9,427 for the 30-year bond and only $3,791 for the 5-year bond. For one year maturity, interest is only $909 of the $10,000 total value.

To recap (by calculator), YTM 10%, we have:

	$10,000 Bond	
Maturity	P	I
1 year	$9,091	$ 909
5	6,210	3,790
30	570	9,430
50	85	9,915
100	1	9,999+
∞	0	10,000

The larger interest component of longer term maturities causes their prices to fluctuate more because of uncertainty about future interest rates.

Bonds sell at more than face value when the market rate of interest falls below the coupon rate; bonds sell below face value when the market rate is above the coupon rate. In these cases, the YTM and CY differ.

Example 2. Bond Selling at Less Than Face Value

Assume 10% coupon—five-year maturity and market rate of interest, 12%.

Contract	f 12%	PV
P $10,000	f 0.567	$5,670
I 1,000	f 3.605	3,605
		$9,275
Discount		725 = $10,000

YTM 12.00%. CY 10.78% ($1,000/$9,275).

The calculation can be checked as follows:

Interest required	$1,200
Interest payable	1,000
Short	$ 200 × f 3.605 = $721 ($725)

The small dollar discrepancies are not significant for the immediate purpose. For actual bond trading, running into the millions, great accuracy is needed:

	Contract	5 years 12% f	PV
	P $10,000	f 0.56742686	$5,674.2686
	I 1,000	f 3.60477620	3,604,7762
			9,279.0448
$1,200			
− 1,000 = $200 ×		f 3.6047762 =	720.9552
			$10,000.0000

The purchaser pays $9,279.0448 to receive $1,000.0000 a year cash and, in effect, sets aside the discount $720.9552 to provide a $200 annuity so that total income is $1,200.0000 for YTM of 12%. The CY is $1,000.0000/$9,279.0448 = 10.77697% (which disregards the recovery of the discount in five years).

Exact calculations, when needed, are provided in bond tables and by calculation. Note that bond tables in the financial press show only CY and not YTM, and the differences may be large, particularly for shorter maturities.

If only the price is known but not the YTM, trial and error is required. An arithmetic approximation may help to start the process.

Market Price	$ 9,275
Face Value	10,000
	19,275/2 = $9637.5 average
Annual Interest	$ 1,000
Discount $725/5 yrs.	145
	$ 1,145 annual average

$1,145.0/$9,637.5 = 11.88%.

This arithmetic average is on the low side (YTM 12%). This method gives a result on the low side for bonds selling at a discount. Thus a first trial at 12% would provide an exact answer in this case.

For example, the market price is $6,000 on a $10,000 bond—10% coupon—20-year maturity.

Interest $ 1,000
Discount $4,000/20   200 = $1,200 average interest
Principal   6,000
                                  10,000
                           $16,000/2 = $8,000 average principal
    $1,200/8000 = 15% *YTM* approximation.

Try 16%

		f 16%	PV	
P	$10,000	f 0.051	$ 510	
I	1,000	f 5.929	5,929	$6,439 High

Try 17%

		f 17%	PV	
P	$10,000	f 0.043	$ 430	
I	1,000	f 5.628	5,628	$6,058 High

Try 18%

		f 18%	PV	
P	$10,000	f 0.037	$ 370	
I	1,000	f 5.353	5,353	$5,723 Low

Interpolate as follows:

17% $6,058 $6,058
18%   5,723   6,000
                   $ 335 $ 58 = 17.3%
18% − 17% = 1% × 17.3% =   0.173%
Add   17.000
Market price $6,000   YTM 17.173

The CY is $1,000/$6,000 = 16.67%. With longer maturities and higher rates, the CY approaches YTM because the discount amount PV is smaller.

Example 3. Bond Selling at More Than Face Value

Assume 10% coupon—five-year maturity and market rate, 8%.

Contract	f 8%	PV
P $10,000	f 0.681	$6,810
I 1,000	f 3.993	3,993

	10,803
Premium	803
Face value	$10,000

YTM 8.00%. CY 9.26%. ($1,000/$10,803)

The calculation can be checked as follows:

Interest required	$ 800
Interest payable	1,000
over	$ 200 × f 3.993 = $799 ($803)

The purchaser pays $10,803 to receive $1,000 a year cash, and the premium of $803 is amortized over five years to reduce the income by $200 ($799/f 3.993) yearly to realize $800 net.

If only the bond price is known, and not the yield to maturity, the arithmetic-average method provides a good approximation.

Interest	$ 1,000.0	
Premium $803/5 years	− 106.6	$839.4 average
Principal	10,803.0	
	10,000.0	
	$20,803.0/2	$10,401.5 average

$839.4/10,401.5 = 8.07%.

For bonds selling at a premium, this method provides an answer a little on the high side. For example, if a $10,000 bond is selling at $13,600 with a coupon rate of 18%, and due in ten years, we have:

Interest payable	$ 1,800	
Premium $3,600/10 years =	360	
		$1,440 average
Principal	13,600	
	10,000	
	$23,600/2	$11,800 average

$1,440/$11,800 = 12.20%

Try 12%:

Contract	f 12%	PV
P $10,000	f 0.322	$ 3,200
I 1,800	f 5.650	10,170
		$13,390 Low

Try 11%:

	Contract	f 11%	PV
P	$10,000	f 0.352	$ 3,520
I	1,800	f 5.889	10,600
			$14,120 High

By interpolation, we have about 11.7%. CY is 13.2% ($1,800/$13,600). To recap ($10,000 bond due in five years, 10% coupon), we have:

Market Rate	Market Price	YTM	CY	
12%	$ 9,275	12%	10.78%	$725 discount
10	10,000	10	10.00	—
8	10,803	8	9.26	803 premium

Note that the bond price is *higher* when the market rate of interest is *less* than the coupon rate; the bond price is *lower* when the market rate of interest is *more* than the coupon rate.

Example 4. Semi-annual Interest Payments

Most bonds pay interest every six months, for example: $20,000, face value; due in ten years; coupon rate, 10% a year (5% each six months):

Annual Basis

	Contract	10 Years (10 Periods) f 10%	PV
P	$20,000	f 3.855	$ 7,710
I	2,000	f 6.145	12,290
			$20,000

Semi-annual Basis

	Contract	20 Periods f 5%	PV
P	$20,000	f 0.3709	$ 7,538
I	1,000	f 12.4620	12,462
			$20,000

Quarterly Basis

Contract		40 Periods f 2.5%	PV
P	$20,000	f 0.3724	$ 7,448
I	500	f 25.1028	12,550
			$20,000

P decreases and I increases with more frequent compounding.

Perpetuities

A few bonds have no maturity and are called "perpetuities," for example, British Consols issued in 1814.

There is no YTM. The CY is the coupon rate divided by the market price. For a $10,000 bond paying 10%: $1,000/$10,000 = 10% if the market price and face value are the same.

By formula, we have:

Contract		f	PV
P	$10,000	—	$ 0
I	1,000	f 10.0	10,000
			$10,000

If the price is $12,500, the CY is $1,000/$12,500 = 8.0%:

Contract		f	PV
P	$10,000	—	$ 0
I	1,000	f 12.5	12,500
			$12,500

If the price is $8,000, the CY is 12.5% ($1,000/$8,000).

Contract		f	PV
P	$10,000	—	$ 0
I	1,000	f 8.0	8,000
			$ 8,000

By calculation, a 10% annuity of $10,000 has a PV, by years, as follows:

Years	PV	20-Year Increase
1	$ 9,091.00	—
2	17,355.00	—

Years	PV	20-Year Increase
5	$ 37,908.00	—
10	61,446.00	—
30	94,269.00	$32,823.00
50	99,148.00	4,879.00
70	99,873.00	725.00
90	99,981.00	108.00
110	99,997.00	16.00
130	99,999.58	2.58
150	99,999.94	0.36
∞	100,000.00	0.06

Thus in perpetuity, the % f is the interest-rate reciprocal:

5%	=	f 20.00
10	=	f 10.00
20	=	f 5.00
30	=	f 3.33
40	=	f 2.50
50	=	f 2.00

Callable Bonds

Some bonds can be called in by the issuer before the final maturity date, at times and premiums specified in the bond indenture. For this privilege, the issuer pays a slightly higher interest rate than that for straight (non-callable) bonds.

YTM can be computed to the first call date. A $10,000 bond with a 10% coupon rate and due in 20 years has a 10% YTM and 10% CY if the market price is $10,000. If the bond can be called in 5 years at $11,000 (premium of one-year interest), the YTM, by short-cut, is:

Interest	$1,000
Premium $1,000/5 years =	200
	$1,200

Principal $11,000
        10,000
$21,000/2 = $10,500 = 11.43%
By calculation   = 11.58%

At $10,000 original market price, the YTM is 11.58% for a call at $11,000 in five years, compared with YTM 10% held to maturity. The issuer would call the bond only if the interest rate dropped below 10% enough to make it profitable, as described in Chapter 7, "Bond Refunding and Defeasance."

If the market rate dropped to 7%, the bond price would be:

	Contract	5 years f 7%	PV
P	$10,000	f 0.713	$ 7,130
I	1,000	f 4.100	4,100
			$11,230

However, with the bond callable at $11,000, the market price would not rise higher. Thus the bondholder has a theoretical "market loss" of $230. He would receive $11,000 from the call to reinvest at 7%, or $770, in place of the $1,000 interest on the bond. But he would have received some extra income for five years because of the higher rate attaching to callable bonds. The callable bonds issued at 10% could have been issued at a somewhat lower rate as straight bonds.

If the bonds are never called (not unusual), the bondholders enjoy the extra interest for the life of the bonds, and the company has the extra cost for a privilege not exercised.

Some recent bond issues have incorporated a put provision whereby the company agrees to buy the bond back at stated times and amounts, thus providing a price floor. This protects the buyer and lowers the coupon rate.

All of these factors are weighed by the issuer in designing bond offerings in support of financing plans.

Discount—Zero Coupon

A bond that pays no interest is called a "zero coupon bond." It has no CY. The YTM is determined from the price relative to the face value and years to maturity.

For example, a $1,000 bond selling for $400 has a YTM of 14% if due in seven years (f 0.3996).

Due In	YTM
1 year	150.0%
5	20.1
6	16.5
7	14.0
9	10.7
12	7.9
15	6.3
20	4.7

A $1,000 bond with an 8% YTM would be priced at $500 if due in 9 years—at $215 if due in 20 years—at $857 if due in 2 years.

Some bonds sell at a discount and also pay a low rate of interest. A $10,000 bond paying 6% and due in ten years would sell at a discount if the market rate is 15%.

	Contract	f 15%	PV
P	$10,000	f 0.247	$2,470
I	600	f 5.019	3,012
	Price		$ 5,482
	Discount		4,518
	Face value		$10,000

Check: $1,500
− 600

$900 × f 5.019 = $4,517 ($4,518)

Or:

$$\$4,518/\text{f } 5.019 = \$900 + \$600 = \$1,500$$

BOND TRADING

Bond prices fluctuate with interest rates and offer trading opportunities similar to the stock market. Assume the following: purchase a $10,000 bond for $10,000; due in 10 years; coupon rate, 10%; YTM and CY, 10%.

Example 1

Sell it in three years for $7,579—market rate, 16% (7 years to maturity).

	Contract	7 years f 16%	PV
P	$10,000	f 0.354	$3,540
I	1,000	f 4.039	4,039
			$7,579

Market loss, $2,421

Interest collected, $3,000

Total dollar gain, $579 for three years

The realized YTM for three years is about 2%.

	Contract	3 years f 2%	PV
P	$ 7,529	f 0.942	$ 7,139
I	1,000	f 2.884	2,884
			10,023
			$10,000 (about 2.1% YTM)

Example 2

Sell it in three years for $13,602—market rate, 4%

	Contract	7 years f 4%	PV
P	$10,000	f 0.760	$ 7,600
I	1,000	f 6.002	6,002
			$13,602

Market gain, $3,602

Interest collected, $3,000

Total dollars gain, $6,602 for three years

The realized YTM for three years is almost 20%:

	Contract	3 years f 20%	PV
P	$13,602	f 0.574	$ 7,876
I	$ 1,000	f 2.106	2,106
			9,982
			$10,000 (about 19.9% YTM)

These two examples show wide swings—from 10% down to 2% or up to 20%—in realized YTM for three years.

The bonds held to maturity would have a yield of 10% when purchased at face value.

If this bond is purchased at $7,579 and sold in one year at $9,000, the gain is $1,421, plus $1,000 interest, or $2,421—a 32% yield.

PREFERRED STOCK

If a company has only one type of stock, it is properly called "capital stock." A second type of stock is given some preference and called "preferred stock."

The capital stock is now called "common stock" and is subject to preferences given to the preferred issue. This distinction in nomenclature is little observed in practice. There may be a second class of common, with different voting rights.

Preferred shares have preference over the common in receiving dividends and are usually cumulative (and without profit participation). No common dividend can be paid until all preferred dividends are paid. Other preferences extend to liquidating values and to protection under default conditions. Preferred stock may be convertible into common, and it may be callable.

Preferred stock is similar to bonds without maturity, but the dividends must be declared by the board of directors. Failure to meet a dividend has highly negative fnancial effects but generally not as severe as defaulting interest on bonds.

A preferred with a stated value of $1,000 could specify annual dividends of 10% or $100, cumulative. The yield is 10.0% ($100/$1,000) as with a perpetual bond. If the price drops to $800, the yield is 12.5% ($100/$800). If the price rises to $1,111, the yield is 9.0% ($100/$1,111). Preferreds trade at competitive market yields, reflected in the market price.

Common stock is the residual recipient of earnings after interest and preferred dividends, both of which exercise leverage on ROE.

Preferred dividends, unlike interest, are not tax deductible to the issuer. However, corporations owning stock (preferred and common) can exclude 85.0% of cash dividends from taxable income. The effective tax rate, for example, could be 6.9%.

Dividend income	$1,000	
Exclude 85%	850	
Taxable	150	
Tax rate, 46%	69	Net rate 6.9%
Net	$ 81	+ $850 = $931 kept.

Or, 15% of 46% = 6.9%. This treatment applies only to qualified domestic corporations.

COMMON STOCK

Financial markets are called "efficient" if they are open to all, public information is readily available to everyone quickly at small cost, trading costs are low, regulation is effective, and many traders deal actively in large volumes for many securities.

Studies have established market efficiency in the sense that no past market performance can be related to future performance (random walk), and that all available information is rapidly reflected in security prices. There is a degree of inefficiency to the extent that insiders use their knowledge to trade in the market for personal gain before the information is made public; this is subject to close scrutiny and regulation.

The markets react speedily to new developments, which are unpredictable and constantly changing. Trading reflects individual viewpoints about the future and shifting risk attitudes. Consequently, market prices are volatile, random, unpredictable.

This subject is in the field of personal finance but some basic approaches are sketched from the viewpoint of the financial manager as a corporate planner, not as an individual investor. No attention is given to topics such as fundamental analysis, technical analysis, portfolio analysis, or other topics of personal finance.

Diversification of Risk

The return, or profitability, on a stock is measured by the change in price, up or down, and dividends, if any, for a period. Return on a stock portfolio is the weighted average of the return for each stock (G = gain; L = loss):

One Year

Stock	Cost	Price	G/L	Div.	Total	Return
#1	$1,000	$1,140	G $140	G $ 60	G $200	20%
#2	1,000	1,000	0	G 100	G 100	10
#3	1,000	940	L 60	0	L 60	− 6
	$3,000	$3,080	G $ 80	G $160	G $240	8%

The portfolio return is 8%—a weighted average of 20% + 10% + −6% (a wide range). Portfolio composition is a matter of individual preference, and return and risk positions vary widely.

The riskiness of a portfolio is not a weighted average and requires complex mathematical formulation to express (co-variance). The risk factor for a single stock is relatively high. However, a careful selection of some 10 to 20 stocks can eliminate most of the risk of the individual companies—known as unsystematic risk. Systematic risk refers to swings of the entire market, which cannot be hedged.

Definition of the market theoretically requires recognition of all assets. As a practical matter, specific market indices must be selected. Investors arrange and rearrange their asset holdings to meet changing personal situations and changing evaluations of the future.

Because investors can readily diversify away company (unsystematic) risk, the market pays no risk premium for individual stocks. However, if a company has a material change in its risk posture, regardless of reason, individual portfolios may be affected enough to require some buying and selling, causing expense for the investor.

Dividend Model Valuation

One approach to stock valuation, long in use, requires estimate of:

Current price	P_0
Future price	P_1
Future dividend	D_1

Current prices are constantly fluctuating, dividends are not dependably predictable, and future prices are not predictable, as borne out by the efficient market theorem. The formulation is as follows, with an example of an estimate for one year:

$$P_0 \qquad \$40$$
$$P_1 \qquad 44$$
$$D_1 \qquad \underline{\quad 2\quad}$$

$$P_1\ 44 + D_1 2 \quad = \quad \frac{\$46}{P_0\ \ \$40} = 115\% = 15\%\ Ke$$

Ke is the rate of return, or yield, on common stock.

Rewritten, we have:

$$\frac{D_1\ \$\ 2}{P_0\ \$40} = 5\%$$

$$P_1\ \$44 - P_0\ \$40 = \frac{\$\ 4\ G}{P_0 = \$40} = 10\%\ G$$

or:

$$\frac{D_1\ \$\ 2}{P_0\ \$40} = 5\% + 10\%\ G = 15\%\ Ke$$

or:

$$\frac{D_1\ \$2.00}{Ke\ \ 0.15 - G\ 0.10} = \frac{\$2.00}{\$0.05} = \$40.00\ P_0$$

Investors seeking a higher return than 15% will not buy—the stock is "overpriced." If 15% is acceptable, or a lower rate, they will buy or hold. These ongoing evaluations create an ever-changing market as requirements and expectations change.

Another investor might expect P_1 $46.00 and D_1 $2.40:

$$P_1\$46.00 + D_1\$2.40 = \frac{\$48.40}{P_0 \quad \$40.00} = 121\% = 21\%Ke$$

or:

$$\frac{D_1 \; \$ \; 2.40}{P_0 \; \$40.00} = 6\% + \frac{P_1 \; \$46.00 - P_0 \; \$40.00 \quad \$6}{P_0 \; \$40.00} = 15\% \; G = 21\% \; Ke$$

or:

$$\frac{D_1 \; \$2.40}{Ke \; 0.21 - G \; 0.15} = \frac{\$2.40}{.06} = \$40.00 \; P_0$$

Still another investor might estimate P_1 $42.00 and D_1 $1.60:

$$\frac{D_1 \; \$ \; 1.60}{P_0 \; \$40.00} = 4\% + \frac{P_1 \; \$42,00 - P_0 \; \$40.00 \quad \$2}{P_0 \; \$40.00} = 5\% \; G = 9\% \; Ke$$

All expectations interact on the market price.

These models use a one-year period for clarity and convenience of expression; yet the same model applies to all periods. Some dividends are always expected in time. Otherwise, the company is considered to have no value and so is bankrupt, with all equity wiped out. Dividends will, at some time, be declared from earnings, or the company will be sold or merged and the equity redeemed in cash or stock of another company. Or the company could be liquidated, with the residual proceeds going to equity.

The valuation model used for bonds can also be applied to stocks:

P in 5 years	$80
D $5 per year for 5 years	
Required Ke	16%
P_0	?

	5 years f 16%	PV
Price $80	f 0.476	$38.08
Dividend $5	f 3.274	16.37
		P_0 $54.45

If the stock is currently priced at a lower figure, the *Ke* will exceed 16%; if the price is higher, the *Ke* will be lower than 16%.

The model can be used to determine a future price for a given yield: For five years: P_0 $50; *Ke,* 20%; and D, $5.

Set-Up Model

	5 years f 20%	PV
Price ?	f 0.402	?
Dividend 5	f 2.990	$14.95
		$50.00

Solving

Price $87.20	f 0.402	$35.05
Dividend $5.00	f 2.990	14.95
		$50.00

The price in five years must be $87.20 to provide *Ke* 20% ($35.05/f 0.042).

It is prudent to estimate a range of likely future outcomes. For example, a stock now selling at $40 is expected to reach prices of $60 to $80 in three to five years, without dividends.

Future Price	Price $40		Yield—*Ke*%		
	Gain	Percent	5 years	4 years	3 years
$60	$20	50	8.4	10.7	14.5
70	30	75	11.8	15.0	20.5
80	40	100	14.9	18.9	26.0

The *Ke* range from 8.4% to 26.0% is wide. The critical element is attaching probabilities to the possible outcomes. If all are considered to be equal, statistics may be applied. The mean is 15.63% (total *Ke* 140.7 divided by 9), the variance is 23.59, and one standard deviation is 4.86. (Supporting details not given.)

For one standard deviation the yield range is:

$$15.63\% + 4.86\% = 20.49\%$$

$$15.63\% - 4.86\% = 10.77\%$$

There is thus a 68.0% chance of *Ke* between 10.8% and 20.5% (a 95.0% chance of *Ke* between 5.9% and 25.4% for 2 standard deviations). These calculations seem to have scant value for the investor, and they are arbitrary at best. Of more concern is the skew, or likelihood of being below a required *Ke,* such as

12%. The table shows three of nine rates below 12%, or one chance in three of sub-par results—a long shot for most people.

Estimated yields are comparable with other securities of all types. For instance, AA bonds with five-year maturities may have YTM of 12.5% and standard deviation of 2.5—a range of 10% to 15%. Choices of risk and return are made in a portfolio context. Risk evaluation for investors is akin to risk evaluation by managers for investment decisions, described in Chapter 6.

These approaches to security valuation underscore its subjective nature and the limits of quantitative analysis. Managers must base company financial plans on goals and policies and deal with the financial markets on an ad hoc basis. The objective in financing, as in investing, is to improve profitability and liquidity within prudent risk limits, regardless of the vagaries of the markets.

Models using both EPS and dividends require estimation of yield on retained earnings, that is, net income less dividends. This treatment is provided as a matter of technical interest but does not add any more certainty or clarity to the results for either the investor or manager.

For example, assume that Ke and E/P agree at 12% and that the yield is 20% on retained earnings (RE):

P_0	$50		
D_1	$ 6	$6/$50 = 12% Dividend	
EPS	$ 6	$50/$6 = 8.33 P/E	$6/$50 E/P = 12%
RE	$ 0		(EPS $6 − D_1 $6)
RE (%)	20%	= G $0	Dividend 12% + G $0 = 12% Ke

E/P ($6/$50) 12% and Ke (12% + 0) 12% agree.

Assume now that the dividend is 80% of $6 EPS, or $4.80, with $1.20 (20%) retained to earn 20%. Growth becomes 20% retained × 20% rate = 4% G. For several assumed prices:

	A	B	C	D	E
P_1	$75.0	$67.00	$60.00	$50.00	$30.00
D $4.80 =	6.4%	7.16%	8.0%	9.60%	16.0%
G%	4.0%	4.00%	4.0%	4.00%	4.0%
Ke%	10.4%	11.16%	12.0%	13.60%	20.0%
P/E ratio (EPS $6)	12.5	11.16	10.0	8.33	5.0
E/P (%)	8.0%	8.96%	10.0%	12.00%	20.0%

A—P_0 jump from $50 to $75 reflects bullish growth prospects.
   P/E jumps from 8.33 to 12.5.
   E/P drops to 8% from 12%, the P/E reciprocal.

B—Equal Ke and P/E at 11.16% contrived to show that the equality is only by coincidence.

C—Ke at 12% = Ke with no dividend. P/E higher. P_1 higher to reflect growth prospects.

D—Same P_1 at \$50. Ke up to 13.6% from 12.0%. P/E and E/P unchanged. Growth outlook discounted.

E—P_1 falls from \$50 to \$30—a 40% drop. P/E down to 5, and Ke and E/P equal at 20%. Bear market, or highly unfavorable news about the company or industry.

Continuing with the same example, but with lowered dividends and a higher RE, we have:

	A1	B1	C1	D1
EPS	\$ 6.00	\$ 6.00	\$ 6.00	\$ 6.00
Div.	\$ 3.60	\$ 2.40	\$ 1.20	\$ 0.00
RE	\$ 2.40	\$ 3.60	\$ 4.80	\$ 6.00
RE (%)	40%	60%	80%	100%
G (at 20%)	8%	12%	16%	20%
P_1	\$90.00	\$96.00	\$96.00	\$ 90.00
Div. (%)	4.0%	2.5%	$1\frac{1}{4}$%	0%
Ke	12.0%	14.5%	$17\frac{1}{4}$%	20.0%
P/E	15	16	16	15
E/P	$6\frac{2}{3}$%	$6\frac{1}{4}$%	$6\frac{1}{4}$%	$6\frac{2}{3}$

A—The increase in RE to 40% from 20% lifts the price to \$90 from \$75 to reflect higher earnings prospects. Ke rises to 12% from 10.4% and P/E rises from 12.5% to 15%.

B—The price rises again (from \$67 to \$96) to reflect greater growth with more RE (60%). Ke and P/E are higher, reflecting a favorable market response.

C—With RE at 80%, the P_1 remains at \$96, as the market has doubts about the successful utilization of the added RE. Compared with A1 P/E remains at 16, but Ke rises to 17.25% from 14.5%.

D—With all earnings retained, the P_1 drops to \$90 and P/E to 15, as in A. Ke rises to 20%.

These illustrations help to point up the great variety of possible results, regardless of the models used.

As a technical footnote, P_1 can be decomposed into its dividend $P(D)$ and growth $P(G)$ components, starting with the assumption that EPS and D are equal: Continuing with the data:

	A1	B1	C1
P_1	\$90.00	\$96.000	\$96.0000
D component:			
D \$6 ÷ Ke (decimal)	\$6.00/0.12	\$6.000/0.145	\$6.0000/0.1725
= $P(D)$	\$50.00 =	\$41.379 =	\$34.783

These are the stock prices assuming *EPS* \$6 − *D* \$6 = RE − \$0, and *Ke* as above.

The G component is:

Balance of P_1	\$40.00	\$54.6210	\$61.2170
RE	\$ 2.40	\$ 3.6000	\$ 4.8000
× 20% *G*	\$ 0.48	\$ 0.7200	\$ 0.9600
÷ *Ke* (decimal)	0.12	0.1450	0.1725
= *PV*	\$ 4.00	\$ 4.9655	\$ 5.5652
less RE	− 2.40	− 3.6000	− 4.8000
= *NPV*	\$ 1.60	\$ 1.3655	\$ 0.7652
÷ Div. % (decimal)	0.04	0.0250	0.0125
= *P(G)*	\$40.00	\$54.6200	\$61.2160
Ratio of *P(G)* to *P(D)*	80%	132%	176%

These are the components attributable to the RE (EPS − *D*), assuming 20% yield on the RE (investment).

CAPM Valuation

The capital asset pricing model (CAPM) is a method (model) for valuing (pricing) capital assets, which include both securities and operating assets. Application of CAPM to operating assets is not developed to a practical level.

Use of the CAPM for securities valuation requires these steps:

1. Determine yields for the "market." Theoretically, this should include all securities. In practice, a substitute is used such as the Standard and Poor's 500 or Wilshire index (5,000 stocks), or whatever is most suitable for the purpose.

2. Determine realized yields for the security to be valued for a selected period and for selected time intervals (e.g., months).

3. Plot the "market" yields and security yields by years, or quarters, or months. Determine the regression line for the security; this is the variability of the security relative to the market (known as the "characteristic line").

4. The variability of market yield is defined as 1.0. The variability of the security relative to 1.0 is called "beta (β)". If the security yield varies directly with the market yield, the β is 1.0, or the same as the market. A β of 2.0 signifies double the market variability and β 0.5, one-half. (This analysis is based on standard deviations.)

5. Determine the current risk-free rate—*Rf*. Treasury bill rates can be used.

6. Determine the current market yield—*Rm*.

7. Write the equation: $Ke = (Rm - Rf) \times \beta + Rf$. For example (common stock): *Rm* 15%, *Rf* 9%, Stock β 1.5. (15% − 9%) = 6% × 1.5 = 9% + 9% = 18% = *Ke*.

The *Ke* of 18%, with β 1.5, compares with the market rate (*Rm*) of 15% and risk-free rate (*Rf*) of 9%. If another stock has a β of 0.5:

$$(15 - 9) = 6 \times 0.5 = 3 + 9 = 12\% \ Ke \ (Rm = 15\%)$$

If another stock has a β of 1.0:

$$(15 - 9) = 6 \times 1.0 = 6 + 9 = 15\% \; Ke \; (Rm = 15\%)$$

This equation (model) deals directly with Ke in terms of company (unsystematic) risk relative to market (systematic) risk. Omitted are stock price, dividends, EPS, growth. But the two approaches are designed to provide the same answer.

CAPM: $(15 - 9) = 6 \times 1.5 = 9 + 9 = 18\% \; Ke$ (or any combination = 18%)

DIVIDEND MODEL: $\dfrac{D_1 \; \$4}{P_0 \; \$50} = 8\% + \dfrac{P_1 \$55 - \$50 = \$5/\$50}{10\%G} = 18\% \; Ke$

(or any combination = 18%)

CAPM contains no dollar amounts. The dividend model disregards risk. In practice, the answers will not agree (as a rule) by varying ranges, but attention is focused on the basis for the difference.

The CAPM is illustrated with a graph (figure 1) that shows an Rm, Rf, and β which is risk as determined by a company's characteristic line.

The difference between Rm and Rf is critical, and it varies significantly over time. In the example given, Rm 15% − Rf 9% = 6%:

				Rf%	Ke%
6%	β	1.0 =	6 + 9		= 15
6%		1.5 =	9 + 9		= 18
6%		0.5 =	3 + 9		= 12

If Rm drops to 14% and Rf rises to 10%, the difference is 4%:

				Rf%	Ke%	Ke% Above
4%	β	1.0 =	4 + 10		= 14	(15)
4%		1.5 =	6 + 10		= 16	(18)
4%		0.5 =	2 + 10		= 12	(12)

If Rm rises to 16% and Rf drops to 8%, the difference is 8%:

				Rf%	Ke%	Ke% Above	Ke% Above
8%	β	1.0 =	8 + 8		= 16	(15)	(14)
8%		1.5 =	12 + 8		= 20	(18)	(16)
8%		0.5 =	4 + 8		= 12	(12)	(12)

The *Rm* − *Rf* differences illustrated (6 − 4 − 8) can be even greater in practice, from zero (or below) to well over 15%.

Stock yields (*Ke*) and risk (β) are evaluated by investors in a portfolio context based on their individual preferences (utilities). Yields are a weighted average but risk is measured by co-variance among the holdings. Risk of individual stocks can be diversified away by the investor, so he will not pay a premium for a risky stock. Company managers evaluate risk (in investment and financing decisions) according to their personal utilities. A change in a company's risk position—either more or less risk exposure—could affect investors' portfolio risk

Figure 1
Security Market Line (SML) (all financial assets)

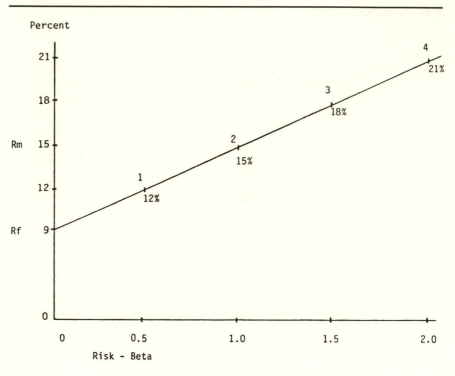

	Rm	Rf		β		Rf	%
1	15 - 9	= 6	x 0.5	= 3 + 9	= 12	Ke
2	15 - 9	= 6	x 1.0	= 6 + 9	= 15	Ke
3	15 - 9	= 6	x 1.5	= 9 + 9	= 18	Ke
4	15 - 9	= 6	x 2.0	= 12 + 9	= 21	Ke

and result in sales and purchases. All portfolios remain fully exposed to market risk (systematic).

Historical betas are used as a guide to future betas for investment decisions. Estimated future betas are supplied by several financial houses, together with standard deviations to indicate probable ranges. To illustrate:

Base		Standard Deviation	High	Low
$Rm\%$	15.0	± 3.0	18.0	12.0
$Rf\%$	9.0	± 2.0	7.0	11.0
	6.0	± 5.0	11.0	1.0
β	× 1.0	± 0.2	× 1.2	× 0.8
	= 6.0		= 13.2	= 0.8
$Rf\%$	9.0	± 2.0	11.0	7.0
$Ke\%$	15.0		= 24.2	= 7.8

Thus the Ke of 15% could range from 7.8% to 24.2%; even wider ranges can occur. The Ke range probabilities for the dividend model are also wide, as illustrated above.

Certain qualifiers to the CAPM are noted:

Rm and Rf are constantly changing and are not predictable.

βs (characteristic lines) also change and must be forecast as probable ranges—usually wide.

Estimated βs compared with actual βs show a bias—the actual βs are somewhat less pronounced.

Use of the CAPM for physical assets is not established.

AN EXERCISE IN MODELS

The effect on stock prices of growth rates and risk levels (β) can be shown by the CAPM and dividend model. Assume that a company has a Ke 20% and a β of 1.5; dividend is $3; price, $15; and growth zero.

CAPM: $(Rm\ 16\% - Rf\ 8\%) = 8\% \times \beta\ 1.5 = 12 + 8 = 20\%\ Ke$

$\dfrac{\text{Div. }\$\ 3}{P_0\ \ \$15} = 20\% + G\ 0\% = 20\%\ Ke$

The company has investment opportunities at three levels: G 5% or G 10% or G 15%. The effects of growth on risk may be at three levels:

A—Increased Risk (β 1.5 − 1.75 − 2.0)
B—Risk not affected (β 1.5 − 1.5 − 1.5)
C—Decreased risk (β 1.5 − 1.25 − 1.00)

A—Increased Risk

CAPM: 1—8% $\times$ β 1.50 = 12% + 8% = 20% Ke (above)
2—8% $\times$ β 1.75 = 14% + 8% = 22% Ke (+2%)
3—8% $\times$ β 2.00 = 16% + 8% = 24% Ke (+4%)

Dividend rates are determined by $Ke - G$:

	A-1	A-2	A-3
	Ke 20%	Ke 22%	Ke 24%
	G 5%	G 10%	G 15%
=	D 15%	D 12%	D 9%

Dividend dollars are increased by G rates:

$$D \quad \$3.00 + 5\% =$$
$$\frac{D_1 \ \$3.15}{D\% \ \$0.15} = 21.00 \ P_1$$

$$D \quad \$3.00 + 10\% =$$
$$\frac{D_1 \ \$3.30}{D\% \ \$0.12} = \$27.50 \ P_1$$

$$D \quad \$3.00 + 15\% =$$
$$\frac{D_1 \ \$3.45}{D\% \ \$0.09} = \$38.33 \ P_1$$

Compare	$15.00 P_0		$15.00 P_0		$15.00 P_0
Increase	$ 6.00		$12.50		$23.33
Percent	40		83		155

	A-2 to A-1	A-3 to A-2
P_1	$27.50	$38.33
P	21.00	27.50
Increase	$ 6.50	$10.83
Percent	31	39

B—Risk Not Affected

With β unchanged at 1.5, the Ke is unchanged (20%).

CAPM: 8% $\times$ β 1.5 = 12% + 8% = 20% Ke (above)

Dividend rates are:

	B-1	B-2	B-3
	Ke 20%	Ke 20%	Ke 20%
	G 5%	G 10%	G 15%
	D 15%	D 10%	D 5%

$$\frac{D_1}{D\%}\frac{\$3.15}{\$0.15} = \$21.00\,P_1 \qquad \frac{D_1}{D\%}\frac{\$3.30}{\$0.10} = \$33.00\,P_1 \qquad \frac{D_1}{D\%}\frac{\$3.45}{\$0.05} = \$69.00\,P_1$$

Compare	$15.00 P_0		$15.00 P_0	$15.00 P_0
Increase	$ 6.00		$18.00	$54.00
Percent	40		120	360

		B-2 to B-1	B-3 to B-2
	P	$33	$69
	P	21	33
	Increase	$12	$36
	Percent	57	109

C—Decreased Risk

CAPM: 1—8% + β 1.50 = 12 + 8 = 20% *Ke*   (above)
2—8% + β 1.25 = 10 + 8 = 18% *Ke*
3—8% + β 1.00 = 8 + 8 = 16% *Ke*

Dividend rates are:

	C-1	C-2	C-3
Ke	20%	18%	16%
G	5%	10%	15%
D	15%	8%	1%

$$\frac{D_1}{\$0.15}\frac{\$3.15}{} = \$21.00\,P_1 \qquad \frac{D_1}{\$0.08}\frac{\$3.30}{} = \$41.25\,P_1 \qquad \frac{D_1}{\$0.01}\frac{\$3.45}{} = \$345.00\,P_1$$

Compare	$15.00 P_0		$15.00 P_0	$ 15.00
Increase	$ 6.00		$26.25	P_0
Percent	40		175	$330.00
				2,220

		C-2 to C-1	C-3 to C-2
		$41.25	$345.00
		21.00	41.25
	Increase	$20.25	$303.75
	Percent	96	736

To recap, we have:

A—Increased Risk

	β	G (%)	Ke (%)	D (%)	P_1	P Increase (%) Base	Cum.
1	1.50	5	20	15	$ 21.00	40	—
2	1.75	10	22	12	27.50	83	31
3	2.00	15	24	9	38.33	155	39

B—Risk Not Affected

	β	G (%)	Ke (%)	D (%)	P_1	P Increase (%) Base	Cum.
1	1.50	5	20	15	$ 21	40	—
2	1.50	10	20	10	33	120	57
3	1.50	15	20	5	69	360	109

C—Decreased Risk

	β	G (%)	Ke (%)	D (%)	P_1	P Increase (%) Base	Cum.
1	1.50	5	20	15	$ 21.00	40	—
2	1.25	10	18	8	41.25	175	96
3	1.00	15	16	1	345.00	2,200	736

A-1, B-1, and C-1 are the same.

Large changes in G and β are assumed to intensify the dynamic effect of the interrelationships on Ke and P. In practice, G and β change slowly, with occasional exceptions.

Market reactions and stock prices are not predictable, but this exercise in models states in literal terms the factors constantly at work in the economy.

CHAPTER 10

Financial Leases

A FINANCING CHOICE

DISCUSSION

Financial leases (also called "capital leases") are the equivalent of buying and borrowing the purchase cost, for repayment over the life of the asset. Legal title remains with the lessor throughout the lease term and at its termination, unless otherwise agreed. The lessee has full rights to possession and use of the asset for the lease period. The lessor pays taxes and insurance, unless otherwise agreed. The lessee pays for operation and maintenance but may contract with the lessor to provide maintenance as a separate contract.

Operating leases are for periods less than the asset life; the lessor pays taxes and insurance, provides maintenance, and retains title. The lessee has usage rights for the lease term.

Financial leases must be capitalized and depreciated by the lessee, and the lessor records a sale and long-term receivable, matched by the lessee's long-term payable. These entries are governed by accounting regulations, which are detailed, complex, and controversial. The purpose is to achieve recognition of the economic equivalent of ownership. Leases must be disclosed in the financial statements and footnotes.

Tax regulations are directed toward ensuring that the transaction is a bona fide lease rather than a sale.

When the lessee acquires property from the lessor (either the manufacturer or a dealer) under a financial lease it is called a "direct financing lease," the subject matter of this chapter. Other varieties include: *sale and lease back,* where the owner of property (real estate) sells it and leases it back; *leveraged leases,* where third parties provide substantial financing to the lessor; *sales type leases,* where the manufacturer sells from inventory at a profit. These variations relate primarily to the lessor and are not presented.

The decision to acquire an asset is a capital expenditure decision and is independent of the financing decision. A financial lease is the equivalent of a purchase and a loan for the purchase cost over the life of the lease, which is equal (or close) to the economic life of the asset. A company may be tempted to avoid this required accounting treatment and record the transaction as an operating lease to show less debt and appear more solvent. However, the footnote disclosure precludes any misconception of the facts, and studies show that the market is not misled by what is called "off balance sheet" financing.

Financial leases are analyzed by discounting the incremental cash flows of the lease proposals at the current net borrowing rate (also used for capital expenditure analysis). The NPV (net present value) of the lease is compared with the cost of borrowing, as illustrated in detail. Lease analysis can be made by other methods, and the subject is highly complex and technical. It is a controversial subject not explored here.

Negotiable factors aside from payment terms include: payment of taxes, insurance, maintenance—usually paid by the lessor; salvage value, which usually stays with the owner/lessor; and investment tax credits, which are allowable to the legal purchaser (based on the tax code).

The financial cost of a lease to the lessee is generally higher than the borrowing cost but may be preferred for a number of reasons:

The lessee has no other available source of credit.

The lease cost is the cheapest source of financing at the time.

The lease terms are less restrictive than those for other financing sources.

The lease can be kept off the Balance Sheet to make it appear more solvent by avoiding capitalization and increase in the D/E ratio.

The future value of the asset is doubtful.

The investment tax credit and accelerated depreciation cannot be fully utilized because of losses.

There is considerable uncertainty about the period of the asset's usefulness so that a shorter lease or an operating lease is preferred. The extra cost is the opportunity cost for the risks avoided.

Lessors, compared with many lessees, have access to cheaper credit, can utilize all tax benefits, and can realize more from salvage because of their size, experience, and specialized knowledge. Also, lessors may offer attractive terms because of competition, in effect offering price reductions in the form of cheaper credit, as illustrated later.

Example 1—Lease Break-Even

Asset cost, $24,000		Annual gain, $12,000
3-year life, SL depr. ($8,000)		Tax, 40%
No salvage		Bank rate, 20% (f 2.106), Net 12% (f 2.402)

A. Purchase Analysis:

	Books	Cash	Yield
Gain	$12,000	$12,000	$\dfrac{\$24,000}{\$10,400}$ = f 2.308
Depr.	− 8,000		
	4,000		= 14.36% (cf. 12.00%)
Tax	− 1,600	− 1,600	NPV:
NI	2,400		$10,400 × f 2.402 = $24,981
Depr.	+ 8,000		− 24,000
			NPV $ 981
Cash	$10,400 =	$10,400	Purchase approved. (Independent of financing source)

B. Asset Cost NPV:

Cost	$24,000.00	Cash outlay
Depr. $8,000 × tax 40%		
= $3,200 × f 2.402	− 7,686.40	PV tax reduction
Cost NPV	$16,313.60	

C. Lessee—Lease Equivalent:

Cost NPV	$16,313.60
÷ f 2.402	$ 6,791.67
÷ 0.6	$11,319.46 before tax payment.

Tax at 40% = $4,527.79
 Also, from B and C we have:

<table>
<tr><td></td><td></td><td></td><td colspan="2">Or</td></tr>
<tr><td>Annual payment</td><td>$11,319.46</td><td></td><td></td><td></td></tr>
<tr><td>less tax</td><td>− 4,527.79</td><td></td><td></td><td></td></tr>
<tr><td>Net payment</td><td>$ 6,791.67</td><td>=</td><td>$ 6,791.67</td><td></td></tr>
<tr><td>× f 2.402</td><td>16,313.60</td><td>=</td><td>+ 3,200.00</td><td>tax on depr.</td></tr>
<tr><td>add PV tax reduction</td><td>+ 7,686.40</td><td></td><td>9,991.67</td><td>× f 2.402</td></tr>
<tr><td>Cost</td><td>$24,000.00</td><td>=</td><td>$24,000.00</td><td></td></tr>
</table>

From A we have:

$$\text{Cost } \frac{\$24,000}{f\ 2.402} = \$\ 9,991.67 \quad \text{cash break-even}$$

$$\text{NPV } \frac{\$\ \ \ 981}{f\ 2.402} = \frac{408.41}{\$10,400.08} \qquad\qquad \$10,400 \text{ cash}$$

The NPV comparison is:

Asset cost NPV	$16,313.60—B
Lease cost NPV:	
$6,791.67 × f 2.402	16,313.60—C
Cost break-even	$ 0.00

The rate comparison is:

$$\text{Lease: } \frac{\text{Cost}\quad \$24,000.00}{\text{Cash B/E}\quad \$\ 9,991.67} = f\ 2.402 = 12\%$$

Bank rate—12%—given.
 Rate break-even.

D. Lessor—Lease Equivalent:

Asset cost (price)	$\dfrac{\$24,000}{\text{f } 2.402}$ =	$ 9,991.67
less tax on depr.	($8,000—40%)	3,200.00
Net		6,791.67
add tax on payment		4,527.79
Before tax payment		$11,319.46

Lessor and lessee have the same payment to earn 12% after tax. Restated we have:

$6,791.67 × f 2.402 = $16,313.60
add PV tax reduction   7,686.40 (B)
Cost (price) $24,000.00

Proof

Receive	$11,319.46	
Less tax on payment	4,527.79	
Net	6,791.67	
Plus tax on depr.	3,200.00 =	$ 9,991.67
× f 2.402		$24,000

E. Cost of Bank Loan at 20%

$\dfrac{\$24,000}{\text{f } 2.106}$ = $11,396.011 annual payment before tax

The Interest schedule is:

	Pay	Interest at 20%	Principal Reduction	Principal Balance, $24,000
1	$11,396	$ 4,800	$ 6,596	$17,404
2	11,396	3,481	7,915	9,489
3	11,396	1,898	9,498	— 9 dif.
	$34,188	$10,179	$24,009	(rounding)

($24,000/f 2.1064815 = $11,393.406 − $11,396. = $2.594)

The cost schedule is:

Interest	Depr.	Total	40% tax	**$11,396** Less Tax = Cash—Net	12% PVf	Cash PV
1 $ 4,800	$ 8,000	$12,800	$ 5,120	$ 6,276	0.893	$ 5,604.47
2 3,481	8,000	11,481	4,592	6,804	0.797	5,422.79
3 1,898	8,000	9,898	3,959	7,437	0.712	5,295.14
$10,179	$24,000	$34,179	$13,671	$20,517		16,322.40

Rounding correction   −   8.80

NPV cost of borrowing $16,313.60

NPV asset cost $16,313.60 B

NPV Lease $16,313.60 C

The lessor and lessee are in complementary positions.

Example 2—Lease Quotes

Data are from Example 1.

Asset cost, $24,000   Annual gain, $12,000

3-year life, SL depr. (8,000)   Tax, 40%

No salvage   Bank rate, 20% (f 2.106),

     Net 12% (f 2.402)

A. Lessor Quotes, $11,600:

NPV:

Pay $11,600

less tax   − 4,640 $6,960

add tax on depr.   + 3,200 $10,160

× f 2.402   24,404.32

Cost   24,000.00

NPV—negative   −$ 404.32

The extra cost is $404.32 for the lease quote of $11,600 (cf. $11,319.46 break-even quote).

$$\text{Rate: } \frac{\$24,000}{\$10,160} = f\ 2.3622 = 12.974\%$$

	Lease (%)	Bank (%)
After tax	12.974	12
Before tax	21.623	20

The lessor rate is higher.

B. Lessor Quotes, $11,000 (Break-even Quote $11,319.46):

NPV
Pay	$11,000		
less tax	4,400	$6,600	
add tax on depr.		+ 3,200	$ 9,800
× f 2.402			23,539.60
Cost			24,000.00
NPV—positive			+$ 460.40

The gain on the lease quote is $460.40 NPV.

$$\text{Rate:} \quad \frac{\$24,000}{\$ 9,800} = f\ 2.449 = 10.876\%$$

	Lease (%)	Bank (%)
After tax	10.876	12
Before tax	18.127	20

The lessor rate is lower.

These two examples demonstrate the simplest way to compare a lease quote with the best alternative borrowing rate, for both rate and NPV. Salvage and accelerated depreciation were excluded from these examples for clarity.

Example 3—Salvage Evaluation

Data are from Example 1.

Asset cost, $24,000	Annual gain, $12,000
3-year life, SL depr. (8,000)	Tax, 40%
No salvage for lessee	Bank rate, 20% (f 2.106),
	Net 12% (f 2.402)

A. Lessee is quoted $9,000 and property title remains with lessor at end of three years:

NPV
Pay	$9,000		
less tax	3,600	$5,400	
add tax on depr.		+ 3,200	$ 8,600
× f 2.402			20,657
Cost			24,000
NPV			+$ 3,343

The lease advantage over bank cost is $3,343 NPV.

Rate: $\dfrac{\$24,000}{\$ 8,600}$ = f 2.7907 = 3.705% (bank 12%)

The lessee's minimum value for retention of title is $3,343 at the 12% rate:

NPV $3,343.00/f 0.712 (3 years, 12%) = $4,695.22 after tax
$4,695.22/0.6 = $7,825.37 before tax at end of 3 years

This is a break-even salvage value computation.

Check

Cost	$24,000		
less salvage	− 3,343	NPV	$20,657
$20,657/f 2.42			8,600
less tax on depr.			− 3,200
			5,400
add tax on payment			+ 3,600
Payment			$ 9,000

If the lessee is confident that the salvage value at the end of three years on the $24,000 asset cost will exceed $7,825 before tax (almost 33%), borrowing from the bank is preferable at 20%. Otherwise, the lease is cheaper if salvage value under $7,825 is likely. For example, if the lessee values the salvage at $9,000 (break-even value $7,825):

PV:

Salvage	$9,000		
less tax	3,600	$5,400 × f 0.712	$ 3,844.80
Cost			24,000.00
Net			20,155.20
$20,155.20/f 2.402			8,391.00
less tax on depr.			− 3,200.00
			5,191.00
Tax on payment			+ 3,460.66
Payment			$8,651.66

This payment compares favorably with the lessor quote of $9,000.

B. A new example of salvage:

Asset cost, $24,000	Tax, 40%
8-year life, SL depr. ($3,000)	Loan, 20% f 3.837
	Net, 12% f 4.968
	Year 8 f 0.404

The lessor quotes $5,500:

NPV
Payment	$5,500		
less tax	− 2,200	$3,300	
add tax on depr.	(40%—$3,000)	+ 1,200	$ 4,500
× f 4.968	=		22,356
Cost			24,000
Lease advantage		NPV	$ 1,644

$$\text{Rate:} \quad \frac{\$24,000}{\$ 4,500} = f\ 5.333 = 10.008\% \text{(bank, 12\%)}$$

The salvage equivalent is:

NPV 1,644/f 0.404 = $4,069/0.6 = $6,782 before tax at end of eight years.

The break-even salvage value is $6,782 on the asset costing $24,000, at the end of eight years (about 28%).

Check

Salvage	$6,782	
less tax	2,713	
Net	$4,069 × f 0.404	$ 1,644
Pay—net	$4,500 × f 4.968	$22,356
Cost		$24,000

If the lessee ascribes a salvage value over $6,782, it gains by the bank loan at 12% net. If salvage is valued at zero by the lessee, the lessor terms are 10% net, compared with the bank rate of 12%.

Example 4—Accelerated Depreciation

Data are from Example 1 and SYD depreciation.

Asset cost, $24,000	Annual gain, $12,000
3-year life, SL depr. (8,000)	Tax, 40%
No salvage	Bank rate, 20% (f 2.106),
	Net 12% (f 2.402)

Use SYD (sum of years digits) depreciation.

Year		SYD	Tax	f	PV Tax	Example 1B	
1	$\frac{3}{6}$	$12,000	$4,800	0.893	$ 4,286.40		
2	$\frac{2}{6}$	8,000	3,200	0.797	2,550.40		
3	$\frac{1}{6}$	4,000	1,600	0.72	1,139.20		
		$24,000	$9,600				
	Tax PV				$ 7,976.00	$ 7,686.40	+$289.60
Asset cost					24,000.00	24,000.00	0.00
NPV					$16,024.00	$16,313.60	+$289.60

The payment gain is:

SYD NPV $16,024/f 2.402 $6,671.11
Example 1C   6,791.67
Payment gain $ 120.56

The rate gain is:

SYD NPV $6,671.11 + $3,200 tax = $9,871.11
$24,000.00/$9,871.11 = f 2.4313 = 11.3% (Bank, 12%)
Before tax, 18.8% (Bank, 20%)

Any accelerated form of depreciation provides a larger tax deduction earlier, although the total is the same for the full life.

EXAMPLES OF ALTERNATE PAYMENT TERMS

A—Price Cutting

Lease terms below current interest rates are a form of price cutting. For example, if the payment terms are offered with zero interest, the price is $24,000 with payments of $8,000 each for three years. If the appropriate interest (borrowing) rate is 20%, the payment PV is $8,000 × f 2.106 = $16,848.

Price $24,000
PV payment   16,848
Reduction $ 7,152 = 29.8%

The equivalent to these terms is a cash offer of $16,848.

A manufacturer with a cost of 70% is affected as follows.

Assume:	Full	Lease	Or Cash Offer	
Price	$24,000	$24,000	$24,000	Price
Cost	16,800	16,800	7,152	Discount
Gross margin	7,200	7,200	16,848	Net
Lost interest	0	7,152	16,800	Cost
Net margin	$ 7,200	$ 48	$ 48	
Percent	30%	0.2%		

Manufacturers offering cut-rate lease terms should reflect the difference as a price reduction and show the financing at the current interest rate; this is particularly important when there are separate divisions.

Check: Net price $16,848/$8,000 a year = f 2.106 = 20%

The required payment at 20% is $24,000/f 2.106 = $11,393.
If the appropriate rate is 15%, the f is 2.283 for three years, and the payment is:

$24,000/f 2.283 = $10,512 payment

compared with $11,393 for 20%.
If the payment terms exceed the current interest rate, there is, in effect, a price increase. When buyers are primarily interested in payment terms, such as monthly mortgage installments, price reductions are often reflected in the lease quotes rather than by selling-price reduction.

B—Real Estate

Real estate is sometimes offered at a low interest rate to appeal to buyers who are reluctant to commit to current high rates and who relate monthly payments to budgetary limits.

Real estate price	$120,000
Terms	20 years at 9%
Payments	$ 13,145 ($120,000/f 9.129)

If the current interest rate is 15%, the payments should be $19,172 ($120,000/f 6.259).
The payment reduction is:

At 15%	$19,172
At 9%	13,145
Reduction	$ 6,027 = 31.4%

Translated into a price reduction, it is:

Payment $13,145 × f 6.259 (15%, 20 years) =	$ 82,275
Cash price	120,000
Reduction	$ 37,725 = 31.4%

Check: Net price $82,275/f 6.259 = $13,145.

If the sale can be made at $85,000 cash, and the buyer can obtain a loan at 14% (f 6.623), the payments are $12,834 ($85,000/f 6.623) compared with the seller's quote of $13,145, a saving of $311 per year.

C—Automobiles

Auto sales frequently relate more directly to the payment terms than to selling price, and competitive selling focuses on low interest rates.

Auto price	$18,000
Terms	5 years at 6%—f 4.212
Pay	$ 4,273.50 ($18,000.00/f 4.212)

If current interest rates are 18% (f 3.127), the payments should be $5,756.32 ($18,000/f 3.127)

$$\$5,756.32 - \$4,273.50 = \$1,482.82, \text{ or } 25.8\%.$$

In terms of price reduction, we have:

$4,273.50 × f 3.127 =	$13,363
Sales price	18,000
Reduction	$ 4,637 = 25.8%

If the auto can be bought for $13,800 cash and a bank loan obtained at 15%, the payment would be $4,116.75 ($13,800/f 3.352), $156.75 less than the quote of $4,273.50.

D—Magazines

Magazine subscriptions at reduced rates for extended periods can be translated into effective interest rates. Four rates for a subscription of five years are compared with the annual rate of $18.

1. 1 year $18 × 5 years = $90. Offer $72.

5 years	$72
1 year	18
4 years	$54

$54/$18 = f 3.00 = 12.6%

2. Offer $63 (rather than $72).

5 years	$63
1 year	18
4 years	$45

$45/$18 = f 2.50 = 21.9%

3. Offer $54 (rather than $63).

5 years	$54
1 year	18
4 years	$36

$36/$18 = f 2.0 = 34.9%

4. Offer $45 (rather than $54).

5 years	$45
1 year	18
4 years	$27

$27/$18 = f 1.5 = 55.2%

A magazine with a one-year rate of $30 offers three years for:

1.

3 years	$80
1 year	30
2 years	$50

$50/$30 = f 1.23 = 13.1%

2.

3 years	$75
1 year	30
2 years	$45

$45/$30 = f 1.5 = 21.5%

3.

3 years	$70
1 year	30
2 years	$40

$40/$30 = f 1.333 = 31.9%

4.

3 years	$65
1 year	30
2 years	$35

$35/$30 = f 1.167 = 44.9%

If the one-year rate is $40 and the two-year rate is $60, the extra outlay now of $20 saves $40 in one year, or 50%—no discounting for one year.

CHAPTER 11

Claims on Common Stock

EQUITY GAMBLES

CONVERTIBLE BONDS

Bonds convertible into common stock, under stated conditions, have lower interest rates because purchasers value the right to acquire stock at a future date by conversion when the conversion rate per share may be less than the market price. Preferred stocks convertible into common are similar to convertible bonds and are not illustrated. If conversion never occurs, the company has saved interest, but the stock price has not risen to the conversion rate. The possibility that conversion to stock might take place with a price rise overhangs the market for common for the life of the bonds. Bondholders have realized less interest income for a right that failed to become profitable.

If the stock price rises enough to induce conversion, stock is issued in exchange for the bonds, and no cash changes hands. Thus a convertible bond is a method for selling stock for possible future issuance at a price (conversion rate) higher than the current market price. This avoids the higher flotation costs and dilution of EPS required by a current sale of common stock. An alternative is to sell non-convertible bonds (higher interest) now and plan to sell stock at a later date when it is hoped that the price will be higher. This is a difficult financing decision.

Convertible bonds are also callable so that the issuer can call the bonds, under stated conditions, for repayment and retirement. Also, the company can call the bonds when the stock market price exceeds the conversion rate, thus forcing conversion. For instance, if the bonds are convertible at a stock price of $30, and the market has reached, say, $35 per share, the bondholder will convert to stock rather than turn in the bonds for cash, as illustrated later. The call enables the company to achieve full bond retirement and issue stock on a planned date. Without a call, some speculators would continue to hold the bonds, possibly up to expiration date, in hopes of a further stock price increase.

A convertible bond has a minimum market value that depends on interest rates and stock prices. For example: Convertible bond, $10,000; coupon rate, 10%; due in ten years; callable at $110; convertible into 500 shares of stock ($20). The bond was issued at face value, with 10% YTM and CY, lower than the non-convertible bond rate of 13%. The conversion rate for the bond is $20 per share. The stock market price at time of issue was $17. If the bond market interest rate one year later is 12%, the bond value with nine years to maturity is:

	Contract	f 12% 9 years	PV	
P	$10,000	f 0.361	$3,610	
I	1,000	f 5.328	5,328	$8,938

This is the investment value.

If the stock market price is now $16, the conversion value is—500 shares @ $16.00 = $8,000, or $938 less than the investment value. However, if the stock price is now $18.50, the conversion value is—500 shares @ $18.50 = $9,250, or $312 more than the investment value.

To recap we have:

Conversion value at $16	$8,000
A—Investment value	$8,938
B—Conversion value at $18.50	$9,250

A—Market value will not go below investment value.
B—Market value will not go below conversion value.

Thus there are two floors, and the values change constantly with changes in rates of interest and stock prices.

With the expectation of higher stock prices, the market value for the bond will exceed its floor value—a premium. The premium dollars can be expressed as a percentage of the floor value. With the expectation of higher stock prices, premium dollars increase but at a lesser rate as the prices rise. Eventually, the bond is converted to stock by the holders, or it is called, or it matures and is redeemed.

Four possible outcomes are described:
1. The bond matures and $10,000 is paid. YTM is 10%. The bondholder has lost the difference between the 10% and the non-convertible (13%) bond rate at the time of issue, and the company has gained that amount. The market price of the stock has failed to rise above $20 ($17 at time of issue). The break-even price is $20 (500 shares @ $20 = $10,000).
2. Convert at $21 in one year.

500 shares at $21 =	$10,500	
Bond cost	10,000	
Gain	500	
Interest	1,000	
Gain	$ 1,500	15% Yield

Use of one year avoids discounting.
3. Convert at $24 in one year.

500 shares at $24 =	$12,000	
Bond cost	10,000	
Gain	2,000	
Interest	1,000	
Gain	$ 3,000	30% Yield

4. Convert at $30 in one year.

500 shares at $30 =	$15,000	
Bond cost	10,000	
Gain	5,000	
Interest	1,000	
Gain	$ 6,000	60% Yield

The owner of the convertible can hold for conversion or sell at a premium, which reflects market expectations for the stock. A purchaser, in turn, would look for a yield based on his acquisition cost. For example: The original bond owner can convert and gain 15%, as in No. 2 above, or sell the bond for $11,000 and gain 20%:

Sell bond	$11,000		
Plus interest	1,000	$12,000	
Cost		10,000	
Gain		$ 2,000	20% Yield

The purchaser pays $11,000 and converts one year later at $24, as in No. 3 above.

Convert at $24	$12,000		
Plus interest	1,000	$13,000	
Cost		11,000	
Gain		$ 2,000	18.2% Yield

Alternatively, he could sell at $12,500

Sell bond	$12,500		
Plus interest	1,000	$13,500	
Cost		11,000	
Gain		$ 2,500	22.7% Yield

The new buyer paying $12,500 could convert a year later at $30,000 as in No. 4 above:

Convert at $30		$15,000	
Plus interest	1,000	$16,000	
Cost		12,500	
Gain		$ 3,500	28% Yield

Or he might sell at a price over $15,000, and so on. If the market moves down, however, holders have a loss in market value and, again, must elect to sell, and cut the losses, or hold in hope of a price reversal.

With a 10% call premium, the bondholder would receive $11,000, the equivalent of a $22 price ($11,000/500 shares). The company might call the bond when the price reaches $25 and conversion value is $12,500. Holders would then convert into stock worth $12,500 rather than turn in the bonds for redemption at $11,000. This is known as using the call to force conversion. The call possibility limits the value of the convertible. Also, the company can encourage conversion by raising the dividend rate, because only stockholders receive the added dividends. The call is not made until the market price ($25 and $22 above) exceeds the conversion price ($20) by a safe margin to guard against a decline after the call and before conversion.

The financial effect of conversion on the company is illustrated with the assumption of a call but no call premium.

Debt	Before Call	After Call
Straight bonds—16⅔%	$30,000	$30,000
Convertible bonds—14%	10,000	—
	$40,000	$30,000
Equity		
2,000 shares ($20)	$40,000	$40,000
500 shares ($20)	—	10,000
2,500 shares ($20)	—	50,000
Capital (Net Assets)	$80,000	$80,000
EBIT (Earnings Before Interest and Tax)	$24,000	$24,000
Interest—16⅔%	5,000	5,000
14%	1,400	—
	6,400	5,000
EBT (Earnings Before Tax)	17,600	19,000
Tax at 50%	8,800	9,500
EAT (Earnings After Tax)	$ 8,800	$ 9,500

Liquidity

D/E (Debt/Equity ratio) $40/$40 = 100%	$30/$50 = 60%	Better
× Interest Earned $24/$6.4 = 3.75	$24/$5 = 4.8	Better

Profitability

ROA	$24 − $12 = $12/$80 = 15%	$12/$80 = 15%	Same
ROE	$8.8/$40 = 22%	$9.5/$50 = 19%	Worse
EPS	$8.8/2,000.0 = $4.40	$9.5/2,500.0 = $3.80	Worse

ROE and EPS decline at the same rate because book value per share is unchanged—$40,000/$2,000 = $20; $50,000/$2,500 = $20.

EPS must be reported as both primary and fully diluted, when applicable, according to technical and complex rules (not fully resolved). The reported EPS then anticipates stock issuance for conversion of convertibles, or stock options (known as "common stock equivalents"). If the effect is to increase EPS, rather than the usual decrease effect, it is disregarded (called "anti-dilutive"). Also, changes in EPS under 3% may be ignored. These reporting requirements are not illustrated.

The result illustrated above can be compared with a possible alternative financing plan: Issue non-convertible bonds at 16% rate (convertibles 14%), callable at $110. Call the bonds and issue stock at a price to achieve net of $20 per share (equivalent of convertibles) for 500 shares.

One year later:
Call bonds at $110 $11,000
Extra interest (2%)   200
                            $11,200
Divide by 500 shares = $22.40
Issue cost for new stock   8%
$22.40 ÷ $0.92 = $24.35

Per share price is $24.35 to break even with alternative of issuing convertible bonds at $20 per share conversion rate.

Five years later:
Call bonds at $110 $11,000
Extra interest (10%)   1,000
                            $12,000
Divide by 500 shares = $24.00
$24.00 ÷ $0.92 = $26.09

This break-even approach helps to define a difficult problem in planning capital structure. The gamble is between the known lower interest with convertible bonds and speculative higher stock prices. The interest saving is fully realized if there is no conversion, and with conversion the opportunity to sell stock at the higher market price is foregone.

WARRANTS

A *warrant* is a right (option) to buy stock in the company issuing the warrant, which specifies the number of shares for each warrant, the exercise price per share, and the period (some are perpetual). The exercise price for the warrant is set about 15% to 20% over the market price at the time of issue. If the stock price does not rise above the exercise price, the warrant is not exercised, and expires without value. If exercised, the company receives the exercise amount and issues stock. The warrant holder pays the exercise amount and receives stock with a higher market value. The possibility of rising stock prices gives value to the warrant over its conversion value.

Warrents are issued for a number of reasons: with bond or preferred issues to aid their sale; as management compensation; in mergers to meet equity needs. The company receives nothing when the warrant is issued but receives cash equal to the conversion value for stock issued, at which time the market value is higher.

If one warrant equals five shares at $20 (exercise price) and the market price rises to $22, the gain on conversion is 5 shares × $2 ($22 − $20) = $10, or 10%. In totals, $110 ÷ $100 = 10% gain. If the stock price goes up to $30, the gain is 5 × $10 = $50, or 50%. In both cases, the company issues 5 shares at $20, or $100.

The expectation of stock price increases over the exercise price gives warrants their value—a premium similar to that for convertibles. For example: Warrant— one share at $50. Assumed stock market prices and prices of warrants to illustrate leverage.

A—Price Table

	Stock Price	Min. Value	Warrant (W) $50		
			Price	Premium	Percent to Min.
1	$ 50	$ 0	$10	$10	∞
2	60	10	18	8	80.0
3	70	20	26	6	30.0
4	80	30	34	4	13.3
5	90	40	42	2	5.0
6	100	50	50	0	0.0

B—Leverage on Base Prices

	Stock Price Increase over $50	Percent to $50	W Price Increase Based on $10	Percent (Ratio 4:1)
1	$ 0	0	$ —	—
2	10	20	8	80
3	20	40	16	160
4	30	60	24	240
5	40	80	32	320
6	50	100	40	400

C—Leverage on Progressive Prices

	Stock Prices	W Prices	Ratio
1	$ 50	$10	$\frac{80.0}{20.0} = 4.00$
2	60 + $10 = 20.0%	18 + $8 = 80.0%	
2	$ 60	$18	$\frac{44.4}{16.7} = 2.66$
3	70 + $10 = 16.7%	26 + $8 = 44.4%	
3	$ 70	$26	$\frac{30.8}{14.3} = 2.15$
4	80 + $10 = 14.3%	34 + $8 = 30.8%	
4	$ 80	$34	$\frac{23.5}{12.5} = 1.88$
5	90 + $10 = 12.5%	42 + $8 = 23.5%	
5	$ 90	$42	$\frac{19.0}{11.1} = 1.73$
6	100 + $10 = 11.1%	50 + $8 = 19.0%	

B and C illustrate a range of results a warrant purchaser might have. But if stock prices decline, the warrant price would drop even faster. Warrant trading reflects investor expectations, but the company is not affected.

STOCK RIGHTS

Stock with a pre-emptive right entitles the stockholders to purchase a share of a new stock issue that preserves their percentage of ownership. If a company is issuing, say, 100,000 new shares, the owner of 1.5% of the currently issued stock would have the right to buy 1,500 shares of the new issue at the offering price. This price is set below the expected market price after the new issue is sold. He can either use the rights to buy stock at the offering price or sell the rights, if they have a market. Otherwise, the rights expire.

The company issues stock at the rights price for all rights received. No entry is needed for expired rights. Shares authorized for issue but not exchanged for rights (plus cash) can be sold at market. Stockholders who do not have pre-emptive rights can buy on the open market, or by subscription to the offering, along with the general public.

As part of its financial planning, a company may decide on a stock issue, as follows: capital needed, $15,000; presently, 800 shares outstanding at a price of $100, or $80,000. What will the market price be with a new stock issue? This depends on the market's evaluation of the company and its use of the additional funds, recognizing that it will take considerable time for new investments to become profitable. The present price of $100 might be discounted to $95, or by 5%. Such evaluations are made primarily by investment bankers.

The decisions to date are summarized in table form:

	Shares	Price	Amount
Present	800	$100	$80,000
New			15,000
Total	1,000	95	$95,000

Thus the price assumption of $95 indicates a total of 1,000 shares, with 200 to be issued at $75, as follows:

	Shares	Price	Amount
Present	800	$100	$80,000
New	+ 200	75	15,000
Total	1,000	$ 95	$95,000

The price of new shares with rights thus becomes $75, compared with the estimated market price of $95. (If the market price were expected to remain at

$100, total shares would be 950, additional shares 150, and rights price $100, thus affording no benefit.)

A right (*R*) is issued for each share currently outstanding. (This is called a "New York right." A "Philadelphia right" is issued for each new share to be issued.) Thus with 800 shares outstanding, 800 rights are issued, and 4 rights are required (with $75) for each new share (800/200).

The value of a right is derived from the table:

	Present price	$100	
	less new price	95	$5 *R*
Or:	New price	95	
	less *R* price	75	$20/4*R* = $5 *R*
Or:	Present price	100	
	less *R* price	75	$25/4 + 1 = 5 = $5 *R*

Rights have a market value arising from stock price expectations:

Market price rises to $115 from $95, increase of $20 = 21.1%.

R price increases from $5 to $10, or by 100% ($115 − $75 = $40/4 = $10 *R*).

Market price drops to $85 from $95, decrease of $10, or 10.5%.

R price decreases from $5.00 to $2.50, or by 50% ($85 − $75 = $10/4 = $2.50 *R*)

At a stock price of $75, the *R* value is zero ($75 − $75 = 0)

Rights may be publicly traded. The shareholder can sell his rights or exercise them. If he holds them, they may expire without value.

A stockholder can either exercise the rights at $75 or sell them at $5 without changing the price ($95) of his shares: own 32 shares; receive 32 rights; buy 8 shares at $75 or sell R at $5.

Exercise *R:*	
Own 32 shares at $100	$3,200
Buy 8 shares at $75	600
Total 40 shares at $95	$3,800
Sell *R:*	
Own 32 shares at $100	$3,200
Sell 32 *R* at $5	− 160
Total 32 shares at $95	$3,040
Difference: 8 shares at $95 =	$ 760

To illustrate further the large effect of pricing stock on rights value:

	Shares	Price	Amount
Present	800	$100.000	$80,000
New	+166⅔	90.000	15,000
Total	966⅔	$ 98.276	$95,000

Number of $R = 800/166\frac{2}{3} = 4.8\ R$ per share
R value $= \$100 - \$98.276 = \$1.724$
or $= \$98.276 - \$90.000 = \$8.267/4.8 = \$1.724\ R$

The price of $98.276 is a discount of only 1.724% on the current price of $100,000, indicating an expected bullish response to the offer.

Total $R = 4.800 \times \$1.724 = \$8.276$ compares with $20.000 ($4 R × $5) in the first example.

A weaker market may have this effect:

	Shares	Price	Amount
Present	800	$100.000	$80,000
New	+ 250	60.000	15,000
Total	1,050	$ 90.476	$95,000

Number of $R = 800/250 = 3.2\ R$ per share

R value $= \$100 - \$90.476 = \$9.524$ or $= \$90.476 - \$60.000 =$
$\$30.476/3.2 = \$9.524$

The price of $90.476 is a discount of 9.524%, a pessimistic forecast of market response.

Total $R = 3.2 \times \$9.524 = \$30.476$

To recap we have:

Stock Prices						Percent
Present	New	With R	Total R Value	No. of R	Value Per R	Discount on Stock Price
$100	$ 90.476	$ 60	$30.476	3.2	$9.524	9.524
100	95.000	75	20.000	4.0	5.000	5.000
100	98.276	90	8.276	4.8	1.724	1.724
100	100.000	100	0.000	(5⅓)	0.000	0.000

The last line shows the upper limit in pricing, with no discount and R value zero ($5\frac{1}{3} = 800/150$). The first line, with a discount close to 10%, is a lower limit. Pricing would fall between these two limits in most cases.

Once the R value is determined, each stockholder knows its value in the acquisition of new shares, but market values can be expected to fluctuate, as illustrated.

STOCK OPTIONS (CALLS AND PUTS)

Call and put stock options are contracts entered into by individuals dealing with one another, principally through organized, public exchanges and clearinghouses. Options are growing rapidly in volume and have increasing significance in all fields of finance. Stock options issued by companies on their common stock as management compensation, or for other purposes, are not described here. The subject is complex, and part of personal finance, but needs to be understood by financial managers as part of capital structure.

The options markets contribute to market efficiency and to the pricing of securities closer to their basic values. Options trading offers opportunities for leverage and hedging to experienced traders. Currency options are discussed in Chapter 13.

A *call option* is a right to buy a specified stock (usually 100 shares) at a stated price (known as the "exercise price" or the "striking price") within a given period (usually less than a year). (European options can be exercised only at the end of the period.) The call option has value if the stock market price is over, or is expected to exceed, the exercise (striking) price. The holder of the option can call (buy) at the exercise price and sell at the market price (higher), and realize the difference, less his cost for the option and commissions. The option seller (writer) has received the option price but must sell at the exercise price if the option is called. If there is no call, the option expires, the seller gains the price of the option, and the buyer has an equal loss. (All of the transactions are actually handled through a clearinghouse; the investors do not deal with one another.) Options are most frequently offered for periods of three, six, and nine months for the more active stocks and in a selected range of exercise prices set by the exchange.

A *put option* is a right to sell a specified stock—the reverse of a call option. The option owner has paid for the right to sell (put) at the exercise price. He expects the stock price to decline so he can sell (put) at the exercise price when it is above the market price, realizing the difference, less his cost and commission. The option seller (writer) must buy stock at the exercise price, now higher than the market price. If the option expires, the seller gains the option price, which is the loss of the buyer.

Call Option—Buyer and Seller

Example 1a

Stock price now $100; in 6 months $110

Option exercise price, $60—option exercised

Option cost, $40 (commission excluded)

Option Buyer		Option Seller		Stock—No Option	
Now—buy Option	$ 40	Buy stock	$100	Buy Stock	$100
6 mos.—call stock	60	Sell option	40		
Total cost	100	Net cost	60		
Sell stock	110	Sell stock	60	Sell Stock	110
Gain—6 mos.	$ 10		$ 0		$ 10
Annual rate	2 × $10 = $20/$40 = 50%		0	2 × $10 = $20/$100 = 20%	

The stock purchase provides a 20% gain compared with the 50% gain for the option purchase. The stock buyer who sells an option has no gain or loss.

Example 1b

The data are the same, but the option cost is $50 (not $40):

Option Buyer		Option Seller		Stock—No Option	
Buy option	$ 50	Buy Stock	$100	Buy Stock	$100
Call stock	60	Sell Option	50		
Total cost	110	Net Cost	50		
Sell stock	110	Sell Stock	60	Sell Stock	110
Gain	$ 0		$ 10		$ 10
Annual rate	0	2 × $10 = $20/$50 = 40%		2 × $10 = $20/$100 = 20%	

The roles are reversed—the option seller gains 40% and the buyer has no gain. The stock purchase again yields 20%, while the option purchase shows no gain. The stock purchaser who sold the option doubles his gain to 40%, over the 20% with no option.

At option prices over $50.0000, the buyer loses money. At option prices under $40.0000, the seller loses. Between $40.0000, and $50.0000, there is a break-even point, which is $45.4545, with a 20% gain in all cases.

Option Buyer		Option Seller		Stock—No Option	
Buy option	$ 45.4545	Buy stock	$100.0000	Buy stock	$100
Call stock	60.0000	Sell option	45.4545		
Total cost	105.4545	Net cost	54.5455		
Sell stock	110.0000	Sell stock	60.0000	Sell stock	110
Gain	$ 4.5455		$ 5.4545		$ 10
Annual rate	× 2 = $9.091 = 20%	× 2 = $10.909 = 20%		× 2 = $20 = 20%	

This equality is a basis for making a choice among the alternatives. Stock price expectations move option prices up and down as conditions change.

Call Option Probabilities

Example 2

An investor can use $1,000 to buy 10 shares of stock at $100. He thinks there are equal probabilities that the price will be $130 or $110 or $90 within a year. Or the $1,000 can buy 100 call options at $10, with an exercise price of $100, exerciseable within a year

Future Price 10 Shares	$130	$110	$90	Total
Total value	$1,300	$1,100	$ 900	$3,300
Stock cost (10 shs. @ $100)	1,000	1,000	1,000	3,000
Gain (loss)	$ 300	$ 100	$ (100)	$ 300
Percent gain (loss)	30	10	(10)	10

With equal probabilities, the weighted average gain is 10%.
   The option alternative is:

Future Price 100 Shares	$130	$110	$90	Total
Total value	$13,000	$11,000	$ 9,000	$33,000
Exercise cost (100 shs. @ $100)	10,000	10,000	10,000	30,000
Gain	3,000	1,000	No Call	4,000
Option cost (100 @ $10)	1,000	1,000	1,000	3,000
Gain (loss)	$ 2,000	$ 0	($1,000)	$ 1,000
Percent gain (loss)	200	0	(100)	$33\frac{1}{3}$

At the $130 price, the option yields 200%, (compared with 30%). At $110, the option breaks even because the stock price gain equals the option cost, (compared with the 10% gain). At $90, the option is not exercised—the holder would not pay the exercise price of $100 when the market price is $90. The option cost is lost—100% (compared with the 10% loss). The weighted average is $33\frac{1}{3}$%, compared with 10%.
   The dramatic difference between the two choices is highlighted:

Future Price	$130	$110	$90	Net
Stock gain (loss)	$ 300	$100	$ (100)	$ 300
Option gain (loss)	2,000	0	(1,000)	1,000
Change	+$1,700	−$100	−$ 900	+$ 700

Great gains involve high risk. The option choice entails two chances in three of a worse result, with a one to three shot at a high payoff.

Put Option Probabilities

Example 3

Use $1,000 to buy put options for 500 shares at $2 each; exercise price is $100, for a one-year term.

Future Price 500 Shs.	$130	$110	$90	Total
Total value	$65,000	$55,000	$45,000	$165,000
Exercise cost	50,000	50,000	50,000	150,000
(500 shs. @ $100)				
Gain	No put	No put	5,000	5,000
Option cost	1,000	1,000	1,000	3,000
(500 shs. @ $2)				
Gain (loss)	$(1,000)	$(1,000)	$ 4,000	$ 2,000
Percent gain (loss)	(100)	(100)	400	66⅔

At market prices over $100 (exercise price) the put option would not be exercised. At the market price of $90, the put option provides a sale at $100, a gain of $10 per share, or $5,000 for 500 shares. There are two chances in three for the loss of the option cost—$1,000—with a one in three chance for a very large gain—400%. The put option at 66⅔% is double the call option at 33⅓%.

The comparison of the put option results with the stock purchase is:

Future Price	$130	$110	$90	Total
Stock gain (loss)	$ 300	$ 100	$ (100)	$ 300
Option gain (loss)	(1,000)	(1,000)	4,000	2,000
Change	−$ 1,300	−$ 1,100	+$ 4,100	+$1,700

The option choice offers one to three odds for a great gain but with two in three chances for large losses.

Example 4

Invest $1,000 in call options and $1,000 in put options, at the same time (called a straddle).

Future price	$130	$110	$90	Total
Call option gain	$3,000	$ 1,000	No Call	$4,000
Put option gain	No Put	No Put	$5,000	5,000
Combined	3,000	1,000	5,000	9,000
Option cost	2,000	2,000	2,000	6,000
Gain (loss)	$1,000	$(1,000)	$3,000	$3,000
Percent gain (loss)	50%	(50%)	150%	50%

Break-even prices are found at both $120 and $96:

Future Price	$120		$96
Call gain (100 shs. × $20)	$2,000	Put gain (500 shs. × $4)	$2,000
Option cost	2,000	Option cost	2,000
	$ 0		$ 0

At prices between $120 and $96, there is a loss, but there are gains for prices over $120 and below $96. The maximum loss is $2,000, the cost of the options.

Many stock and option combinations are possible and have names such as "spreads," "strangles," "strips," "straps," and "butterflies." Stock and option prices are related through interest (risk free) and risk, related to time.

PUBLISHED OPTION PRICES

The following examples are close approximations of published figures, slightly modified for clarity and simplification.

Example A

Assume stock price, $112.50; six-month call option; exercise price—$100, $110, $120; Rf interest rate, 7.47%; and six months, 3.735% (f 0.964).

				Change
Stock price	$112.50	$112.500	$112.500	SAME
Exercise price	− 100.00	− 110.000	− 120.000	UP
Parity value	+ 12.50	+ 2.500	− 7.500	DOWN
6 months' discount on exercise price	+ 3.60	+ 3.960	+ 4.320	UP
	($100.00 − $96.40)	($110.00 − $106.04)	($120.00 − $115.68)	
Time value	+ 16.10	+ 6.460	− 3.180	DOWN
Risk premium	+ 1.40	+ 3.915	+ 8.305	UP
Actual option price	$ 17.50	$ 10.375	$ 5.125	DOWN

Option Price $17.50

The cost of the right to buy stock at $100.00 (now $112.50) within the next six months contains three parts. Exercised today, the gain is $12.50—parity value. Interest on the $100.00 for six months is $3.60 (by risk-free discounting). The $100.00 does not have to be paid for six months—$100.00/$96.40 = $103.735. Parity value plus interest = $16.10—the time value. The risk premium of $1.40 reflects the chance (a statistical abstraction) that the price can go higher than $112.50, with no limit on the upside potential. The downside risk is limited to the option cost—$17.50.

Assume that the exercise price is $100 and the stock price in six months is:

Price	(up 10%)	(up 6%)	(up 4.44%)	(no change)	(down 12%)
	$123.75	$119.25	$117.50	$112.50	$ 99.00
Exercise at	100.00	100.00	100.00	100.00	100.00
Gain	+ 23.75	+ 19.25	+ 17.50	+ 12.50	no call
Option	− 17.50	− 17.50	− 17.50	− 17.50	− 17.50
Net	+ 6.25	+ 1.75	0	− 5.00	− 17.50
× 2	+$ 12.50	+$ 3.50	$ 0	−$ 10.00	−$ 35.00
=	71.4%	20%	0%	(57.1%)	(200%)

This selected price range illustrates the basis for the risk premium of $1.40.

Option Price $10.375

The option price has decreased $7.125 with the $10 increase in the exercise price:

Parity value down	−$10.00	
Interest up	+ 0.36	−$9.640
Risk premium up		+ 2.515
Net change		−$7.125

Option Price $5.125

This is $5.25 less than the previous option price.

Parity value down	−$10.00	
Interest up	+ 0.36	−$9.64
Risk premium up		+ 4.39
Net change		−$5.25

Increased risk premiums attach to the higher exercise prices, but the total option cost is lower. Thus there is less investment in the option and less total loss possible, offset by less upside potential with a higher exercise price.

This relationship can be illustrated with the stock price of $119.25 in the foregoing schedule. This price shows a 20% profit. The stock required to provide 20% profit for the higher exercise prices can be derived:

Annual profit (%)	20.00	20.0000	20.0000
Option cost ($)	17.50	10.3750	5.1250
= Year gain ($)	3.50	2.0750	1.0250
6 months gain ($)	1.75	1.0375	0.5125
Total gain (add option cost) ($)	19.25	11.4125	5.6375
Exercise price ($)	100.00	110.0000	120.0000
Stock price ($)	119.25	121.4125	125.6375
% increase from $112.50	6.00	7.9200	11.6800

Stock price increase ($)		121.4125	125.6375
		119.2500	121.4125
		2.1625	4.2250
	+	1.813%	+ 3.480%
Option price decrease ($)		17.5000	10.3750
		10.3750	5.1250
	−	7.1250	− 5.2500
	−	40.710%	− 50.600%

When the exercise price is $110 rather than $100, a 20.00% profit can be realized only if the price moves higher by 1.8%, but the option cost has dropped 40.70%. When the exercise price is $120, rather than $110, a 20.00% profit can be realized only if the price moves higher by 3.48%, but the option cost has dropped by 50.60%. The decrease in downside risk is matched by a higher sales price requirement to reach the same 20.00%.

Also, comparing the option cost of $120 with that of $100, we have:

Stock price increase		$125.6375
		119.2500
		6.3875
	+	5.36%
Option price decrease		17.5000
		5.1250
	−	12.3750
	−	70.7%

Example B

This illustration is the same as Example A except that the call has only three days to go, so discounting is omitted:

Stock price	$112.50	$112.50	$112.5000
Exercise price	− 100.00	− 110.00	120.0000
Parity value	+ 12.50	+ 2.50	− 7.5000
Discount	0.00	0.00	0.0000
Time value	+ 12.50	+ 2.50	− 7.5000
Risk premium	+ 0	+ 0.50	+ 7.5625
Actual option price	$ 12.50	$ 3.00	$ 0.0625

The smallest trading fraction is $\frac{1}{16}$ or 0.0625.
Compare this with Example A:

6-month option price	$17.50	$10.375	$5.1250
6-month change	$5.00	$ 7.375	$5.0625
Accounted for by:			
Time	$ 3.60	$ 3.960	$4.3200
Risk	1.40	3.415	0.7425
	$ 5.00	$ 7.375	$5.0625

Example C

This illustration is the same as Example A but with a six-month put option. Exercise prices are $100, $110, and $120 with six months interest, 3.735% (f 0.964). The discount is negative because the option holder has to wait six months to receive the option price.

Stock price	−$112.50	−$112.50	−$112.50
Exercise price	+ 100.00	+ 110.00	+ 120.00
Parity value	− 12.50	− 2.50	+ 7.50
Discount (negative)	− 3.60	− 3.96	− 4.32
Time value	− 16.100	− 6.460	+ 3.18
Risk premium	+ 17.475	+ 10.210	+ 5.32
Actual option price	$ 1.375	$ 3.750	$ 8.50

Assume that the exercise price is $120 and the stock price in six months is:

Price	(down 6⅔%)	(down 2.22%)	(down 0.09%)	(no change)	(up 10%)
	$105.00	$110.00	$111.50	$112.50	$123.75
Exercise at	120.00	120.00	120.00	120.00	120.00
Gain	+ 15.00	+ 10.00	+ 8.50	+ 7.50	No Put
Option Cost	− 8.50	− 8.50	− 8.50	− 8.50	− 8.50
Net	+$ 6.50	+$ 1.50	$ 0.00	−$ 1.00	−$ 8.50
× 2 = year	+$ 13.00	+$ 3.00	$ 0.00	−$ 2.00	−$ 17.00
Annual % on cost	152.90	35.30	0.00	− 23.50	− 200.00

This selected price range illustrates the basics for risk premiums and can be compared with the similar schedule for the six-month call option—Example A.

Example D

This illustration is the same as Example C except that the put expires within a few days, so discounting is omitted:

Stock price	−$112.5000	−$112.5000	−$112.50
Exercise price	+ 100.0000	+ 110.0000	+ 120.00
Parity value	− 12.5000	− 2.5000	+ 7.50
Discount	0.000	0.0000	0.00
Time value	− 12.5000	− 2.5000	+ 7.50
Risk premium	+ 12.5625	+ 3.1875	0.00
Actual option price	$ 0.0625	$ 0.6875	$ 7.50

The smallest trading fraction is $\frac{1}{16}$ or 0.0625.

Compare this with Example C:

6-month option price	$1.3750	$3.7500	$8.50
6-month change	$1.3125	$3.0625	$1.00
Accounted for by:			
Time	−$3.6000	−$3.9600	−$4.32
Risk	+ 4.9125	+ 7.0225	+ 5.32
	$1.3125	$3.0625	$1.00

THE OPTION PRICING FORMULA

The formula for pricing stock options can be stated as:

$$\text{Stock price} + \text{put} = \text{call} + \text{PV exercise price}$$

Or:

$$\text{Stock price} + \text{put} - \text{call} = \text{PV exercise price}$$

Applied to six-month options for Examples A and C we have:

Stock price	$112.500	$112.500	$112.500
add put	+ 1.375	+ 3.750	+ 8.500
	113.875	116.250	121.000
deduct call	− 17.500	− 10.375	− 5.125
= PV exercise price	$ 96.375	$105.875	$115.875

By calculation we have:

$100 × f 0.964	$96.400		
$110 × f 0.964		$106.040	
$120 × f 0.964			$115.680
Difference	+ $ 0.025	+$ 0.165	−$ 0.195

Similar results are obtained for Examples B and D:

Stock price	$112.5000	$112.5000	$112.5000
add put	+ 0.0625	+ 0.6875	+ 7.5000
	112.5625	113.1875	120.0000
deduct call	− 12.5000	− 3.0000	− 0.0625
= PV exercise price	100.0625	110.1875	119.9375
Exercise price (not discounted)	100.000	110.0000	120.0000
Difference	−$ 0.0625	−$ 0.1875	+$ 0.0625

Published reports of option trading generally show the stock price, exercise price, and call and put option prices, by month of maturity. The PV exercise price is not given, nor is the discount rate. For the examples given, the discount rate used was derived to reach the degree of equality shown. The derived interest rate is 7.47% with continuous compounding, or 7.20% annually.

To illustrate price volatility and changing relationships, the option prices for the next day are presented in comparison with those given. The stock price dropped from $112.50 to $111.25, a decrease of $1.25 (1.11%).

Exercise Price	$100		$110		$120	
6 mo. calls—down	16\frac{7}{8}$	(17\frac{1}{2}$)	$10	(10\frac{3}{8}$)	5\frac{1}{8}$	(5\frac{1}{8}$)*
Current calls—down	11$\frac{1}{4}$	(11$\frac{1}{2}$)	2$\frac{1}{4}$	(3.0)	$\frac{1}{16}$	($\frac{1}{16}$)*
6 mo. puts—up	1$\frac{3}{4}$	(1$\frac{3}{8}$)	4$\frac{3}{8}$	(3$\frac{3}{4}$)	9$\frac{3}{8}$	(8$\frac{1}{2}$)
Current puts—up	$\frac{1}{16}$	($\frac{1}{16}$)*	1$\frac{1}{16}$	(1$\frac{1}{16}$)*	8$\frac{3}{4}$	(7$\frac{1}{2}$)

*No change.

The relationship of the change in the stock price to the change in the option price is called the "hedge ratio" (not illustrated).

Option theory is being increasingly applied to securities valuation and the design of security offerings, such as the use of calls and puts in bond issues.

CHAPTER 12

Capital Structure

RAISING THE REQUISITE FUNDS

WHAT IT IS AND ISN'T

Capital structure refers to the composition of the funds needed to operate the company (assets). It includes all borrowing, which comprises all money that must be repaid with interest (including financial leases); preferred stock; common stock; and retained earnings. The total—capital—equals all assets, net of spontaneous (cost-free) credit such as payables and accruals and deferred credits. (*Note:* the term *financial structure* is sometimes used to refer to capital structure plus spontaneous credit, not a useful construct because it combines two incongruous elements.)

Capital structure depends on financial planning to meet the company's goals for growth and profitability, within acceptable risk limits. The valuation of securities is described in separate chapters (9 and 11) from the viewpoint of the investor. The company designs and markets securities to obtain funds much in the manner of product marketing. The objective is to obtain the best mix of funds in terms of cost, control, liquidity, and risk, over time, relative to the planned financing needs. The company is a money buyer, selling securities designed to appeal to money sellers.

Risk refers to both liquidity and maintaining effective management control relative to each security. Closely interrelated to financing cost and risk are the profitability and risk of investments, and both affect liquidity. The challenge is to achieve the best balance among these factors over time to support goals and improve yield on common equity—ROE.

The cost of funds to the company is the obverse of the yield to investors. The expression "cost of capital" is frequently used but lacks clarity in meaning and is better discontinued. It can have several uses, each of which is separately defined:

Cost of Funds—weighted average cost of actual or planned capital structure at either book or market values

Rate of Return—yields to investors for individual securities and portfolios

Discount Rate—the rate used to discount future cash flows to determine NPV for investment decisions, both capital expenditures and net current assets; also called "investment rate," "hurdle rate," and "cut-off rate."

The discount rate to be used, as established in this chapter, is the current (marginal) borrowing rate, less the current (marginal) tax rate. This is a minimum rate relative to leverage and the correct rate to determine the basis for risk evaluation. (Any risk element in the discount rate contaminates the results.) The discount rate provides the basis for growth and profitability, and it is not derived from the cost of funds—a separate concept. There is a disturbing and dangerous persistence of the concept that the discount rate should be "the cost of capital" (variously defined), despite the refutation of this idea years ago.

BORROWING

Effect of Interest Rates

Assume the following:

<table>
<tr><td>Capital structure:</td><td></td><td></td><td></td><td colspan="3" align="center">ROA</td></tr>
<tr><td>Debt</td><td>$ 5,000</td><td></td><td></td><td colspan="2">EBIT</td><td>$ 1,500</td></tr>
<tr><td>Equity</td><td>5,000</td><td></td><td></td><td colspan="2">Tax—40%</td><td>− 600</td></tr>
<tr><td>Capital</td><td>$10,000</td><td></td><td></td><td colspan="2">Net</td><td>$ 900</td></tr>
<tr><td>D/E ratio</td><td>100%</td><td></td><td></td><td colspan="2">Net Assets</td><td>$10,000 = 9%</td></tr>
</table>

Interest rates:	5%	10%	15%	20%	25%	30%
EBIT	$ 1,500	$1,500	$1,500	$1,500	$1,500	$1,500
Interest	250	500	750	1,000	1,250	1,500
EBT	1,250	1,000	750	500	250	0
Tax	500	400	300	200	100	0
EAT	$ 750	$ 600	$ 450	$ 300	$ 150	$ 0
ROE	15%	12%	9%	6%	3%	0%
(EAT/Equity)						
ROA (above)	9%	9%	9%	9%	9%	9%
Interest Coverage	6	3	2	1.5	1.2	1.0
(EBIT/Interest)						

Interest coverage is EBIT divided by Interest. ROE is EAT divided by Equity. ROA is EBIT less tax divided by Net Assets, which equal Capital.

Borrowing under 15% provides positive leverage—ROE greater than ROA. Over 15% interest, the equity return is less, or negative leverage. At 30% interest takes all earnings.

The table above reflects a D/E ratio of 100% and EBIT of $1,500. Changes in these factors are considered separately for emphasis.

Note: These computations are based on management needs. Published ROA and ROE are often computed differently and without disclosure of the bases used. ROI (Return on Investment) is often used ambiguously.

Effect of EBIT

Assume the following:

Capital structure:			
Debt	$ 5,000	Interest rate	15% ($750)
Equity	5,000	Tax rate	40%
Capital	$10,000		
D/E ratio	100%		

EBIT	$ 750	$1,000	$1,250	$1,500	$1,750	$2,000
Interest	750	750	750	750	750	750
EBT	0	250	500	750	1,000	1,250
Tax	0	100	200	300	400	500
EAT	0	150	300	450	600	750
ROE	0	3%	6%	9%	12%	15%
ROA: EBIT	$750	$1,000	$1,250	$1,500	$1,750	$2,000
Tax	− 300	− 400	− 500	− 600	− 700	− 800
Net	$450	$600	$750	$900	$1,050	$1,200
	= 4.5%	6%	7.5%	9%	10.5%	12%
Interest coverage	1.0	$1\frac{1}{3}$	$1\frac{2}{3}$	2	$2\frac{1}{3}$	$2\frac{2}{3}$

This example illustrates the need for good estimates of EBIT to support interest coverage and D/E ratios. Below EBIT $1,500, leverage is negative.

EBIT can be squeezed by competitive price pressures and inflationary cost trends. Asset control is also needed to preserve ROA.

Effect of D/E Ratio

Assume the following:

			ROA	
EBIT	$2,000		EBIT	$2,000
Interest rate	10%		Tax—40%	800
			Net	$1,200
			Net Assets	$10,000 = 12%

Debt	$ 0	$ 2,000	$ 3,333	$ 4,286	$ 5,000	$ 5,556
Equity	$10,000	8,000	6,667	5,714	5,000	4,444
Capital	10,000	10,000	10,000	10,000	10,000	10,000
D/E ratio	0%	25%	50%	75%	100%	125%
EBIT	$ 2,000	$ 2,000	$ 2,000	$ 2,000	$ 2,000	$ 2,000
Interest	0	200	333	429	500	557
EBT	2,000	1,800	1,667	1,571	1,500	1,443
Tax	800	720	667	628	600	577
EAT	$ 1,200	$ 1,080	$ 1,000	$ 943	$ 900	$ 866
ROE	12%	13.5%	15%	16.5%	18%	19.5%
ROA	12%	12.0%	12%	12.0%	12%	12.0%
Interest coverage	0	10	6	$4\frac{2}{3}$	4	3.6

With a given EBIT, the higher the D/E ratio, the higher the interest cost (10%) and the lower the interest coverage. ROE climbs with ROA unchanged. The limit on ROE is the threat of higher D/E ratios and interest expense on liquidity.

With declining EBIT and ROA, there is pressure to increase debt to maintain

ROE. Assuming that the D/E ratio of 50% above is acceptable, a declining EBIT
has this effect:

	Last Year (as above)	A This Year	Projections—Next Year		
			B Same D/E 10% Int.	C Higher D/E 10% Int.	D Higher D/E 12% Int.
Debt	$ 3,333	$ 3.333	$ 3,333	$ 5,000	$ 6,000
Equity	6,667	6,667	6,667	5,000	4,000
Capital	$10,000	$10,000	$10,000	$10,000	$10,000
EBIT	$ 2,000	$ 1,800	$ 1,600	$ 1,600	$ 1,600
Interest	333	333	333	500	720
EBT	1,667	1,467	1,267	1,100	880
Tax	667	587	507	440	352
EAT	$ 1,000	$ 880	$ 760	$ 660	$ 528
ROE	15%	13.2%	11.4%	13.2%	13.2%
ROA	12%	10.8%	9.6%	9.6%	9.6%
Interest coverage	6	5.4	4.8	3.2	2.22
D/E ratio	50%	50%	50%	100%	150%

A—The 10% drop experienced in EBIT has lowered ROA and ROE and reduced interest
coverage.

B—The projection of another $200 drop in EBIT for next year results in unacceptable
deterioration of the ratios.

C—An increase in the D/E ratio from 50.0% to 100.0% restores ROE to 13.2% but
leaves ROA at 9.6%. Interest coverage drops to 3.2. ROE is preserved at high
liquidity risk.

D—If the interest rate becomes 12.0%, the D/E ratio must be increased to 150.0% to
maintain ROE at 13.2%, and interest coverage falls to a low 2.22.

These choices place heavy pressure on increasing EBIT rather than facing low
profits or high liquidity risk. With limits on pricing and volume, cost reduction is
mandated, often with jeopardy to long-term profitability.

Financial planning for capital structure requires a range of probable EBIT, as
well as interest and tax rates. Trade-offs between profitability and liquidity are
policy questions governed by management risk attitudes.

Examples

Assume EBIT is projected at $2,000, $2,500, and $3,000, with equal proba-
bilities. The interest rate is 15% and taxes are 40%. The question is whether or
not to increase debt from $2,000 to $4,000, with the D/E ratio going from 25%
to 66⅔%.

	Debt $2,000	Equity $8,000	Total $10,000
Capital: D/E 25%			
EBIT	$2,000	$2,500	$3,000
Interest (15%)	300	300	300
EBT	1,700	2,200	2,700
Tax (40%)	680	880	1,080
EAT	$1,020	$1,320	$1,620
ROE	$12\frac{3}{4}$%	16.5%	$20\frac{1}{4}$
ROA	12%	15%	18%
Interest coverage	$6\frac{2}{3}$	$8\frac{1}{3}$	10

	Debt $4,000	Equity $6,000	Total $10,000
Capital: D/E 66⅔%			
EBIT	$2,000	$2,500	$3,000
Interest (15%)	600	600	600
EBT	1,400	1,900	2,400
Tax (40%)	560	760	960
EAT	$ 840	$1,140	$1,440
ROE	14%	19%	24%
ROA	12%	15%	18%
Interest coverage	$3\frac{1}{3}$	$4\frac{1}{6}$	5

The alternative leaves ROA unchanged (same net assets), but ROE increases and at a faster rate for higher EBIT because of leverage. Interest coverage is cut in half, and D/E goes from 25% to 66⅔%. (When measured on total capital, the ratios are 20% and 40%, a common basis for published figures because it moderates the result.) Again, the choice relates to the degree of confidence in EBIT and risk attitudes.

Management must also deal with lender policies. Banks and other lenders generally charge the prevailing interest rate and establish a current rate for each borrower. With questionable liquidity, the lender looks primarily to protection in loan collection, not a higher rate. Borrower rates are often set at the prime rate for the largest companies, with a premium over prime for others. Protection requirements are tightened for greater collection risk. The restrictions placed on management are the major deterrent to higher borrowing rather than the interest terms only.

Loan terms must be carefully negotiated to preclude unacceptable limits on management freedom of action to protect the company's profits and liquidity with changing circumstances.

Terms may include:

Limitations on further debt, dividends, capital expenditures, mergers, compensation

Pledging of assets, limits on asset sales, and capital leases

Retention of key personnel, key man insurance, limits on bonuses and fringe benefits (no "golden parachutes")

Accelerated debt repayment for any infringement of terms

Maintenance of working capital levels

Detailed reporting requirements; audits by banks and independent accountants

Managers generally keep within prudent liquidity limits and avoid onerous loan terms.

THE COST OF FUNDS

The weighted average cost of funds depends on the relative amount of each type in the capital structure and its cost. The calculation can be made using book amounts or market values, either current or projected. The concern of management is primarily in the future, so the most relevant basis is the projection of funds and costs at estimated market, related to financial planning.

The presentation includes debt, preferred stock, and common stock plus RE (retained earnings)—the major components of capital structure. Excluded are the wide range of variations such as convertibles, leases, warrants, stock rights, and stock options issued by the company.

Example 1

Debt, $8,000 at 16%; net, 8% (tax, 50%)   *Rm 16% Rf 8%*
Common equity (stock plus RE), $12,000   Growth, 8%
Dividend, $5; market price, $50   Beta 1.25

$Ke:$ Dividend model: $\dfrac{D_1}{P_0} \ \dfrac{\$5}{\$50} = 10\% + 8\% \ G = 18\% \ Ke$

CAPM: $Rm \ 16 - Rf \ 8 = 8 \times 1.25 \ \beta = 10 + 8 \ Rf = 18\% \ Ke$

The weighted average cost of funds is:

Debt	$ 8,000	40% at 8%	3.2%
Equity	12,000	60% at 18%	10.8
Capital	$20,000		14.0

D/E ratio 67% (debt to capital 40%)

An alternative is:

Issue, $4,000 preferred at 15% (Pfd.).
Reduce debt to $4,000.

The weighted average cost of funds is:

Debt	$ 4,000	20% at 8%	1.6%
Pfd	4,000	20% at 15%	3.0
Equity	12,000	60% at 18%	10.8
	$20,000		15.4%

D/E ratio 33% omitting preferred $(\frac{4}{12})$
D/E ratio 25% with preferred part of equity $(\frac{4}{16})$
D/E ratio 67% with preferred part of debt $(\frac{8}{12})$

The cost of funds increases from $14.0 to $15.4—a 10% increase. Preferred issues are relatively rare because the dividends are not tax deductible. Preferreds are used most frequently by utilities when necessary to preserve a liquidity position and not impair credit ratings, which could increase borrowing costs more than the extra cost of the preferred issue. Preferreds may also be used in mergers to resolve equity and dividend claims. (Companies owning stock can exclude 85% of dividend income from taxable income for qualifying sources.)

Another alternative is to issue common in lieu of preferred. The flotation costs for a new issue of common are stated below. The rates used for debt and preferred in the prior examples are net of flotation costs, with details omitted. The total equity of $12,000 is for stock already outstanding.

Common is to be sold to realize $4,000. The offering price will be assumed to be $48, or $2 less than the present market price of $50, a 4% discount. Total flotation expenses per share are $6.33 (legal and accounting fees, filing charges, printing costs). The net price is $41.67 ($48.00 − $6.33) and the issuance expense rate is 13.2% ($6.33/$48), which is in line for smaller issues.

$$\text{Dividend model:} \quad \frac{D_1}{P_1} \frac{\$5}{\text{new } \$41.67} = 12\% + 8\% \ G = 20\% \ Ke$$

$$\text{CAPM: } Rm \ 16 - Rf \ 8 = 8 \times 1.50 \ \beta = 12 + 8 \ Rf = 20\% \ Ke$$

Ke increases from 18% to 20% and beta from 1.25 to 1.50.

The weighted average cost of funds is:

Debt	$ 4,000	20% at 8%	1.6%
New Common	4,000	20% at 20%	4.0
Equity	12,000	60% at 18%	10.8
	$20,000		16.4

The average has increased to 16.4% from 15.4% with preferred, and 14.0% with debt only.

Note: A practice that is not correct is to use a lower common equity rate (18%) because dividends require stockholders to pay taxes and incur reinvestment expenses. The investors have individually and collectively allowed for these factors in the market price. The assumption could allow more investments and profits, which in time become dividends, or gains subject to capital gain tax. This approach is hypothetical and invalid.

These three alternatives for capital structure are based on highly variable factors that cannot be reliably forecast—market rates for interest, security prices, flotation costs, taxes. Many companies limit growth to retained earnings and borrowing. With a D/E 50%, for example, every $100 increase in RE supports another $50 in debt. Stock issues are particularly expensive, with flotation costs in a range two to three times that of borrowing. A new stock issue can be evaluated only in the light of current circumstances and the outlook based on financial planning, analyzed later in this chapter.

Example 2

The effect of liquidity on the cost of funds is illustrated with six D/E ratios.

Constants		Variables
Capital	$10,000	D/E ratio
EBIT	3,000	Interest rate—Ke
Tax rate	50%	Interest coverage
ROA	15%	ROE

1. D/E 0

D	$	0	0%	18/9%	0%	EBIT	$3,000
E		10,000	100%	21%	21%	Interest	0
		$10,000			21%	EBT	$3,000
						EAT	$1,500
						ROE	15%
						ROA	15%

Loans are available at 18%. Ke is high at 21% because of the failure to use debt to increase ROE by leverage. This management choice has an opportunity cost in lower stock prices.

2. D/E 25%

D	$ 2,000	20%	18/9%	1.8%	EBIT	$3,000
E	8,000	80%	20%	16.0%	Interest	360
	$10,000			17.8%	EBT	$2,640
Interest coverage $8\frac{1}{3}$					EAT	$1,320
					ROE	16.5%
					ROA	15.0%

Ke drops from 21.0% to 20.0% (stock price rise) with the use of some debt, and ROE jumps to 16.5%. The cost of funds drops to 17.8% from 21.0%.

3. D/E 50%

D	$ 3,333	33⅓%	18/9%	3.0%	EBIT	$3,000
E	6,667	66⅔%	18%	12.0%	Interest	600
	$10,000			15.0%	EBT	$2,400
Interest coverage 5					EAT	$1,200
					ROE	18%
					ROA	15%

Ke drops from 20% to 18% with the increased leverage within acceptable risk limits for liquidity. ROE jumps to 18% and the cost of funds drops to 15%.
4. D/E 67%

D	$ 4,000	40%	18/9%	3.6%	EBIT	$3,000
E	6,000	60%	18%	10.8%	Interest	720
	$10,000			14.4%	EBT	$2,280
Interest coverage 4⅙					EAT	$1,140
					ROE	19%
					ROA	15%

Ke holds at 18.0% and interest remains at 18.0%. The higher ROE, at 19.0%, does not lower Ke because of liquidity risk. The cost of funds is at a new low— 14.4%.
5. D/E 100%

D	$ 5,000	50%	20%/10%	5.0%	EBIT	$3,000
E	5,000	50%	20%	10.0%	Interest	1,000
	$10,000			15.0%	EBT	$2,000
Interest coverage 3					EAT	$1,000
					ROE	20%
					ROA	15%

The interest rate—20.0%—is now higher because of the high D/E ratio at 100.0%, and interest coverage drops to a low 3. Ke rises to 20.0% while ROE increases again—to 20.0%. The cost of funds reverses direction from 14.4% to 15.0%—the same as for D/E 50.0%. These conjectural numbers illustrate the effect of high liquidity risk, which more than offsets the higher ROE. Prudent managers would avoid this situation if at all possible. If there are net losses, equity is reduced and D/E rises (unless debt is reduced). Lower EBIT decreases interest coverage. Leverage may become negative, dropping ROE below ROA. These possible effects cause managers to be cautious in using debt to improve ROE.
6. D/E 150%

D	$ 6,000	60%	22/11%	6.6%	EBIT	$3,000
E	4,000	40%	28%	11.2%	Interest	1,320
	$10,000			17.8%	EBT	$1,680

Interest coverage 2.27   EAT $ 840
                                                ROE   21%
                                                ROA   15%

This position of very high liquidity risk illustrates possible effects on interest and stock price, with *Ke* rising sharply to 28.0%. The cost of funds at 17.8% equals that at D/E 25.0%.

To recap, we have:

	Liquidity		Profitability		Cost of Funds		
	D/E	Int. Cov.	ROE	ROA	Ke	Net Int.	Av.
1.	0	0.00	15.0%	15%	21%	—	21.0%
2.	25	$8\frac{1}{3}$	16.5	15	20	9%	17.8
3.	50	5.00	18.0	15	18	9	15.0
4.	67	$4\frac{1}{6}$	19.0	15	18	9	14.4
5.	100	3.00	20.0	15	20	10	15.0
6.	150	2.27	21.0	15	28	11	17.8

The increasing leverage produces constantly increasing ROE, even with higher interest. The average cost of funds is in a narrow range from D/E 50% to 100%. However, at D/E 100%, both interest and *Ke* are higher. The average cost of funds rises sharply for D/E under 50% and over 100%, considered to be overly conservative or overly risky liquidity positions. The situations depicted vary widely among industries and among companies.

Note: It is important to distinguish between D/E as used here and the debt to capital ratio often publicized (which is misleading):

D	E	Capital	D/E	Debt to Capital
$ 20	+ $80	= $100	25%	20%
$33\frac{1}{3}$	+ $66\frac{2}{3}$	= 100	50	$33\frac{1}{3}$
40	+ 60	= 100	67	40
50	+ 50	= 100	100	50
60	+ 40	= 100	150	60
$66\frac{1}{3}$	+ $33\frac{1}{3}$	= 100	200	67
80	+ 20	= 100	400	80
90	+ 10	= 100	900	90
100	+ 0	= 100	∞	100

EVALUATION

These examples demonstrate the relatively small effect of borrowing on the average cost of funds. Prudent managers prefer to protect liquidity at the sacrifice of some leverage as a hedge against uncertainty. The costs of illiquidity can be high. Market evaluations of the risk-return trade-off are difficult to predict or measure. At some point, liquidity risk outweighs ROE gain, and market prices are depressed (higher Ke).

The company's cost of funds reflects the investors' yields, which arise from market conditions and evaluation of the company's prospects. As a practical matter, funds are raised from outside sources in terms of current needs and market conditions, within the capital structure framework.

Outside financing usually provides large (lumpy) amounts, causing the composition of debt and equity to vary considerably. Also, net income and dividends affect equity. However, such swings have a relatively small effect on the average cost of funds.

Example

D/E 33⅓%   **Low**

D	$ 3,000	25%	20/10%	2.5%	EBIT	$3,600
E	9,000	75%	16%	12.0%	Interest	600
	$12,000			14.5%	EBT	$3,000
Interest coverage 6					EAT	$1,500
					ROE	16⅔%
					ROA	15%

D/E 60%   **Target**

D	$ 4,500	37.5%	20/10%	3.75%	EBIT	$3,600
E	7,500	62.5%	16%	10.00%	Interest	900
	$12,000			13.75%	EBT	$2,700
Interest coverage 4					EAT	$1,350
					ROE	18%
					ROA	15%

D/E 100%   **High**

D	$ 6,000	50%	20/10%	5.0%	EBIT	$3,600
E	6,000	50%	16%	8.0%	Interest	1,200
	$12,000			13.0%	EBT	$2,400
Interest coverage 3					EAT	$1,200
					ROE	20%
					ROA	15%

These relatively wide swings can occur in practice. The target cost of funds of 13.75% changes only ± 0.75% despite the large changes in D/E ratios and interest coverage. ROA remains at 15.00% but ROE ranges from $16\frac{2}{3}$% to 20%, with the target rate at 18%.

The high cost of raising money is moderated by larger issues, and bonds are cheaper than stock. The following table is illustrative of the relationships.

Total Issue in Millions of $	Approximate Issue Costs (%)	
	Bonds	Common Stock
to 10	4.0%+ to 5.0%+	12%+ to 18%+
10–20	3.0%+	9%+
20–50	2.0%+	6%+
50–100	1.4%+	4%+
over 100	1.0%+	3%+

Bonds are thus considerably cheaper to issue than stock. The differential costs for larger amounts are small. Also, stock issues are offered at a price some 2% to 10% under current market prices to insure sale. Funds generated internally by operations have no issue costs and provide the basis for dividends and most of investment funds. A broad estimate could be 90% internal funds and 10% external, mostly bonds, but there are large annual variations and by industry.

Companies work within plans of capital structure but must adapt to constantly changing circumstances—in the company, in the industry, and in the world. Investments, dividends, and capital issues must be decided in the light of existing circumstances and the outlook for the future at the time. The calculation of a weighted average cost of capital—actual or prospective—is not relevant to the decision process; it has no practical usefulness.

Use of the cost of funds—often labeled "cost of capital"—is not correct for discounting cash flows to determine the profitability of investments. It necessarily contains an element of risk, contained in Ke, and such a rate contaminates the discounted amounts and precludes rational risk evaluation. The "cost of capital" rate is not used in practice, and it has been discredited by financial theory. Ke is a result of the investing and financing process, as well as market forces, and cannot logically be used to determine them, as will be demonstrated later in this chapter.

FINANCING—BONDS OR STOCKS?

A company plans to raise $4,000: Issue bonds at 18%, or Sell 100 shares at $40, net. EBIT increases $1,200—$4,800 to $6,000.

	Present (Book Value)		Proposed Bonds			Stock
Bonds	(12%)	$ 2,000	(12%)	$ 2,000	(12%)	$ 2,000
Add		—	(18%)	4,000		—
		2,000		6,000		2,000
Equity	(1,000 shs.)	18,000	(1,000 shs.)	18,000	(1,000 shs.)	18,000
					(100 shs.)	4,000
					(1,100 shs.)	22,000
Capital		$20,000		$24,000		$24,000
EBIT		$ 4,800		$ 6,000		$ 6,000
Interest		240		240		240
				720		
				960		
EBT		$ 4,560		$ 5,040		$ 5,760
EAT (Tax 50%)		$ 2,280		$ 2,520		$ 2,880
ROE (EAT/ Equity)		12.67%		14.0%		13.09%
ROA (EBIT net/capital)		12.00%		12.5%		12.50%
EPS (1,000 shs.)		$ 2.28	(1,000 shs.)	$ 2.52	(1,100 shs.)	$2.6182
D/E ratio		11.10%		33.3%		9.10%
Interest coverage (EBIT/ Interest)		20		$6\tfrac{1}{4}$		25

The EBIT increase of $1,200 is 30.00% of the $4,000 raised by bonds at 18.00%. This favorable leverage raises ROE to 14.00%, from 12.67%, and ROA to 12.50% from 12.00%. For the stock issue, the ROE increases to only 13.09% compared with the present ROE of 12.67%. EPS increases more for the stock issue ($2.6182) than for bonds ($2.52). Thus there is higher EPS and lower ROE with stock, a not uncommon relationship. Thus EPS can be deceptive. Only 100 shares are needed to raise $4,000, an average of $40 a share, while the book rate is $18 ($18,000 divided by 1,000 shares). If the $4,000 required 150 shares (not 100) the EPS would be $2.5043 ($2,880 divided by 1,150 shares) instead of $2.6182 as shown, slightly under the EPS for bonds of $2.52.

The increase in EPS is attractive, but only ROE and ROA measure profits correctly. The bond issue raises D/E and lowers interest coverage significantly but within an acceptable range. The stock issue improves liquidity, as well as EPS, but at the expense of lower ROE.

However, the critical risk factor is the variability of EBIT—operating risk—which in turn affects the degree of acceptable financial risk. Assume that EBIT of $6,000, $7,200, and $8,400 are believed to be equally probable.

	Proposed		Proposed	
	Bonds	**Stock**	**Bonds**	**Stock**
EBIT	$7,200	$ 7,200	$8,400	$ 8,400
Interest	960	240	960	240
EBT	$6,240	$ 6,960	$7,440	$ 8,160
EAT (tax 50%)	$3,120	$ 3,480	$3,720	$ 4,080
ROE	17.33%	15.82%	20.67%	18.55%
ROA	15.00%	15.00%	17.50%	17.50%
EPS	$ 3.12	$3.1636	$ 3.72	$3.7091
D/E ratio	33.30%	9.10%	33.3%	9.10%
Interest coverage	7.5	30.0	$8\frac{3}{4}$	35.0

At EBIT $7,200 (compared with EBIT $6,000) ROA is 15.00%, up from 12.50%. The leverage on ROE for bonds is greater than that for stock—17.33% and 15.82%. EPS for stock at $3.1636 exceeds that for bonds by a smaller margin. D/E ratio is unchanged and interest coverage improves. With the liquidity acceptable for EBIT $7,200, the bonds are favored for higher ROE, despite lower EPS of $0.0436 ($3.1636 − $3.1200).

At EBIT $8,400, ROA is 17.50% and the bonds show a leverage advantage for ROE at 20.67% compared with stock at 18.55%. Also, EPS for bonds is now higher ($3.7200) than that for stock ($3.7091). Thus bonds favor both ROE and EPS. For EBIT over $8,400, this advantage would widen. D/E remains the same, and interest coverage is higher. At this level of EBIT, bonds are clearly more advantageous, given the acceptability of the liquidity risk. The stock choice involves an opportunity cost in both ROE and EPS.

To recap, we have:

	Books	**Bonds**	**Stock**	**Bonds**	**Stock**	**Bonds**	**Stock**
EBIT	$4,800	$6,000	$ 6,000	$7,200	$ 7,200	$8,400	$ 8,400
ROE (%)	12.67	14.00	13.09	17.33	15.82	20.67	18.55
ROA (%)	12.00	12.50	12.50	15.00	15.00	17.50	17.50
EPS	$ 2.28	$ 2.52	$2.6182	$ 3.12	$3.1636	$ 3.72	$3.7091
D/E (%)	11.10	33.30	9.10	33.30	9.10	33.30	9.10
Interest coverage	20	$6\frac{1}{4}$	25	7.5	30	$8\frac{3}{4}$	35

The choice between bonds or stock depends on evaluation of the range of EBIT and trade-offs between liquidity and profit, with separate consideration of ROE and EPS.

Use of break-even analysis may be useful: EBIT = X; tax rate, 50%.

For EPS (EAT/no. of shares) we have:

	Bonds		Stock
1	$\dfrac{0.5\ (X - \$960)}{1{,}000\ \text{shs.}}$	$=$	$\dfrac{0.5\ (X - \$240)}{1.100\ \text{shs.}}$
2	$\dfrac{0.5X - \$480}{1{,}000\ \text{shs.}}$	$=$	$\dfrac{0.5X - \$120}{1{,}100\ \text{shs.}}$
3	$550X - \$528{,}000$	$= 500X - \$120{,}000$	
4	$50X$	$= \$408{,}000$	
5	X	$= \$8{,}160 = \text{EBIT}$	

Proof:

	Bonds		Stock
EBIT	$8,160		$8,160
Interest	960		240
EBT	$7,200		$7,920
EAT	$3,600		$3,960
EPS			
1,000 shs.	$ 3.60		
1,100 shs.			$ 3.60
ROE	$\dfrac{\$\,3{,}600}{\$18{,}000}$	20%	$\dfrac{\$\,3{,}960}{\$22{,}000}$ 18%
ROA	$\dfrac{\$\,4{,}080}{\$24{,}000}$	17%	17%

For ROA ($0.5X$/capital), we have the following; ROA is not affected by interest or the number of shares and so is the same whether bonds or stock are issued:

EBIT	$ 4,800	$ 6,000	$ 7,200	$ 8,400
EBT	$ 4,800	$ 6,000	$ 7,200	$ 8,400
EAT	$ 2,400	$ 3,000	$ 3,600	$ 4,200
Capital	$20,000	$24,000	$24,000	$24,000
ROA	12%	12.5%	15%	17.5%

For ROE (EAT/Equity), we have:

	Bonds		Stock
1	$\dfrac{0.5\ (X - \$960)}{\$18{,}000}$	$=$	$\dfrac{0.5\ (X - \$240)}{\$22{,}000}$
2	$\dfrac{0.5X - \$480}{\$18{,}000}$	$=$	$\dfrac{0.5X - \$120}{\$22{,}000}$
3	$\$11{,}000X - \$9{,}000X$	$= \$2{,}000X$ and	
4	$\$10{,}560{,}000 - \$2{,}160{,}000$	$= \$8{,}400{,}000$	
5	$\$8{,}400{,}000/\$2{,}000X$	$- \$4{,}200\ \text{EBIT}$	

Proof:

		Bonds		Stock
EBIT		$4,200		$4,200
Interest		960		240
EBT		$3,240		$3,960
EAT		$1,620		$1,980
ROE	$(\frac{\$\ 1,620}{\$18,000})$	9%	$(\frac{\$\ 1,980}{\$22,000})$	9%
EPS	(1,000 shs.)	$ 1.62	(1,100 shs.)	$ 1.80
ROA	$(\frac{\$\ 2,100}{\$24,000})$	8.75%		8.75%

For zero leverage (Equal ROA and ROE), we have:

	Book		Bonds		Stock	
EBIT	$2,400		$3,840		$2,880	
Interest	240		$ 960		240	
EBT	$2,160		$2,880		$2,640	
EAT	$1,080		$1,440		$1,320	
ROE	$(\frac{\$\ 1,080}{\$18,000})$	6%	$(\frac{\$\ 1,440}{\$18,000})$	8%	$(\frac{\$\ 1,320}{\$22,000})$	6%
ROA	$(\frac{\$\ 1,200}{\$20,000})$	6%	$(\frac{\$\ 1,920}{\$24,000})$	8%	$(\frac{\$\ 1,440}{\$24,000})$	6%
EPS	(1,000 shs.)	$ 1.08	(1,000 shs.)	$ 1.44	(1,100 shs.)	$ 1.20

EBIT below the break-even amounts reduces ROE below ROA (negative leverage). These break-even points can be useful in risk evaluation. The Stock EBIT exceeds the Book EBIT by ($2,880 − $2,400) $480, or 12% of the $4,000 added to equity. The Bonds EBIT exceeds the Stock EBIT by ($3,840 − $2,880) $960, or 12% of $8,000 (which is $4,000 switched from equity to debt).

The following is another look at EPS:

Stock (as Above)	No. of Shs.	Equity		Average
Books	1,000.00	$18,000	$18.00	
Issues	100.00	4,000	40.00	OVER BOOK
	1,100.00	$22,000	$20.00	
Assume—A:				
Books	1,000.00	$18,000	$18.00	
Issue	222.22	4,000	18.00	SAME AS BOOK
	1,222.22	$22,000	$18.00	

Assume—B:

Books	1,000.00	$18,000	$18.00
Issue	500.00	4,000	8.00 UNDER BOOK
	1,500.00	$22,000	$14.67

A recap follows for EPS including the number of shares in A and B:

	Books	Bonds	Stock	Bonds	Stock	Bonds	Stock
EBIT	$4,800	$6,000	$6,000	$7,200	$7,200	$8,400	$8,400
EAT	$2,280	$2,520	$2,880	$3,120	$3,480	$3,720	$4,080
ROE (%)	12.67	14.00	13.09	17.33	15.82	20.67	18.55
EPS (rounded)							
Books	$ 2.28	$ 2.52	$ 2.62	$ 3.12	$ 3.16	$ 3.72	$ 3.71
A	$ 2.28	$ 2.52	$ 2.36	$ 3.12	$ 2.85	$ 3.72	$ 3.34
B	$ 2.28	$ 2.52	$ 1.92	$ 3.12	$ 2.32	$ 3.72	$ 2.72

Stock - EAT:	$2,880	$3,480	$4,080
Number of shares:			
as above 1,100.00		1,100.00	1,100.00
A 1,222.22		1,222.22	1,222.22
B 1,500.00		1,500.00	1,500.00

EPS for stock less EPS for bonds is as follows:

EBIT	$6,000	$7,200	$8,400
Books	+$ 0.10	+$ 0.04	−$ 0.01
A	− 0.16	− 0.27	− 0.38
B	− 0.60	− 0.80	− 1.00

Stock EPS is thus lower than bond EPS for both A and B in all cases.

This exercise demonstrates that the number of shares issued affects EPS but nothing else. ROE (and ROA) are not affected. For Assume—A, the relationships of the ROEs and EPS are the same. (This is not apt to happen in practice, and examples based on this premise are suspect.) For Assume—B, a low issue price is used for emphasis.

The disparity in EPS between bonds and stock increases rapidly. Managers may be unduly swayed by the effect of financing proposals on EPS. Some may be reluctant to sell stock in a weak market because of the dilutive effect of more shares on EPS, even though the plan is advantageous in all other respects.

THE INVESTMENT DISCOUNT RATE

The discount rate used for cash flows to determine NPV for investment proposals should be the current borrowing rate less taxes. It is a marginal (or cut-off) rate to qualify proposals for minimum profitability and is required for risk appraisal as demonstrated in Chapter 6.

Approved proposals will have yields ranging from the minimum upward. The weighted average for all proposals can be approximated statistically: low yield opportunities are relatively abundant and those with high yields are relatively scarce. This condition reflects competition and the law of diminishing returns.

If all approved proposals are divided into four groups of equal yield ranges, the dollar content will be, from high to low, about 10%, 20%, 30%, and 40% (rather than the arithmetic average of 25%). For illustration, we have:

Yield Range	Dollar Content	Average Yield in Range
20%+	10%	22%
15–20	20	17
10–15	30	12
5–10	40	7
	100%	

The average yield in each range reflects the same skew as that for the dollar percents.

Substituting dollars, we have:

Yield Range	Proposals	Average Yield	Yield
20%+	$ 10,000	22%	$ 2,200
15–20	20,000	17	3,400
10–15	30,000	12	3,600
5–10	40,000	7	2,800
	$100,000		$12,000

The $12,000 total yield is 12% of the $100,000 total for all proposals. The marginal cut-off rate (discount rate) of 5% thus produces a 12% average return. This is ROA. With leverage, ROE could be 15%, for example (although leverage varies widely among companies and over time).

Assume the following:

Capital:	Debt—10%	$ 6,000		
	Equity	14,000		
		$20,000		
EBIT		$ 4,800	ROE	$\frac{\$ 2,100}{\$14,000} = 15\%$
Interest		600		
EBT		$ 4,200	ROA	$\frac{\$ 2,400}{\$20,000} = 12\%$
EAT		$ 2,100		
Interest Coverage		8		
D/E (%)		43		

The yield schedule is now expanded to include cumulative results:

Yield Range	Proposals	Yield %	Yield $	Cumulative Proposals	Cumulative Yield	Cumulative Percent
20%+	$ 10,000	22	2,200	$ 10,000	$ 2,200	22
15–20	20,000	17	3,400	30,000	5,600	$18\frac{2}{3}$
10–15	30,000	12	3,600	60,000	9,200	$15\frac{1}{3}$
5–10	40,000	7	2,800	100,000	12,000	12
	$100,000		12,000			

If the discount rate is:

10%—average yield $15\frac{1}{3}$%—proposals drop $40,000 to $60,000
15%—average yield $18\frac{2}{3}$%—proposals drop $30,000 to $30,000
20%—average yield 22% —proposals drop $20,000 to $10,000
Total reduction in proposals $90,000

The reductions in investments increase yield averages but necessarily reduce growth in profits and revenue. Growth rates are assumed for illustration:

Yield Range	Cum. (%)	Cum. Proposals	Assumed Growth Rate	
20%+	22	$ 10,000	0%	Minimum—replacement
15–20	$18\frac{2}{3}$	30,000	5	Highly selective
10–15	$15\frac{1}{3}$	60,000	12	Substantial
5–10	12	100,000	21	Stretch goal

The schedule could be related to industry performance. If this is running about 15%, the third level at 12% is sub par, and the top rate at 21% is ambitious. Growth-oriented companies will plan operations and financing to accomplish their goals, within policy limits for risk and liquidity.

If the current borrowing rate is 10% net (20% less tax), the company is restricted to the $60,000 maximum, with 12% growth. High interest rates and rising uncertainty seriously restrict investment levels.

Managers make decisions about investing and financing in line with their goals and policies, but attention should also be given to possible market reactions. If the dividend model is:

$$D_1\$2/P_0\$40 = 5\% + G\ 10\% = 15\%\ Ke$$

and the CAPM is:

$$Rm\ 14\% - Rf\ 9\% = 5 \times \beta\ 1.2 = 6 + Rf\ 9\% = 15\%\ Ke$$

The cost of funds is

Debt	$ 6,000	30%	10/5%	=	1.5%
Equity	14,000	70%	15%	=	10.5%
	$20,000				12.0%

The cumulative investment yield of 12% (ROA), based on the 5% discount rate, agrees with the cost of funds. However, to use the cost of funds ("cost of capital") for discounting confuses a weighted average result with the marginal rate needed for analysis. Also, Ke includes a risk factor, which attaches to all equities, that obscures risk analysis, as explored in Chapter 6.

The use of 12% as a discount rate would decrease total investments (based on 5%) from $100,000 to about $50,000, with a growth rate of perhaps 10%, the rate used to arrive at 15% Ke. Presumably, higher growth rates, within acceptable risk and liquidity limits, encourage optimistic market response and boost stock prices. Use of discount rates over 15% would decrease investment and growth and depress stock prices.

Although management may be concerned with the effect of its actions on stock prices, it is not feasible to predict price movements as a basis for decisions. Market efficiency precludes discerning any pattern of predictability from past prices, and future prices are not predictable. Prices adjust rapidly to all new information and also include, to an unknown degree, unpublished (or insider's) information. Market prices are constantly reacting to world and industry developments, as well as to company news. Both the dividend model and the CAPM are broad and uncertain measures of $Ke,$ at best, as described in Chapter 9.

The dividend model, as given, and the growth rates used in the yield schedule, can be incorporated into the projected cost of funds, as a speculative exercise.

$$\frac{D_1}{P_0} \frac{\$\,2}{\$40} = 5\% + G\ 10\% = 15\%\ Ke$$

Assumed Growth Rates	Plus Dividend =	Ke	
0%	5%	5%	1
5	5	10	2
12	5	17	3
21	5	26	4

D	30%	10/5%	1.5%	
E	70	15	10.5	12%

The projected cost of funds is:

D	30%	10/5%	1.5%	
E	70	5 1	3.5	5.0%
D	30	10/5	1.5	
E	70	10 2	7.0	8.5
D	30	10/5	1.5	
E	70	17 3	11.9	13.4
D	30	10/5	1.5	
E	70	26 4	18.2	19.7

The higher the discount rate, the lower the investment total and the lower the related growth. At zero growth (20% discount rate) and 5% dividends, the *Ke* is 5% and the cost of funds is:

D	30%	10/5%	1.5%	
E	70	5	3.5	5.0%

Thus the cost of funds returns to the net borrowing rate.

This exploration helps to clarify the logic of using a marginal rate for analysis to produce a maximum result. The *Ke* and cost of funds are results, rather than analytic factors.

Many companies use internally generated funds plus borrowing to meet financing needs. The internally available funds are free of explicit cost, and stock issues are expensive and speculative. An investment opportunity dependent on a stock issue should be evaluated marginally—the project yield compared with the new stock cost. A stock offering can be evaluated only at the time the issuance is relevant to financial planning in the light of the current situation. As explained above, the effect on the cost of funds is not relevant. Major projects may be deferred pending availability of internal funds or a stronger stock market. Lost project profit is an opportunity cost of the stock issue not made.

CHAPTER 13

Foreign Currencies

DEALING WITH CHANGING RELATIONSHIPS

TOPIC COVERAGE

This chapter deals with some fundamentals of a complex and increasingly important subject, with the continued expansion of world trade in goods and services
and rapidly changing currency relationships. The macro and personal finance
aspects are not covered—each is a large topic. The intent here is to clarify the
basic currency exchange relationships with clear and realistic examples.

Foreign exchange is related to both investing and financing. It is a major
concern for the proliferating multi-nationals and for the many companies en-
gaged in importing and exporting.

Investing assets abroad increases the risk factor substantially for both profitability and liquidity because of ever-changing and unpredictable developments.
Financing abroad offers opportunities for raising funds on more favorable terms
because of freedom from restrictions applicable in the United States.

Foreign currency contracts for specific transactions can be "covered" several
ways—illustrated with forward exchange contracts, currency options, and foreign investment, under Sweden. Rate details are omitted—bid and asked rates,
financial, commercial, official, floating, restricted, or other rates. Illustrations
are based on individual contracts to cover specific transactions. Futures contracts
and hedging are described following Sweden but without illustrations.

CANADA—THE ARITHMETIC OF CURRENCY EXCHANGE

If a U.S. dollar (US $) is worth $1.25 in Canadian dollars (C $), it is written:

$$US \ \$1.00 = C \ \$1.25$$

Or:

$$C \ \$1.00 = US \ \$0.80$$

The relationship is always reciprocal:

$$C \ \$1.25 \times US \ \$0.80 = 1.00$$

If the US $ "strengthens," the C $ "weakens":

$$US \ \$1.00 = C \ \$1.33\tfrac{1}{3}$$

Or:

$$C \ \$1.00 = US \ \$0.75$$

$$\text{Reciprocal: } C \ \$1.33\tfrac{1}{3} \times US \ \$0.75 = 1.00$$

If the US $ "weakens," the C $ "strengthens":

$$US \ \$1.00 = C \ \$1.20$$

Or:

$$C \ \$1.00 = US \ \$0.83\tfrac{1}{3}$$

$$\text{Reciprocal: } C \ \$1.20 \times US \ \$0.83\tfrac{1}{3} = 1.00$$

To recap, we have:

Stronger US $1	Weaker C $1
$US \ \$1.00 = C \ \$ \ 1.20$	$C \ \$1.00 = US \ \$0.83\tfrac{1}{3}$
$US \ \$1.00 = C \ \$ \ 1.25$	$C \ \$1.00 = US \ \$0.80$
$US \ \$1.00 = C \ \$ \ 1.33\tfrac{1}{3}$	$C \ \$1.00 = US \ \$0.75$

In percentages we have:

Weaker C $

$US \ \$0.80/\$0.83\tfrac{1}{3} = 96\%$	decrease 4%
$US \ \$0.75/0.80 = 93\tfrac{3}{4}\%$	decrease $6\tfrac{1}{4}\%$
$US \ \$0.75/0.83\tfrac{1}{3} = 90\%$	decrease 10% combined

Stronger US $

$C \ \$1.25/\$1.20 = 104\tfrac{1}{6}\%$	increase $4\tfrac{1}{6}\%$
$C \ \$1.33\tfrac{1}{3}/\$1.25 = 106\tfrac{2}{3}\%$	increase $6\tfrac{2}{3}\%$
$C \ \$1.33\tfrac{1}{3}/\$1.20 = 111\tfrac{1}{9}\%$	increase $11\tfrac{1}{9}\%$ combined

These relations are now illustrated with examples of imports and exports. Thus an exporter billing C $10,000 for a shipment to the United States could be progressively satisfied with fewer US $:

Total	C Rate	US Rate
US $8,333$\tfrac{1}{3}$	C $1.20	US 0.83\tfrac{1}{3}$
US $8,000	C $1.25	US $0.80
US $7,500	C 1.33\tfrac{1}{3}$	US $0.75

This reduced US $ requirement would encourage imports by the United States. The Canadian exporter would continue to receive C $10,000. If the price is kept at US $8,333$\tfrac{1}{3}$ by the Canadian exporter, the rate of US $0.80 would yield C $10,416$\tfrac{2}{3}$ and the rate of US $0.75 would yield C $11,111$\tfrac{1}{9}$, thus boosting profits.

A U.S. exporter to Canada billing US $10,000 would require the Canadian importer to pay:

Total	US Rate	C Rate
US $12,000	US $0.83⅓	C $1.20
US $12,500	US $0.80	C $1.25
US $13,333⅓	US $0.75	C $1.33⅓

This would discourage Canadian imports from the United States.

If the U.S. company keeps the price at C $12,000 (US $10,000) receipts would be US $9,600 (C $1.25) and US $9,000 (C $1.33⅓), thus impairing profit margins for the U.S. exporter.

The relationships work in the same way for all countries dealing with the United States and with each other. If these relationships in exchange are reversed, the U.S. exporter has the advantage, but imports are discouraged.

With goods and services flowing in both directions among many countries, fluctuating exchange rates pose a thorny problem for money managers.

BRITAIN—THREE COUNTRY RELATIONSHIPS

Assume a stronger US $ relative to the British pound:

$$US \ \$1.00 = £0.66\tfrac{2}{3} \ (£ = US \ \$1.50)$$

$$US \ \$1.00 = £0.69444 \ (£ = US \ \$1.44)$$

$$US \ \$1.00 = £0.74074 \ (£ = US \ \$1.35)$$

These relationships are of the same nature as those described for Canada.

The exchange rates between Britain and Canada can be developed:

$$US \ \$1.00 = C \ \$1.20 + £0.66\tfrac{2}{3} \ so \ £ = C \ \$1.80 \ (\$1.20/\$0.66\tfrac{2}{3})$$

$$US \ \$1.00 = C \ \$1.25 + £0.69444 \ so \ £ = C \ \$1.80 \ (\$1.25/\$0.69444)$$

$$US \ \$1.00 = C \ \$1.33\tfrac{1}{3} + £0.74074 \ so \ £ = C \ \$1.80 \ (\$1.33\tfrac{1}{3}/\$0.74074)$$

Thus the C $ and British £ stay in step—the trading relationships are unaffected. Restated, $C \ \$1.20 = £ \ 66\tfrac{2}{3}$ so:

$$C \ \$1.00 = £0.55555 \ (\$0.66\tfrac{2}{3}/\$1.20)$$

$$C \ \$1.00 = £0.55555 \ (\$0.69444/\$1.25)$$

$$C \ \$1.00 = £0.55555 \ (\$0.74074/\$1.33\tfrac{1}{3})$$

$$Reciprocal \ £0.55555 \times C \ \$1.80 = \$1.00$$

Thus the exchange relationships encourage imports by the United States from Britain and Canada (exports by those countries to the United States) while their trading relationships remain unchanged. The cheaper imports lower the U.S. cost of living. Decreasing exports cause industry dislocations of varying length and intensity.

International travel is affected in the manner illustrated for goods. A Canadian planning to spend C $1,200 on a trip to the United States for US $1,000 would find the cost rising with a stronger US $:

C $1.20	C $1,200
C $1.25	C $1,250
C $1.33⅓	C $1,333⅓

The outlay can be kept at C $1,200 by reductions of US $:

US $0.83⅓	US $1,000
US $0.80	US $ 960
US $0.75	US $ 900

Thus the Canadian must either pay more C $ for a planned trip or reduce its extent.

The weaker C $ encourages U.S. travel to Canada to the same degree:

US $1,000	C $1.20	C $1,200
US $1,000	C $1.25	C $1,250
US $1,000	C $1.33⅓	C $1,333⅓

The same US $ provides greater results, or the same trip can be made for less US $:

C $1,200	US $0.83⅓	US $1,000
C $1,200	US $0.80	US $ 960
C $1,200	US $0.75	US $ 900

Travel from Britain to the United States is adversely affected to an equal degree by the stronger US $:

US $1,000	£0.66.67	£666.67
US $1,000	£0.69444	£694.44
US $1,000	£0.74074	£740.74
£666⅔	US $1.50	US $1,000
£666⅔	US $1.44	US $ 960
£666⅔	US $1.35	US $ 900

Either more £ are needed or fewer $ are available.

U.S. travel to Britain is equally encouraged by the weaker pound, as above:

US $1,000	£0.66⅔	£666⅔
US $1,000	£0.69444	£694.44
US $1,000	£0.74074	£740.74

More £ are available, or the same £ for fewer $, as above.
However, travel between Canada and Britain is not affected:

C $1,200	£0.55555	£666⅔ (C $1.80)
C $1,200	£0.55555	£666⅔ (C $1.80)
C $1,200	£0.55555	£666⅔ (C $1.80)

This degree of parity is rare and fleeting in actual practice.

WEST GERMANY—EXCHANGE RATES, PRICES, PROFITS

The following shows exchange rates with a stronger US $ and weaker mark (M):

$$US \$1.00 = M2.00 \ (M = US \$0.50)$$

$$US \$1.00 = M2.50 \ (M = US \$0.40)$$

$$US \$1.00 = M3.00 \ (M = US \$0.33\tfrac{1}{3})$$

A German car priced at $30,000 would provide the exporter with more marks as the dollar strengthens and more profits. Assuming annual time periods and a cost of M50,000 increasing first to M54,000 (8%) and then to M60,000 (11.1%), or combined 20% for two years we have:

US $ Price	M Rate	M Price	M Cost	M Profit	Percent M Cost	Percent M Price
30,000	2.00	60,000	50,000	10,000	20.0	16.7
30,000	2.50	75,000	54,000	21,000	38.9	28.0
30,000	3.00	90,000	60,000	30,000	50.0	33.3

The German exporter could reduce prices to maintain a profit of 20.0% on cost (or 16.7% on price) as follows:

M Cost	M Add 20%	US $ Rate	US $ Price	Reduction	
50,000	60,000	0.50	30,000	—	
54,000	64,800	0.40	25,920	$4,080	13.6%
60,000	72,000	0.33⅓	24,000	1,920	7.4
				$6,000	20.0%

Thus the German exporter can benefit from some combination of lower sales prices and higher profits, even with large cost increases.

The U.S. exporter to Germany is adversely affected in equal degree. Assuming a constant sales price in Germany of M60,000 and cost increases from $25,000 of 8% to $27,000 the first year, and 11.1% the second year to $30,000, equaling the cost increases in Germany, we have:

M Price	US $ Rate	$ Price	$ Cost	$ Profit (Loss)	Percent Increase On Cost	Percent Increase On Price
60,000	0.50	30,000	25,000	5,000	20.0	16.7
60,000	0.40	24,000	27,000	(3,000)	(11.1)	(12.5)
60,000	0.33⅓	20,000	30,000	(10,000)	(33.3)	(50.0)

For the U.S. exporter to maintain a 20.0% margin on cost (16.7% on sales) would require price increases:

$ Cost	Add 20%	M Rate	M Price	Increase on Price
25,000	30,000	2.00	60,000	—
27,000	32,400	2.50	81,000	M21,000 35.0%
30,000	36,000	3.00	108,000	M27,000 33.3%
				M48,000 80.0%

Such price increases would not be competitive.

JAPAN—SPOT RATES AND FORWARD RATES

Spot rates are the current (now) exchange rates between two countries; spot selling rates exceed spot buying rates by a small margin to provide the dealer with a profit. Spot rates are for transactions expected at once.

Forward rates are the exchange rates quoted at the present time (now) for transactions to be carried out at specified future dates. Time intervals and currency amounts can be specified to meet individual situations. At the time of maturity, the transaction is settled at the contract rate regardless of the spot rate at the time. The movements of exchange rates in direction and extent are random and not predictable.

The spot rate and the forward rate for two currencies are related exactly to the specific period and interest rates in each country. (Interest rates include anticipated inflation or deflation.) For example, $1,000 invested in New York City (NYC) at 20% provides $1,200 in one year. If $1,000 is sent to Tokyo at the rate of $1 = 250 yen, the 250,000 yen invested at 8% provides 270,000 yen in a year. At the year-end, the rate is $1 = 225 yen − 270,000 yen/$1,200. Thus 225 yen is the forward rate for one year with a 250 yen (Y) spot rate. The following schematic illustrates this:

	NYC		Rate	Tokyo
Today invest		$1,000	250Y	250,000Y
Interest	20%	200		8% 20,000
Total		$1,200		270,000Y

270,000Y/$1,200 = 225Y and $1,200/270,000Y = $0.004444.

Thus a forward rate of 225Y ($0.004444) provides parity between the interest rates in NYC and Tokyo. Forward rates fluctuate with changing spot rates and relative interest rates. Arbitrage keeps the relationships in close alignment. For the illustration, taxes, expenses, and exchange restrictions are omitted.

The schematic can also be written to find the interest rate in Tokyo:

	NYC		Rate	Tokyo
Today invest		$1,000	250Y	250,000Y
Interest	20%	200		
Total		$1,200	225	270,000 + 20,000Y

20,000Y/250,000Y = 8%.

With the forward rate known, the interest rate in Tokyo is found to be 8%.

A forward rate can be found with given interest rates; a rate of 12% in Tokyo is used:

	NYC		Rate	Tokyo
Today invest		$1,000	250Y	250,000Y
Interest	20%	200		12% 30,000
Total		$1,200		280,000Y

280,000Y/$1,200 = $233\frac{1}{3}$Y and $1,200/280,000Y = 0.004286Y.

These are break-even calculations.

The schematic helps to find any unknown factor and to explore possible relationships. With $1,000 invested in NYC at 20%, $1,200 is available in one year. If the $1,000 is sent to Tokyo and 250,000Y is invested at 8%, 270,000Y in one year can be exchanged for $1,200 at 225Y as shown above. If the spot rates are higher or lower in one year, the effect can be dramatic:

Assumed Spot Rates in 1 Year	270,000Y Equals $	Gain (Loss) on $1,200		Interest Rate Earned on $1,000
$258\frac{1}{3}$Y — 0.003871	$1,045	$(155)	(12.9)%	4.5%
250 — 0.004000	1,080	(120)	(10.0)	8.0
$241\frac{2}{3}$ — 0.004138	1,117	(83)	(6.9)	11.7
$233\frac{1}{3}$ — 0.004286	1,157	(43)	(3.6)	15.7
225 — 0.004444	1,200	0	0	20.0

Assumed Spot Rates in 1 Year		270,000Y Equals $	Gain (Loss) on $1,200		Interest Rate Earned on $1,000
216⅔	— 0.004615	$1,246	$ 46	3.8	24.6
208⅓	— 0.004800	1,296	96	8.0	29.6
200	— 0.005000	1,350	150	12.5	35.0
191⅔	— 0.005217	1,409	209	17.4	40.9

These possible results illustrate gain and loss ranges compared with keeping the $1,000 in NYC at 20% interest, based on assumed deviations from the current forward rate of 225Y of ± 33⅓Y. The realized interest rate ranges from 20.0% down to 4.5% and up to 40.9%.

The Tokyo investor with 250,000Y is in a similar but reversed position. He can invest locally at 8% to realize 270,000Y in one year or exchange the 250,000Y for $1,000 ($0.004) to invest in NYC at 20%, to realize $1,200. If one year later the spot rate is $0.004444 (225Y), he can convert to 270,000Y with no gain or loss.

		Tokyo	Rate		NYC
Today invest		250,000Y	$0.004000		$1,000
Interest	8%	20,000		20%	200
Total		270,000Y	0.004444		$1,200

However, if the spot rate in one year is $0.004 (unchanged), then we have:

	Tokyo	Rate		NYC
Today invest	250,000Y	$0.004		$1,000
Interest			20%	200
Total	300,000	0.004		$1,200

$$+ \quad 50,000Y = 20\%, \text{ rather than } 8\%.$$
Gain in Yen 30,000/270,000 = 11.1%.

If the spot rate rises to $0.005, we have:

	Tokyo	Rate		NYC
Today invest	250,000Y	$0.004		$1,000
Interest			20%	200
Total	240,000	0.005		$1,200

$$- \quad 10,000Y = (4\%) \text{ rather than } 8\%.$$
Loss in Yen 30,000/270,000 = (11.1%).

The following table presents a direct comparison of the position of the Tokyo investor with that of the NYC investor, as shown in the preceeding table:

Assumed Spot Rate in 1 Year	$1,200 = Y	Gain (Loss) on 270,000Y		Interest Rate Earned on 250,000Y
$0.003871—258⅓Y	310,000Y	40,000Y	14.8%	24%
0.004000— 250	300,000	30,000	11.1	20
0.004138— 241⅔	290,000	20,000	7.4	16
0.004286— 233⅓	280,000	10,000	3.7	12
0.004444— 225	270,000	0	0.0	8
0.004615— 216⅔	260,000	(10,000)	(3.7)	4
0.004800— 208⅓	250,000	(20,000)	(7.4)	0
0.00500 — 200	240,000	(30,000)	(11.1)	(4)
0.005217— 191⅔	230,000	(40,000)	(14.8)	(8)

The realized interest rate ranges from 8.0% down to a loss of 8.0% and up to 24.0%. This range is narrower and lower than that for NYC and is in the opposite direction: at 258⅓Y the NYC rate is 4.5% and the Tokyo rate is 24.0%, and at 191⅔Y the NYC rate is 40.9% and the Tokyo rate is minus 8.0%.

Most forward contracts are for less than one year, and it is necessary to express period interest rates and restate them on an annual basis.

Example—Two Months

Assume a NYC annual rate of 18%, for two months—3%, with a spot rate of 250Y and forward rate, 246Y. Find the interest rate in Tokyo:

		NYC	Rate	Tokyo
Today invest		$1,000	250Y	250,000Y
Interest	3%	30		
Total		$1,030	246	253,380
				+ 3,380Y

$$3,380Y/250,000Y = 1.352\% \times 6 = 8.112\%$$

Or:

$$3,380 \times 6 = 20,280Y/250,000Y = 8.112\%$$

Example—Four Months

Assume a Tokyo rate of 6% per year, or 2% for four months, with a spot rate of $0.004 and forward rate, $0.004082.

		Tokyo	Rate	NYC
Today invest		250,000Y	$0.004000	$1,000.00
Interest	2%	10,000		
Total		260,000Y	0.004082	1,061.32

$$\$\quad 61.32 \times 3 = \$183.96$$
$$\text{or } 18.4\%$$

Example—Six Months

Assume a NYC annual rate of 12%, or 6% for six months and a Tokyo annual rate of 18%, or 9% for six months, with a spot rate of 250Y. Find the forward rate:

		NYC	Rate		Tokyo
Today invest		$1,000	250.000Y		250.000Y
Interest	6%	60		9%	22,500
Total		$1,060	257.075		272,500Y

Or:

$$\$1,060/272,500Y = \$0.003890$$

FRANCE—EXCHANGE RATE EQUATIONS

It is convenient to use equations stated as parities to facilitate finding unknowns from available data. Assume the following (F = franc):

	NYC	Paris
Annual interest rates	14.45%	9.0%
Spot rates	$ = 9.091F	F = $0.1100
One year forward rate	$ = 8.658F	F = $0.1155

	NYC	Rate		Paris
Today invest	$11,000	9.091F ($0.1100)		100,000F
Interest 14.45%	1,590		9%	9,000
Total	$12,590			109,000F

$$109,000F/\$12,590 = 8.658F$$
$$\$12,590/109,000F = \$0.1155$$

Three parities follow:

	Interest Rates	
NYC	114.45%	= 105%
Paris	109.00%	

	NYC	
Spot	$\dfrac{9.091F}{8.658F}$	= 105%
Forward		

	Paris	
Forward	$\dfrac{\$0.1155}{\$0.1100}$	= 105%
Spot		

Or:

$$\frac{114.45\%}{109.00\%} = \frac{9.091F}{8.658F} = \frac{\$0.1155}{\$0.1100} = 105\%$$

Examples of finding unknowns follow:

$$\frac{114.45\%}{109.00\%} = \frac{9.091F}{?} = 8.658F$$

$$\frac{9.091F}{8.658F} = \frac{?}{\$0.1100} = \$0.1155$$

$$\frac{\$0.1155}{?} = \frac{114.45\%}{109.00\%} = \$0.1100$$

$$\frac{?}{109.00\%} = \frac{\$0.1155}{\$0.1100} = 114.45\%$$

$$\frac{114.45\%}{?} = \frac{9.091F}{8.658F} = 109.00\%$$

$$\frac{\$0.1155}{\$0.1100} = \frac{?}{8.658F} = 9.091F$$

SWEDEN—COVERING FORWARD POSITIONS

A U.S. importer owes $10,000, payable in krona (K), in one year, for a purchase billed at 80,000K. The debt could be settled now for $10,000 ($0.125), but one year's interest on $10,000 would be forfeited, say $1,500 or more. If the debt could be paid in one year with $10,000, the U.S. importer would have a known obligation, but the Swedish exporter would bear the exchange risk. The U.S. importer can wait one year and buy 80,000K at the spot rate at that time, but he may gain or lose an indeterminate amount because exchange rates move randomly. For example:

Spot Rate in 1 year		$ Needed to Buy 80,000 K	Gain (Loss) on $10,000
$0.110	(9.091K)	$ 8,800	$1,200
.115	(8.696K)	9,200	800
.120	(8.333K)	9,600	400
.125	(8.000K)	10,000	0
.130	(7.692K)	10,400	(400)
.135	(7.407K)	10,800	(800)
.140	(7.143K)	11,200	(1,200)
0.145	(6.897K)	11,600	(1,600)

To avoid gambling on unpredictable and ever-fluctuating rate changes, the U.S. importer could cover his future liability now in several ways: buy a forward exchange contract, buy a currency option, or invest now in Sweden.

Buy a Forward Exchange Contract

The spot rate is K = $0.125 or $ = 8.0K. The one year forward rate is K = $0.130; $ = 7.692K. Signing this contract today ensures the 80,000K needed in one year at a known cost of $10,400 (80,000K at $0.130) payable in one year. The premium of $400 over the spot rate is similar to an insurance premium.

The forward contract protects against loss for spot rates over $0.125 but forfeits gains for lower rates. At $0.130 the forward contract premium equals the spot rate loss:

Spot Rate in 1 Year	No Cover: Gain (Loss) on $10,000 (80,000K)		Foward Contract Premium	Net Gain (Loss)*
$0.110	$ 8,800	$1,200	$400	$(1,600)
.115	9,200	800	400	(1,200)
.120	9,600	400	400	(800)
.125	10,000	0	400	(400)
.130	10,400	(400)	400	0
.135	10,800	(800)	400	400
.140	11,200	(1,200)	400	800
0.145	11,600	(1,600)	400	1,200

*Loss = premium cost plus gain lost. Gain = premium cost less loss avoided.

The importer has chosen the known cost of $400 to protect against possible greater losses, but he has also forfeited potential gains. The 4% premium for the forward rate (7.692K × 104% − 8.0K) is the interest rate differential between the two countries.

If the U.S. interest rate is 16.0000%, the Swedish rate is 11.5385%, or 11.5400%:

		United States	Rate	Sweden
Today invest		$10,000	8.00000K	80,000.0K
Interest	16%	1,600		
Total		$11,600	7.69231	89,230.8
Check: 116.000%/$111.538 = 104%				+ 9,230.8K = 11.5385%

Forward exchange contracts are available from the larger banks and foreign currency houses, which have full-time staff handling exchange transactions.

The U.S. exporter billing in a foreign currency for future payment can also cover the transaction with a forward contract. Using the data from the example given for the U.S. importer, a U.S. exporter billing 80,000K to be paid in one year could sell a forward exchange contract for $10,400 to cover the sale of 80,000K to be received:

Spot Rate in 1 Year	No Cover: Gain (Loss) on $10,000 (80,000K)		Foward Contract Premium	Net Gain (Loss)*
$0.110	$ 8,800	(1,200)	$400	$ 800
.115	9,200	(800)	400	400
.120	9,600	(400)	400	0
.125	10,000	0	400	(400)
.130	10,400	400	400	(800)
.135	10,800	800	400	(1,200)
.140	11,200	1,200	400	(1,600)
0.145	11,600	1,600	400	(2,000)

*Gain = loss avoided less premium cost. Loss = gain lost plus premium cost.

The known premium of $400 gives the U.S. exporter protection against possible exchange loss and forfeits possible gain. The net gain (loss) result is reversed for the U.S. exporter; at $0.110 he gains $800 while the importer loses ($1,600) and at $0.145 he loses ($2,000) while the importer gains $1,200.

Buy a Currency Option

The importer could buy a currency option to pay 80,000K within one year at the exercise price of $10,000 for, say, a premium of $500 payable at once.

Interest at 16% on $500, or $80, is added because the premium is payable now, and the option extends for a year. The $580 total is comparable with the forward contract premium at $400.

Protection is afforded against exchange losses, and gains may be realized. Break-even (B/E) points are added to the table.

Spot Rate in 1 Year	No Cover: Gain (Loss) on $10,000	Total Option Cost $580			Gain (Loss)
$0.11000	$ 1,200	EXPIRE	G $1,200 −	$580 = $	620
.11500	800	EXPIRE	G 800 −	580 =	220
.11775 (B/E)	580	EXPIRE	G 580 −	580 =	0
.12000	400	EXPIRE	G 400 −	580 =	(180)
.12500	0		G 0 −	580 =	(580)
.13000	(400)	EXERCISE G	400 −	580 =	(180)
.13225 (B/E)	(580)	EXERCISE G	580 −	580 =	0
.13500	(800)	EXERCISE G	800 −	580 =	220
.14000	(1,200)	EXERCISE G	1,200 −	580 =	620
0.14500	(1,600)	EXERCISE G	1,600 −	580 =	1,020

$0.110 and $0.115—The option is not exercised and the gain from the lower spot rates is realized (e.g., $1,200 less $580, or $620 gain).

$0.11775 and $0.13225—Break-even points—$580 both ways.

$0.120—The spot rate gain is realized for $400, offset by the $580, for a loss of $180.

$0.125—The known option cost of $580 is realized—with or without exercising the option. This is the maximum loss.

$0.130, $0.135, $0.140, $0.145—The option is exercised to avoid the spot rate losses, and the $580 cost is deducted. At $0.130 the option is exercised to buy 80,000K for $10,000, rather than pay $10,400 (80,000K × $0.130). The $400 gain is reduced by the $580 for a net loss of $180. At rates over $0.13225, the option provides net gains by avoiding spot rate losses.

The flexibility of the option ensures a maximum loss of the total $580 and gains for spot rate movements in either direction past the break-even points. For spot rates over $0.125, losses are avoided compared with uncovered positions.

The results with the currency option can be compared with those for the forward contract:

Spot Rate in 1 Year	No Cover: Gain (Loss) on $10,000	Net Gain (Loss)		Relative Change for Option
		Forward Contract	Currency Option	
$0.11000	$1,200	$(1,600)	$ 620	+$2,220
.11500	800	(1,200)	220	+ 1,420

| | | Net Gain (Loss) | | |
Spot Rate in 1 Year	No Cover: Gain (Loss) on $10,000	Forward Contract	Currency Option	Relative Change for Option
$ .11775	$ 580	$ (980)	$ 0	+$ 980
.12000	400	(800)	(180)	+ 620
.12500	0	(400)	(580)	− (180)
.13000	(400)	0	(180)	− (180)
.13225	(580)	180	0	− (180)
.13500	(800)	400	220	− (180)
.14000	(1,200)	800	620	− (180)
0.14500	(1,600)	1,200	1,020	− (180)

Thus the currency option permits realization of gains from rate changes, which can be substantial, and the relative extra cost is limited to any excess of the option premium ($580) over the forward rate premium ($400) or negative $180.

The use of currency options to cover forward positions is relatively new and gaining acceptance. The options can be written on an individual basis with financial houses to cover both exports and imports. Some major currencies are traded on the Philadelphia exchange for specified amounts and periods.

The comparative table illustrates the basic choice between profit and risk. With no cover, a wide range of gain or loss is possible and unpredictable—a position appealing only to risk-prone gamblers. For a sure thing—the forward contract—the cost is $400. Losses are avoided, but gains are forfeited. The maximum loss with the currency option is $580, but there are possible gains from large enough rate swings in either direction.

However, the currency option involves an added cost of $180 ($580 − $400) with a 50–50 chance of gain or loss. The gains shown by the illustration are very large, but the probabilities are low. The odds improve with more transactions to cover.

Invest Now in Sweden

The importer could also send dollars to Sweden now to provide the 80,000K payable in one year. With interest in Sweden at 11.54%, 71,723K is needed now (80,000K/111.54%). At 8.0K spot rate, $8,965 must be invested abroad (71,723K/8.0K = $8,965.375):

		United States	Rate		Sweden
Today invest		$ 8,965	8.0000K		71.723K
Interest	16%	1,435		11.54%	8,277
Total		$10,400	7.6923		80,000K

The importer can set aside $8,965 in the United States at 16.00% to provide $10,400 to liquidate the forward contract or send $8,965 to Sweden for investment at 11.54% to provide the 80,000K to be paid to the exporter. However, if investment in Sweden can be made at a higher rate, say 12.20%, then (working the numbers backward) we have:

United States	Rate		Sweden
$8,912.50	8.0K		71,300K
		12.2%	8,700
			80,000K

Thus the importer can meet the obligation with a current cost of $8,912.50, or $52.50 less (or $60.90 in one year at 16%) than the forward contract. Such possible gains exist but are volatile and kept small by arbitrage.

The methods described in general terms are in use, individually tailored to meet specific requirements for each transaction and each company. Again, risk and reward must be evaluated. There are also other methods for covering future currency commitments.

FUTURES CONTRACTS

The forward contracts described can be purchased to meet specific needs—any currency, any period, any amount—at a known cost.

Futures contracts are offered by public, regulated exchanges in major currencies, for specified periods, and in specified amounts. Settlements are made through the clearinghouse; traders do not deal with one another.

HEDGING

A company with investments abroad may have an excess of assets over liabilities (long position) or the reverse (short position). The balance can be managed according to plans and prospects for each country—more or less investment, more or less debt. Also, long and short positions can be hedged (individual contracts are said to be covered) by several methods including futures and options.

Appendix

Table 1
Present Value of $1

Years Hence	1%	2%	4%	6%	8%	10%	12%	14%	15%	16%	18%	20%	22%	24%	25%	26%	28%	30%	35%	40%	45%	50%
1	0.990	0.980	0.962	0.943	0.926	0.909	0.893	0.877	0.870	0.862	0.847	0.833	0.820	0.806	0.800	0.794	0.781	0.769	0.741	0.714	0.690	0.667
2	0.980	0.961	0.925	0.890	0.857	0.826	0.797	0.769	0.756	0.743	0.718	0.694	0.672	0.650	0.640	0.630	0.610	0.592	0.549	0.510	0.476	0.444
3	0.971	0.942	0.889	0.840	0.794	0.751	0.712	0.675	0.658	0.641	0.609	0.579	0.551	0.524	0.512	0.500	0.477	0.455	0.406	0.364	0.328	0.296
4	0.961	0.924	0.855	0.792	0.735	0.683	0.636	0.592	0.572	0.552	0.516	0.482	0.451	0.423	0.410	0.397	0.373	0.350	0.301	0.260	0.226	0.198
5	0.951	0.906	0.822	0.747	0.681	0.621	0.567	0.519	0.497	0.476	0.437	0.402	0.370	0.341	0.328	0.315	0.291	0.269	0.223	0.186	0.156	0.132
6	0.942	0.888	0.790	0.705	0.630	0.564	0.507	0.456	0.432	0.410	0.370	0.335	0.303	0.275	0.262	0.250	0.227	0.207	0.165	0.133	0.108	0.088
7	0.933	0.871	0.760	0.665	0.583	0.513	0.452	0.400	0.376	0.354	0.314	0.279	0.249	0.222	0.210	0.198	0.178	0.159	0.122	0.095	0.074	0.059
8	0.923	0.853	0.731	0.627	0.540	0.467	0.404	0.351	0.327	0.305	0.266	0.233	0.204	0.179	0.168	0.157	0.139	0.123	0.091	0.068	0.051	0.039
9	0.914	0.837	0.703	0.592	0.500	0.424	0.361	0.308	0.284	0.263	0.225	0.194	0.167	0.144	0.134	0.125	0.108	0.094	0.067	0.048	0.035	0.026
10	0.905	0.820	0.676	0.558	0.463	0.386	0.322	0.270	0.247	0.227	0.191	0.162	0.137	0.116	0.107	0.099	0.085	0.073	0.050	0.035	0.024	0.017
11	0.896	0.804	0.650	0.527	0.429	0.350	0.287	0.237	0.215	0.195	0.162	0.135	0.112	0.094	0.086	0.079	0.066	0.056	0.037	0.025	0.017	0.012
12	0.887	0.788	0.625	0.497	0.397	0.319	0.257	0.208	0.187	0.168	0.137	0.112	0.092	0.076	0.069	0.062	0.052	0.043	0.027	0.018	0.012	0.008
13	0.879	0.773	0.601	0.469	0.368	0.290	0.229	0.182	0.163	0.145	0.116	0.093	0.075	0.061	0.055	0.050	0.040	0.033	0.020	0.013	0.008	0.005
14	0.870	0.758	0.577	0.442	0.340	0.263	0.205	0.160	0.141	0.125	0.099	0.078	0.062	0.049	0.044	0.039	0.032	0.025	0.015	0.009	0.006	0.003
15	0.861	0.743	0.555	0.417	0.315	0.239	0.183	0.140	0.123	0.108	0.084	0.065	0.051	0.040	0.035	0.031	0.025	0.020	0.011	0.006	0.004	0.002
16	0.853	0.728	0.534	0.394	0.292	0.218	0.163	0.123	0.107	0.093	0.071	0.054	0.042	0.032	0.028	0.025	0.019	0.015	0.008	0.005	0.003	0.002
17	0.844	0.714	0.513	0.371	0.270	0.198	0.146	0.108	0.093	0.080	0.060	0.045	0.034	0.026	0.023	0.020	0.015	0.012	0.006	0.003	0.002	0.001
18	0.836	0.700	0.494	0.350	0.250	0.180	0.130	0.095	0.081	0.069	0.051	0.038	0.028	0.021	0.018	0.016	0.012	0.009	0.005	0.002	0.001	0.001
19	0.828	0.686	0.475	0.331	0.232	0.164	0.116	0.083	0.070	0.060	0.043	0.031	0.023	0.017	0.014	0.012	0.009	0.007	0.003	0.002	0.001	
20	0.820	0.673	0.456	0.312	0.215	0.149	0.104	0.073	0.061	0.051	0.037	0.026	0.019	0.014	0.012	0.010	0.007	0.005	0.002	0.001		
21	0.811	0.660	0.439	0.294	0.199	0.135	0.093	0.064	0.053	0.044	0.031	0.022	0.015	0.011	0.009	0.008	0.006	0.004	0.002	0.001		
22	0.803	0.647	0.422	0.278	0.184	0.123	0.083	0.056	0.046	0.038	0.026	0.018	0.013	0.009	0.007	0.006	0.004	0.003	0.001	0.001		
23	0.795	0.634	0.406	0.262	0.170	0.112	0.074	0.049	0.040	0.033	0.022	0.015	0.010	0.007	0.006	0.005	0.003	0.002	0.001			
24	0.788	0.622	0.390	0.247	0.158	0.102	0.066	0.043	0.035	0.028	0.019	0.013	0.008	0.006	0.005	0.004	0.003	0.002	0.001			
25	0.780	0.610	0.375	0.233	0.146	0.092	0.059	0.038	0.030	0.024	0.016	0.010	0.007	0.005	0.004	0.003	0.002	0.001				
26	0.772	0.598	0.361	0.220	0.135	0.084	0.053	0.033	0.026	0.021	0.014	0.009	0.006	0.004	0.003	0.002	0.002	0.001				
27	0.764	0.586	0.347	0.207	0.125	0.076	0.047	0.029	0.023	0.018	0.011	0.007	0.005	0.003	0.002	0.002	0.001	0.001				
28	0.757	0.574	0.333	0.196	0.116	0.069	0.042	0.026	0.020	0.014	0.010	0.006	0.004	0.002	0.002	0.002	0.001	0.001				
29	0.749	0.563	0.321	0.185	0.107	0.063	0.037	0.022	0.017	0.014	0.008	0.005	0.003	0.002	0.002	0.001	0.001					
30	0.742	0.552	0.308	0.174	0.099	0.057	0.033	0.020	0.015	0.012	0.007	0.004	0.003	0.002	0.001	0.001	0.001					
40	0.672	0.453	0.208	0.097	0.046	0.022	0.011	0.005	0.004	0.003	0.001	0.001										
50	0.608	0.372	0.141	0.054	0.021	0.009	0.003	0.001	0.001	0.001												

Table 2
Present Value of an Annuity of $1

Years (N)	1%	2%	4%	6%	8%	10%	12%	14%	15%	16%	18%	20%	22%	24%	25%	26%	28%	30%	35%	40%	45%	50%
1	0.990	0.980	0.962	0.943	0.926	0.909	0.893	0.877	0.870	0.862	0.847	0.833	0.820	0.806	0.800	0.794	0.781	0.769	0.741	0.714	0.690	0.667
2	1.970	1.942	1.886	1.833	1.783	1.736	1.690	1.647	1.626	1.605	1.566	1.528	1.492	1.457	1.440	1.424	1.392	1.361	1.289	1.224	1.165	1.111
3	2.941	2.884	2.775	2.673	2.577	2.487	2.402	2.322	2.283	2.246	2.174	2.106	2.042	1.981	1.952	1.923	1.868	1.816	1.696	1.589	1.493	1.407
4	3.902	3.808	3.630	3.465	3.312	3.170	3.037	2.914	2.855	2.798	2.690	2.589	2.494	2.404	2.362	2.320	2.241	2.166	1.997	1.849	1.720	1.605
5	4.853	4.713	4.452	4.212	3.993	3.791	3.605	3.433	3.352	3.274	3.127	2.991	2.864	2.745	2.689	2.635	2.532	2.436	2.220	2.035	1.876	1.737
6	5.795	5.601	5.242	4.917	4.623	4.355	4.111	3.889	3.784	3.685	3.498	3.326	3.167	3.020	2.951	2.885	2.759	2.643	2.385	2.168	1.983	1.824
7	6.728	6.472	6.002	5.582	5.206	4.868	4.564	4.288	4.160	4.039	3.812	3.605	3.416	3.242	3.161	3.083	2.937	2.802	2.508	2.263	2.057	1.883
8	7.652	7.325	6.733	6.210	5.747	5.335	4.968	4.639	4.487	4.344	4.078	3.837	3.619	3.421	3.329	3.241	3.076	2.925	2.598	2.331	2.108	1.922
9	8.566	8.162	7.435	6.802	6.247	5.759	5.328	4.946	4.772	4.607	4.303	4.031	3.786	3.566	3.463	3.366	3.184	3.019	2.665	2.379	2.144	1.948
10	9.471	8.983	8.111	7.360	6.710	6.145	5.650	5.216	5.019	4.833	4.494	4.192	3.923	3.682	3.571	3.465	3.269	3.092	2.715	2.414	2.168	1.965
11	10.368	9.787	8.760	7.887	7.139	6.495	5.937	5.453	5.234	5.029	4.656	4.327	4.035	3.776	3.656	3.544	3.335	3.147	2.757	2.438	2.185	1.977
12	11.255	10.575	9.385	8.384	7.536	6.814	6.194	5.660	5.421	5.197	4.793	4.439	4.127	3.851	3.725	3.606	3.387	3.190	2.779	2.456	2.196	1.985
13	12.134	11.343	9.986	8.853	7.904	7.103	6.424	5.842	5.583	5.342	4.910	4.533	4.203	3.912	3.780	3.656	3.427	3.223	2.799	2.468	2.204	1.990
14	13.004	12.106	10.563	9.295	8.244	7.367	6.628	6.002	5.724	5.468	5.008	4.611	4.265	3.962	3.824	3.695	3.459	3.249	2.814	2.477	2.210	1.993
15	13.865	12.849	11.118	9.712	8.559	7.606	6.811	6.142	5.847	5.575	5.092	4.675	4.315	4.001	3.859	3.726	3.483	3.268	2.825	2.484	2.214	1.995
16	14.718	13.578	11.652	10.106	8.851	7.824	6.974	6.265	5.954	5.669	5.162	4.730	4.357	4.033	3.887	3.751	3.503	3.283	2.834	2.489	2.216	1.997
17	15.562	14.292	12.166	10.477	9.122	8.022	7.120	6.373	6.047	5.749	5.222	4.775	4.391	4.059	3.910	3.771	3.518	3.295	2.840	2.492	2.218	1.998
18	16.398	14.992	12.659	10.828	9.372	8.201	7.250	6.467	6.128	5.818	5.273	4.812	4.419	4.080	3.928	3.786	3.529	3.304	2.844	2.494	2.219	1.999
19	17.226	15.678	13.134	11.158	9.604	8.365	7.366	6.550	6.198	5.877	5.316	4.844	4.442	4.097	3.942	3.799	3.539	3.311	2.848	2.496	2.220	1.999
20	18.046	16.351	13.590	11.470	9.818	8.514	7.469	6.623	6.259	5.929	5.353	4.870	4.460	4.110	3.954	3.808	3.546	3.316	2.850	2.497	2.221	1.999
21	18.857	17.011	14.029	11.764	10.017	8.649	7.562	6.687	6.312	5.973	5.384	4.891	4.476	4.121	3.963	3.816	3.551	3.320	2.852	2.498	2.221	2.000
22	19.660	17.658	14.451	12.042	10.201	8.772	7.645	6.743	6.359	6.011	5.410	4.909	4.488	4.130	3.970	3.822	3.556	3.323	2.853	2.498	2.222	2.000
23	20.456	18.292	14.857	12.303	10.371	8.883	7.718	6.792	6.399	6.044	5.432	4.925	4.499	4.137	3.976	3.827	3.559	3.325	2.854	2.499	2.222	2.000
24	21.243	18.914	15.247	12.550	10.529	8.985	7.784	6.835	6.434	6.073	5.451	4.937	4.507	4.143	3.981	3.831	3.562	3.327	2.855	2.499	2.222	2.000
25	22.023	19.523	15.622	12.783	10.675	9.077	7.843	6.873	6.464	6.097	5.467	4.948	4.514	4.147	3.985	3.834	3.564	3.329	2.856	2.499	2.222	2.000
26	22.795	20.121	15.983	13.003	10.810	9.161	7.896	6.906	6.491	6.118	5.480	4.956	4.520	4.151	3.988	3.837	3.566	3.330	2.856	2.500	2.222	2.000
27	23.560	20.707	16.330	13.211	10.935	9.237	7.943	6.935	6.514	6.136	5.492	4.964	4.524	4.154	3.990	3.839	3.567	3.331	2.856	2.500	2.222	2.000
28	24.316	21.281	16.663	13.406	11.051	9.307	7.984	6.961	6.534	6.152	5.502	4.970	4.528	4.157	3.992	3.840	3.568	3.331	2.857	2.500	2.222	2.000
29	25.066	21.844	16.984	13.591	11.158	9.370	8.022	6.983	6.551	6.166	5.510	4.975	4.531	4.159	3.994	3.841	3.569	3.332	2.857	2.500	2.222	2.000
30	25.808	22.396	17.292	13.765	11.258	9.427	8.055	7.003	6.566	6.177	5.517	4.979	4.534	4.160	3.995	3.842	3.569	3.332	2.857	2.500	2.222	2.000
40	32.835	27.355	19.793	15.046	11.925	9.779	8.244	7.105	6.642	6.234	5.548	4.997	4.544	4.166	3.999	3.846	3.571	3.333	2.857	2.500	2.222	2.000
50	39.196	31.424	21.482	15.762	12.234	9.915	8.304	7.133	6.661	6.246	5.554	4.999	4.545	4.167	4.000	3.846	3.571	3.333	2.857	2.500	2.222	2.000

271

THE PRESENT VALUE TABLES (PV)

The formulas are as follows:

Table 1: PV $100—3 years—10%

$$\frac{1}{(1.10)^3} = \frac{1}{1.331} = f\ 0.7513148 \times \$100 = \$75.13$$

Table 2: PV $100 Annuity—3 years—10%

$$\frac{1 - \dfrac{1}{(1.10)^3}}{0.10} = \frac{1 - 0.7513148}{0.10} = \frac{0.2486852}{0.10}$$

$$= f\ 2.486852 \times \$100 = \$248.68$$

Table 1

Percent	Dollars
100.0%	$ 75.13
+ 10.0	+ 7.51
110.0	82.64
+ 11.0	+ 8.27
121.0	90.91
+ 12.1	+ 9.09
133.1%	$100.00

Table 2

$248.68		
− 75.13	$ 75.13	(1/1.331)
173.56		
− 82.64	+ 82.64	(1/1.21)
$ 90.91	+ 90.91	(1/1.10)
	$248.68	

f = PV for $1 per table, or by calculation.

The number of decimal points used depends on the degree of accuracy needed for the problem. Hand-held calculators are available at low cost and perform many financial and statistical functions. Computer programs provide a wide range of financial calculations.

To compute f by use of triangulation, we have:

Given 10%—5 years = f 0.621

Given 10%—f 0.621 = 5 years

Given f 0.621—5 years = 10%

$$\text{By formula } \frac{1}{(1.00)^5} = \frac{1}{1.6105} = \text{f } 0.6209 = \text{f } 0.621$$

Table			Other Amounts		
Ratio: $1	$1,000.00	$1,610.00	$621.00	$12,345.00	$20.00
Given 10% and 5 years = f 0.621 =	$ 621.00	$1,000.00	$385.64	$ 7,666.25	$12.42

Restated, we have:

1 is to f 0.621 as

$1,000 is to $621 and

$1,610 is to $1,000, etc.

Total PV = amount times f

For interpolation, to find the years for f 0.652 and 10%, the closest years are:

4 years	f 0.683	f 0.683
		− f 0.652
5 years	− f 0.621	—
	= f 0.062	= f 0.031 = $\frac{31}{62}$ = 0.5 = 4.5 years

Given five years and f 0.607, the rate is:

10%	f 0.621	f 0.621
		− f 0.607
11%	− f 0.593	—
	= f 0.028	= f 0.014 = $\frac{14}{28}$ = 0.5 = 10.5%

These are linear interpolations, but the tables are logarithmic. To limit error, interpolation should be kept within a narrow range.

For example, find the years given 10% and f 0.652:

		Beginning Year		Year				Years	Cum.
Yr.4 − Yr.5	=	f − 0.652	=	Range	=	Extension	=	Result	Difference
f 0.683 − f 0.621 f 0.062		0.031	50%	1		0.50		4.50	0.00
$\dfrac{\text{Yr. 3 − Yr. 7}}{\text{f } 0.751 − \text{f } 0.513}$ f 0.238		0.099	42	4		1.68		4.68	0.18
$\dfrac{\text{Yr. 2 − Yr. 9}}{\text{f } 0.826 − \text{f } 0.424}$ f 0.402		0.174	43	7		3.01		5.01	0.51
$\dfrac{\text{Yr. 1 − Yr. 11}}{\text{f } 0.909 − \text{f } 0.350}$ f 0.559		0.257	46	10		4.60		5.60	1.10

Find the rates given five years and f 0.607:

f 10% − 11%	=	Beginning Year f − 0.607	= ×	Percent Range	Rate Extension	= Result	Cum. Difference
f 0.621 − f 0.593	f 0.028	0.014	50%	1	0.50	10.5%	0.0
8% − 13% / f 0.681 − f 0.543	f 0.138	0.074	54	5	2.70	10.7	0.2
6% − 15% / f 0.747 − f 0.497	f 0.250	0.140	56	9	5.04	11.0	0.5
4% − 17% / f 0.822 − f 0.456	f 0.366	0.215	59	13	7.67	11.7	1.2

These examples show the cumulative effect of wider ranges on the degree of error.

Note that the tables do not have a column for 0% (zero)—it would be $1 for all years in Table 1, and for Table 2 the dollars would equal the years:

$$\text{Year } 0 = \$\ 0$$
$$1 = \ 1$$
$$2 = \ 2$$
$$3 = \ 3$$
$$10 = \ 10$$
$$30 = \ 30$$

Also, there is no line for 0 years (zero)—it would be $1 for all rates because it is the present time.

POINTERS FOR TABLE 1

The Rule of 72 (An Approximation)

A single amount doubles when the number of years times the percentage rate equals 72. For example, $1 becomes $2 in 9 years at 8% (9 × 8 = 72). Three pairs from the tables are:

	Difference from 1.000	Correct Amount
72 = 4% × 18 years = f 0.494 × 2 = 0.988 −	0.012	$2.026
72 = 18% × 4 years = f 0.516 × 2 = 1.032 +	0.032	1.939
72 = 6% × 12 years = f 0.497 × 2 = 0.994 −	0.006	2.012
72 = 12% × 6 years = f 0.507 × 2 = 1.014 +	0.014	1.974
72 = 8% × 9 years = f 0.500 × 2 = 1.000	0.000	1.999
72 = 9% × 8 years = f 0.502 × 2 = 1.004 +	0.004	1.993

Over the 4 and 18 limits, the errors are larger. For instance, at 36% an amount doubles in 2.254 years (not 2.000 years), and in 2 years at 36% an amount becomes $1.8496 (not $2.0000).

Some examples of this handy rule are:

a. "Management is happy to report that sales have doubled in just nine years." Is 8% annual growth a good record? (9 × 8 = 72)

b. "The present stock price of $50 is expected to double in eight to ten years, and the current dividend is $1." Annual growth rates are 9.0% to 7.2%, and the dividend rate is 2.0%, or 11.0% to 9.2% combined. This is not so attractive if AA bonds pay 12.0%.

c. "Your funds have quadrupled in 18 years." Doubling in 9 years is 8%; doubling again for another 9 years is again 8%. This would be compared to comparable funds, but 8% sounds low.

d. "A bond for $1,000 pays no interest and matures in five years." If the price is $500, the rate is 14.40%. If the bond matures in ten years and the price is $250, the rate is also 14.40%. (By calculation the true rate is 14.87%.)

e. "Borrow $2,000 now and repay $4,000 in four years." The rate is 18% (by calculation, 18.92%).

Finding Factors Not Given by the Table

The tables are logarithmic and factors (f) can be found by *adding* any two years and *multiplying* the f for each year: the resulting f relates to the sum of the two years.

Examples in the Table

Find f for 10% for 15 years:

```
Year   7              f. 0.513
plus   8    times     f. 0.467
=     15              = 0.239571
             (by calculation 0.239392) = f 0.239 (table)
```

Or:

```
Year   5              f 0.621
plus  10    times     f. 0.386
=     15              = 0.239706
             (by calculation 0.239392) = f 0.239 (table)
```

Thus any combination of years adding to 15, and their f's multiplied, gives the answer.

Examples Not in the Table

Find f for 10% for 32 years:

Year 16   f 0.218
plus 16   times   f 0.218
=   32   = 0.047524 by calculation f 0.047362

Find f for 2% for 60 years:

Year 30   f 0.552
plus 30   times   f 0.552
=   60   = 0.304704 by calculation 0.304782

More decimals provide greater accuracy, as needed.

Discount and Accumulation

The great power of time and interest rates is illustrated using $10,000 and three decimals (use table f and move four decimals). At 0%, $10,000 is $10,000 for all periods. At 0 time, $10,000 is $10,000 for all rates.

		Discount	Accumulation
At 1% Year	5	$9,510	$ 10,515
	15	8,610	11,614
	30	7,420	13,477
At 15% Year	5	$4,970	20,121
	15	1,230	81,301
	30	150	666,667
At 30% Year	5	$2,690	$ 37,174
	15	200	500,000
	30	10	10,000,000
30% by calculation for:			
Year 15		$ 195.37	$ 511,859
Year 30		3.82	26,199,957

If you hope to inherit $10,000 in 30 years, it is worth only $3.82 at 30%, $150 at 15%, and $7,420 at 1%. If you invest $10,000 now it becomes $13,447 in 30 years at 1%, but at 15% it becomes $666,667. Also, $1 for 100 years becomes:

at 5% = $ 132
at 10 =   13,780
at 15 =   1,174,313
at 20 =   82,817,977

Note that error rates increase rapidly with higher percentages and a longer number of years based on three decimal tables.

Time Periods Other Than One Year

Frequency	Times per Year	Rate	f	$10,000 Discount	Accumulation	Increase	Cum.
Annual	1	24.00000%	0.806000	$8,060	$12,400	—	—
Semi-annual	2	12.00000	.797000	7,970	12,544	$144	$144
Quarterly	4	6.00000	.792000	7,920	12,625	81	225
Monthly	12	2.00000	.788000	7,880	12,682	57	282
Daily	365	0.06575	0.786700	7,867	12,711	29	311
				(or 7,866.90)	(or 12,711.49)		(311.49)
"Continuous" (e = 2.718282)			0.786628	7,866	12,712	1	312
				(or 7,866.28)	(or 12,712.49)		(312.49)

The difference between daily and "continuous" compounding is only $1 on $10,000, per year at 24%. Daily compounding is more than annual by $311 per year but only $29 more than the monthly rate. Also, if $12,400 is provided by $10,000 at 24% per annum, what rate provides $12,400 on a monthly basis? Not 2%, but 1.8088%. If $10,000 accumulates to $12,400 at 2%, how many periods are there? 10.863.

Uneven Future Amounts

The annuity table can be used only for an equal amount, equal periods, and one rate—that is how the table is constructed. Otherwise, the single amount table—Table 1—must be used. For example:

		10% f	PV	30% f	PV
1 year	$ 100	0.909	$ 91	0.769	$ 77
2 years	1,000	.826	826	.592	592
3 years	10,000	0.751	7,510	0.455	4,550
	$11,100		$8,427		$5,219

With dollars reversed we have:

		10% f	PV	30% f	PV
1 year	$10,000	0.909	$9,090	0.769	$7,690
2 years	1,000	.826	826	.592	592
3 years	100	0.751	75	0.455	46
			$9,991		$8,328
Increase			$1,564		$3,109

An annuity example is:

		10% f	PV
1 year	$1,000	f 0.909	$ 909
2 years	1,000	f 0.826	826
3 years	1,000	f 0.751	721
		f 2.486	$2,486

With the annuity table we have:

$$\$1,000 \quad \times \quad \text{f } 2.486 \quad = \quad \$2,486$$

POINTERS FOR TABLE 2

Table 2 f's are simply the sum of Table 1 f's. Also, the difference between the Table 2 f's for two consecutive years is the f for the single year. These points are evident by inspecting the tables.

Table 1	20%f
Year 1	0.833
2	.694
3	.579
4	0.483
	2.589 = f on table 2 for 20%—4 years

Table 2	20%f
Year 4	2.589
3	2.106
	0.483 = f on Table 1 for year 4—20%

Decimal discrepancies can be disregarded.

The year 1 is the same for both tables—an annuity for a year is a single amount. Beyond one year, annuity PV's are greater than 1.0. Note the absence of a column for zero percent, and of a line for zero time.

The triangulation as described for Table 1, given the following, is:

$$10\%\text{—5 years} = \text{f } 3.791$$

$$5 \text{ years—f } 3.791 = 10\%$$

$$10\%\text{—f } 3.791 = 5 \text{ years}$$

The ratio as described for Table 1 is:

10%—5 years

$1 is to f 3.791 as

$10.00 is to $37.91, and

$100.00 is to $379.10, and

$60.00 is to $227.46, and

$3,791.00 is to $14,371.68, and

$263.78 is to $1,000.00 $\left(\dfrac{\$1,000.00}{\text{f } 3.791} = \$263.78\right)$

For interpolation, given five years and f 3.475, what is the rate?

12%	f 3.605	f 3.605
—	—	f 3.475
14%	f 3.433	—
	f 0.172	f 0.130 = f 0.130/f 0.172 = 0.7558% × 2%
		= 1.51% = 13.51% (12.00% + 1.51%)

Given five years and f 3.400, what is the rate?

15%	f 3.352	f 3.352
—	—	f 3.400
14%	f 3.433	—
	f 0.081	f 0.048 = f 0.48/f 0.81 = 0.59%
		= 14.41% (15.00% − 0.59%)

Also, f 3.400 − f 3.433 = f 0.033/f 0.081 = .41% and 14% + 0.41% = 14.41%.

Given 12% and f 5.600, how many years are there?

10 years	f 5.650	f 5.650
—	—	f 5.600
9 years	f 5.328	—
	f 0.322	f 0.050 = $\dfrac{\text{f } 0.050}{\text{f } 0.322}$ = 0.15% = 9.85 years

Also, f 5.600 − f 5.328 = 272/322 = 0.85% = 9.85 years.

Note the powerful effect of time and rates—$1,000 annuity discounted:

	0%	4%	15%	30%
5 years	$ 5,000	$ 4,452	$3,352	$2,436
30 years	30,000	17,292	6,566	3,332
Increase	$25,000	$12,840	$3,214	$ 896

Thus a $1,000 annuity extended to 30 years from 5 years at 15% has a PV increase of only $3,214 for the added 25 years, compared with $3,352 for the first 5 years. When the rate doubles from 15% to 30% and the period goes from 5 to 30 years, the amounts are almost unchanged—$3,352 and $3,332. An annuity of $1,000 for 30 years would require now (PV) $17,292 at 4% but only $6,566 at 15%.

To show accumulation, with $1,000 deposited annually, we have:

	For 5 Years	For 30 Years
0%	$5,000	$ 30,000
4	5,416	56,085
15	6,742	434,745
30	9,043	8,729,986

Examples

Bank Loans

To borrow $25,890 for four years at 20% and repay $10,000 annually (4 years × $10,000 = $40,000), we have:

$$\frac{\$25,890}{\$10,000} = f\ 2.589 - 4 \text{ years} = 20\%$$

The proof is:

Year	Repay	20% Interest	Reduce Principal	Principal Balance
				$25,890
1	$10,000	$ 5,178	$ 4,822	21,068
2	10,000	4,213	5,787	15,281
3	10,000	3,056	6,944	8,337
4	10,000	1,666	8,334	3
	$40,000	$14,113	$25,887	$ 0

(Exact payment—$10,001.025)
(Exact f—2.5887346)

Mortgages

To borrow $90,000 for 30 years we have:

$$\text{At } 6\% \ \frac{\$90,000.00}{f\ 13.760} = \$6,540.70 \text{ payment}$$

$$30 \times \$6,540.70 = \$196,221.00 - P\ \$90,000.00 = I\ \$106,221.00$$

If only $5,000 can be paid each year, for 30 years at 6%, principal is limited to $68,800 ($68,800/$5,000 = f 13.760). If $5,400 is paid each year (interest only) there is no reduction of principal. If $90,000 at 6% is borrowed for 60 years (not 30) the payments are $5,569 (not $6,540). The added 30 years reduce the payment by only $971.

$$At\ 14\%\ \frac{\$90,000.00}{f\ 7.003} = \$12,851.64\ payment—30\ years$$

$$30\ years \times \$12,851.64 = \$385,549.00 - P\ \$90,000.00 = I\ \$295,549.00$$

The total interest paid is $295,549.00 (cf. $106,221.00 at 6%). Interest alone is $12,600.00 per year—$90,000.00 × 14%. If only $12,000.00 can be paid each year, principal is limited to $84,036.00 at 14% ($84,036.00/$12,000.00 = f 7.003). If $90,000.00 is borrowed at 14% for 60 years (not 30) the payments are $12,604.86 (not $12,851.64), a reduction of only $247.00.

$$At\ 22\%\ \frac{\$90,000.00}{f\ 4.534} = \$19,850.02\ payment—30\ years$$

$$30\ years \times \$19,850.02 = \$595,500.00 = P\ \$90,000.00 = I\ \$505,500.00$$

The first year payment of $19,850.02 includes $19,800.00 interest (22% × $90,000.00) and the principal reduction is only $50.02. If only $18,000.00 can be paid each year for 30 years at 22%, principal is limited to $81,612.00. If $90,000.00 is borrowed at 22% for 60 years (not 30) the payments are $19,800.13 (not $19,850.02), a reduction of $49.89 for the 30 year increase.

Magazine Subscriptions

Assume an annual subscription of $20, or five years for $80 (not $100). What is the savings rate?

$$\frac{1\ year}{For\ \$20}\ or\ \frac{5\ years}{For\ \$80} = \frac{+4\ years}{+\$60\ investment}\ \ \$60/\$20 = f\ 3.0$$

Save $20 per year for four years = f 3.0 = 12.6%.
If the five-year rate is $70 we have:

$$\frac{1\ year}{For\ \$20}\ or\ \frac{5\ years}{For\ \$70} = \frac{4\ years}{\$50\ investment}\ \ \$50/\$20 = f\ 2.5$$

Save $20 per year for four years = f 2.5 = 21.9%.

If the five-year rate is $90 we have:

For $\dfrac{1 \text{ year}}{\$20}$ or For $\dfrac{5 \text{ years}}{\$90} = \dfrac{4 \text{ years}}{\$70 \text{ investment}}$ $\$70/\$20 = f\ 3.5$

Save $20 per year for four years $= f\ 3.5 = 5.6\%$.

Asset Investment

Assume a machine cost of $60,000, a 20-year life, no salvage, and a cash gain as follows:

Cash	f	Yield
$12,000	5.0	19.4%
10,000	6.0	15.8
8,000	7.5	11.9
6,000	10.0	7.8
4,000	15.0	2.9
3,000	20.0	0
2,000	30.0	loss $20,000 ($-3.6\%$)

Similarly, the machine cost could vary, with cash gain and life constant; the life could vary, with cost and cash gain constant. In practice, all three factors are subject to some estimated range. Probabilities must be assigned for all possible outcomes to provide a basis for risk evaluation.

Pensions

Assume a fund balance of $120,000, age 65. The annual pension for various rates and lives is:

		8%		12%		16%
10-year life	(f 6.710)	$17,884	(f 5.650)	$21,239	(f 4.833)	$24,830
15-year life	(f 8.559)	14,020	(f 6.811)	17,618	(f 5.575)	21,525
20-year life	(f 9.818)	12,222	(f 7.469)	16,066	(f 5.929)	20,240

The annual pension range shown is from $12,222 to $24,830. Higher fund balances available at retirement pay more benefits in the same proportion.

To save $120,000 for the pension fund would require annual saving for:

		at 8%		at 12%
40 years	=	$ 463.22	=	$ 156.44
30	=	1,059.29	=	497.24
20	=	2,622.26	=	1,665.45
10	=	8,283.53	=	6,838.10

EXAMPLES—BOTH TABLES

Asset Investment—Disposal Value

With no disposal, value-asset cost of $70,000, for 10 years, and a cash gain of $10,000, f 7.0 = yield 7.07%.

With salvage at 10% of cost, or $7,000 before tax, or $3,500 after tax, the yield can be found by trial and error. It will be higher than 7.07%, so try 9%:

	Cash	10 Year f 9%	PV
Gain	$10,000	6.418	$64,180
Disposal	3,500	0.423	1,480
			$65,660 LOW

Try 8%:

	Cash	f 8%	PV
Gain	$10,000	6.710	$67,100
Disposal	3,500	0.463	1,620
			$68,720 LOW

Try 7.5%:

	Cash	f 7.5%	PV
Gain	$10,000	6.864	$68,640
Disposal	3,500	0.485	1,697
			$70,337 HIGH

Interpolate as follows:

7.5%	$70,337	$70,337
—	—	$70,000
8.0%	68,720	—
	$ 1,617	$ 337

$$\frac{\$\ 337}{\$1,617} = 0.208\% \times 0.5\% = 0.104\% = 7.604\% \text{ or } 7.60\%$$

Yield is increased by only 0.53% (7.60% − 7.07%) by the salvage estimate of 10.00% before tax on cost.

If the estimated disposal is revised to 40% of cost, or $28,000 before tax and $14,000 net, the yield is 9%:

	Cash	10 Year f 9%	PV
Gain	$10,000	6.418	$64,180
Disposal	$14,000	0.423	5,922
			$70,102—about 9.04% for $70,000

The 40.00% salvage estimate provides 9.04%, but the 10.00% estimate yields only 7.60%. With no salvage, the yield is 7.07%. If the required yield (company discount rate) is 8.00%, salvage over 18.00% must be estimated to justify the project.

Because cost is fully depreciated, any salvage value is fully taxable. Yields depend on salvage values at a future date, for used assets in an unpredictable market and with unknown tax effects.

Bonds—Sold at Face Value

Assume a face value of $10,000 at 10% interest for 10 years.

	Contract	10-Year Maturity f 10%	PV
Principal (P)	$10,000	f 0.386	$3,860
Interest (I)	1,000	f 6.145	6,145 $10,005 ($10,000)

The contract is to repay the $10,000 principal (PV $3,860), plus $1,000 interest for ten years (PV $6,145). The yield to maturity (YTM) is 10%, and the current yield (CY) is 10%. YTM and CY are always the same for bonds selling at face value, regardless of maturity.

	Contract	5-Year Maturity f 10%	PV
P	$10,000	f 0.621	$6,210
I	1,000	f 3.791	3,791 $10,001 ($10,000)

The $10,000 total PV is unchanged, but the interest component is much less, $3.791. Cf. $6,145. Yields are unchanged. YTM is 10%. CY is 10%.

	Contract	30-Year Maturity f 10%	PV
P	$10,000	f 0.057	$ 570
I	1,000	f 9.427	9,427 $9,997 ($10,000)

Interest is now over 94% of the PV. YTM 10% and CY 10% are the same for all maturities.

For a 50-year maturity, interest is $9,915.0000 and principal is $85.0000. For 100 years, interest is $9,999.2700. At 150 years, interest is $9,999.9938.

Bonds—Market Price Below/Over Face Value

If the market rate of interest rises to 15%, the 10% bonds due in 10 years fall in price, by about 25%:

	Contract	10 Years f 15%		PV	
P	$10,000	f 0.247		$2,470	
I	1,000	f 5.019		5,019	
				$7,489	
			Discount	2,511	$10,000

The YTM is 15.00% (market rate) but the CY is 13.35% $\left(\dfrac{\$1,000}{\$7,489}\right)$. The CY disregards the recovery of the discount ($2,511) at maturity ten years later and thus is lower.

The following are alternative calculations:

$$\begin{array}{ll} \text{Contract interest} & \$1,000 \\ \text{Market rate} & \underline{1,500} \\ + \$ 500 \times \text{f } 5.019 = \$2,510 \text{ discount} \end{array}$$

Or:

$$\text{Discount } \$2,511/\text{f } 5.019 = \$500 \text{ annuity}$$

A buyer at $7,489 has, in effect, withheld $2,511 to provide an annuity of $500 on top of the $1,000 cash to provide the $1,500 market rate.

If the market rate falls to 5%, the 10% bonds rise in price by about 38%:

	Contract	10 Years f 5%		PV	
P	$10,000	f 0.614		$ 6,140	
I	1,000	f 7.722		7,722	
				$13,862	
			Premium	3,862	$10,000

The YTM is 5.00% and CY is 7.21% $\left(\dfrac{\$ 1,000}{\$13,862}\right)$, higher than the YTM because the loss of the $3,862 premium at maturity is disregarded.

The following are alternative calculations:

Contract interest $1,000
Market rate   500
                    — $ 500 × f 7.722 = $3,861 premium

Or:

$$\$3,862/f\ 7.722 = \$500\ \text{annuity}$$

The seller has required a premium ($3,862) to provide an annuity ($500) to reduce his contract cost to the market rate.

Bonds—Market Price Quoted

If face value bonds for $10,000 sell at $6,667, with 10% interest, and ten-year maturity, the YTM requires trial and error. The CY is $1,000/$6,667 or 15%. The YTM must be higher.

Try 16%:

	Contract	10 Years f 16%	PV
P	$10,000	f 0.227	$2,270
I	1,000	f 4.833	4,833
			$7,103 HIGH by $436

Try 18%:

	Contract	10 Years f 18%	PV
P	$10,000	f 0.191	$1,910
I	1,000	f 4.494	4,494
			$6,404 LOW by $263

Try 17%:

	Contract	10 Years f 17%	PV
P	$10,000	f 0.208	$2,080
I	1,000	f 4.659	4,659
			$6,739 HIGH by $72

To interpolate we have:

17% PV $6,739 $6,739
Market price   —   6,667
18% PV   6,404   —
              $ 335 $ 72 $\frac{\$72}{\$335} = 0.21\% = 17.21\%$

By calculation the rate of 17.21% produces a PV of $6,666.64.

Selecting a close first trial rate can be aided by an arithmetic short-cut:

Average price $ 6,667
                + 10,000
                $16,667/2 = $8,333.50

Average interest $1,000.00
Discount $3,333/10 years +   333.30
                                $1,333.30

$$\text{Rate: } \frac{\$1,333.30}{\$8,333.50} = 16.0\%$$

This procedure produces an answer below the true YTM (17.2%) when the bonds are sold at a discount. Thus the 16.0% could suggest a first trial at 17.0% because 16.0% is low.

When bonds sell at a premium, the arithmetic procedure gives an answer that is high. The average price is divided by the contract interest, less the average premium.

Discount Bonds—Zero Coupon

These bonds do not pay interest and thus have no CY. YTM depends on bond price and years to maturity. For a $10,000 face value bond we have:

YTM 12%

Maturity	1 Year	5 Years	10 Years	20 Years
Price (PV)	$8,929	$5,674	$3,220	$1,037

10-Year Maturity

YTM	1.2%	6.0%	12.0%	24.0%
Price (PV)	$8,876	$5,584	$3,220	$1,164

With the rule of 72, assuming a bond face value of $1,000 and a price of $500 (doubling), we have:

Maturity	YTM	Calculated
4 years =	18%	(18.9%)
6 years =	12	(12.2)
8 years =	9	(9.1)
9 years =	8	(8.0)
12 years =	6	(5.9)
18 years =	4	(3.9)

Some discount bonds pay a low rate of interest: Assume a bond face value of $1,000; interest, 6%; maturity, eight years; and YTM 15%.

	Contract	8 Years f 15%	PV
P	$1,000	f 0.327	$327.00
I	60	f 4.487	269.22
			$596.22 market price

Bond Interest Paid Twice a Year

Assume a face value of $10,000, ten years, and 10% interest. The annual basis is:

	Contract	10 Years f 10%	PV
P	$10,000	f 0.3855	$ 3,855
I	1,000	f 6.1450	6,145
			$10,000

The semi-annual basis is:

	Contract	20 Periods f 5%	PV	Cf.
P	$10,000	f 0.377	$ 3,770	−$85
I	500	f 12.460	6,230	+ 85
			$10,000	$ 0

The interest component increases $85.
If the market rate is 16% YTM we have:

Annual Basis

	Contract	10 Years f 16%	PV
P	$10,000	f 0.227	$2,270
I	1,000	f 4.833	4,833
			$7,103

Semi-annual Basis

	Contract	20 Periods f 8%	PV	Cf.
P	$10,000	f 0.215	$2,150	−$120
I	500	f 9.818	4,909	+ 76
			$7,059	−$ 44

If the market rate is 4% YTM we have:

	Annual Basis				Semi-annual Basis			
		10 Years				**20 Periods**		
	Contract	f 4%	PV		Contract	f 2.0%	PV	Cf.
P	$10,000	f 0.676	$ 6,760	P	$10,000	f 0.673	$ 6,730	−$30
I	1,000	f 8.111	8,111	I	500	f 16.351	8,175	+ 64
			$14,871				$14,905	+$34

Callable Bonds

Assume a face value of $100,000; 20 years; interest, 15%; and callable in five years at $115. Determine YTM. If the bond had no call and sold at face value, YTM would be 15% and CY 15%. With a call, yield can be determined for the call date by trial and error. Try 18% for five-year maturity (call):

	Contract	**5 Years** f 18%	PV
P	$115,000	f 0.437	$50,255
I	15,000	f 3.127	46,905
			$97,160 − $2,840 under

Try 17% for five years:

	Contract	**5 Years** f 17%	PV
P	$115,000	f 0.456	$ 52,440
I	15,000	f 3.199	47,985
			$100,425 +$ 425 over
			$3,265 total

$$\$425/\$3,265 = 0.13\% = 17.13\% \text{ YTM for 5 years}$$

Thus if the bond is bought at $100,000 now with five years to the first call date, the YTM is 17.13% (calculates to $100,009).

If the five-year call is for $110, try 16%:

	Contract	**5 Years** 16%	PV
P	$110,000	f 0.476	$ 52,360
I	15,000	f 3.274	49,110
			$101,470

Estimated YTM is higher—about 16.4% by extrapolation.

If the five-year call is for $105, try 16% or 15%:

	Contract	f 16%	PV		Contract	f 15%	PV
P	$105,000	f 0.476	$49,980	P	$105,000	f 0.497	$ 52,185
I	15,000	f 3.274	49,110	I	15,000	f 3.352	50,280
			$99,090				$102,465
			− 910				+ 2,465
							910

$2,465/$3,375 = 0.73% = 15.73% YTM by interpolation $ 3,375

With no call premium the YTM is 15%. To Recap, we have:

Call Price	YTM
$115	17.13%
110	16.44
105	15.73
100	15.00

Further analysis of callable bonds and refunding relative to both the bond issuer and bond holder is given in Chapter 7.

ANNUALIZED FUTURE RATES

YTM is an annualized rate based on bond maturity; individual rates for each year are disregarded. For example, a $10,000 discount bond due in two years with 12% YTM has a market value of $7,971.94:

Current cost (PV)		$ 7,971.94	
Year 1 Interest	12%	956.63	(accumulation)
Year 1 Amount		$ 8,928.57	
Year 2 Interest	12%	$ 1,071.43	(accumulation)
Year 2 Amount		$10,000.00	

If the two-year rate is 12% and the year 1 rate is 12%, the year 2 rate is 12%. But if the year 1 rate is different, the year 2 rate also differs.

	Year 1 Rate	Bond Cost	Year 1 Interest	Year 1 Amount	Year 2 Discount	Year 2 Rate
	9%	$7,971.94	$ 717.47	$8,689.41	$1,310.59	15.08%
	10	7,971.94	797.19	8,769.13	1,230.87	14.04
	11	7,971.94	876.91	8,848.85	1,151.15	13.01
PARITY	12	7,971.94	956.63	8,928.57	1,071.43	12.00
	13	7,971.94	1,036.35	9,008.29	991.71	11.01
	14	7,971.94	1,116.07	9,088.01	911.99	10.03
	15	7,971.94	1,195.79	9,167.73	832.27	9.08

The buyer of the two-year bond at 12.00%, when the year 1 rate is 9.00%, is locking in 15.08% for year 2, but if the year 1 rate is 15.00% he is committing to 9.08% for year 2. This table illustrates a possible range of current expectations for interest rates one year hence.

Thus YTM for year 1 is at the current market rate (known) plus future annual rates (unknown). Rates change constantly to reflect expectations based on several factors—liquidity preferences, inflation, risk, market factors—all part of macro-finance.

INTEREST RATES—NOMINAL AND REAL—AND INFLATION

Interest—the price of money—has several components:

1. The actual rate in effect—called the "nominal rate" (unfortunately).
2. Inflation rate—expected annual change in price levels.
3. Basic rate—called the "real rate" reflecting demand and supply without inflation or risk. Risk is a premium over zero risk (federal issues) based on the degree of uncertainty of the future yield and is omitted here.

With two factors given, the third is determinable:

Rates	Given	Find
1. Actual	15.0%	
2. Inflation	9.0%	
3. Basic	?	$115/109 = 105.5 = 5.5\%$
1. Actual	15.0%	
2. Inflation	?	$115/105.5 = 1.09 = 9\%$
3. Basic	5.5%	
1. Actual	?	$1.09 \times 105.5 = 1.15 = 15\%$
2. Inflation	9.0%	
3. Basic	5.5%	

These relationships vary widely over time and among countries. The only known rate is the actual rate ("nominal"). There is substantial disagreement about the expected rate of inflation as well as the basic rate. This is a subject for macro-finance.

Index

About the Author

SHERMAN L. LEWIS had many years of practical experience in management and consulting for major firms, followed by an academic career in finance and accounting.